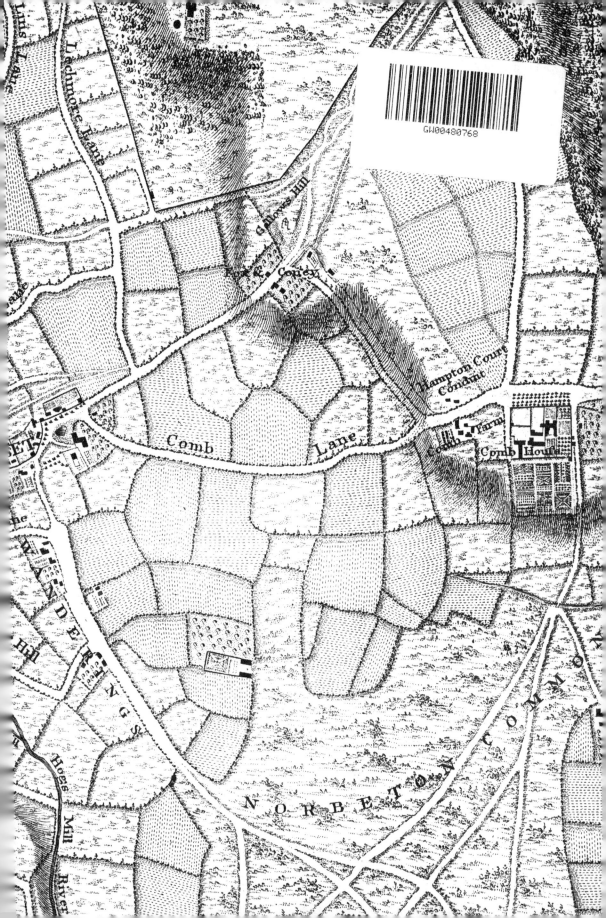

GW00480768

The Book of Kingston
has been published
in a Limited Edition
of which this is

Number *191*

ENDPAPERS — FRONT: John Roque's Map of Kingston, c1745;
BACK: Kingston Bridge and the River Thames, c1828. (KM & HS)

Kingston's Coat of Arms. A 1912 copy of Kingston's arms and seals, as
recorded by the Heralds in 1623. (KM & HS)

THE BOOK OF
KINGSTON

BY
SHAAN BUTTERS MA DPhil

BARON
MCMXCV

PUBLISHED BY BARON BIRCH FOR QUOTES LIMITED
AND PRODUCED BY
KEY COMPOSITION, SOUTH MIDLANDS LITHOPLATES,
CHENEY & SONS, HILLMAN PRINTERS (FROME) LTD,
AND WBC BOOKBINDERS LTD

© Shaan Butters 1995

All rights reserved. No part of this publication may be reproduced,
stored in a retrieval system, or transmitted, in any form or by any
means, electronic, mechanical, photocopying, recording or
otherwise, without the prior permission of Quotes Limited.

Any copy of this book issued by the Publisher as clothbound or as a
paperback is sold subject to the condition that it shall not by way of
trade or otherwise, be lent, re-sold, hired out or otherwise circulated
without the Publisher's prior consent, in any form of binding or
cover other than that in which it is published, and without a similar
condition including this condition being imposed on a
subsequent purchaser.

ISBN 0 86023 562 9

Contents

Acknowledgements

There are several people to thank: June Sampson, whose own carefully researched books and articles bring old Kingston to life, for her example and encouragement; Paul Hill at Kingston Museum for sharing his expert knowledge of the artefacts; Les Kirkin, who took the photographs at the Museum; and all the helpful, long-suffering staff at Kingston Museum and Heritage Service, especially Tim Everson, the Local History Officer, and Jill Lamb, Assistant Borough Archivist. All Kingston local historians must also be in the debt of the late Joan Wakeford for her painstaking, accurate research and the quality of her critical judgement. I am grateful to a number of specialists for discussing particular points with me: John Penn (Kingston University), John Blair (The Queen's College, Oxford), Susan Reynolds, Michael Wood, Nick Fuentes, Philip Emery, Freddie Rushmore, and also staff at the Museum of London. General thanks to David Robinson, Surrey County Archivist, and Rachel Watson, Northamptonshire County Archivist; and to Joan and Amanda Akester and Anne and Jeffery Butters for reading the manuscript. I salute my family's patience, and reserve my biggest 'thank you' for Tim Everson, who has not only given so much professional help, but is also my husband.

Notes on the Sources

Much archival material for Kingston, including charters, chamberlains', churchwardens' and bridgewardens' accounts, and council minutes, is held as part of Kingston Borough Archives, which at present may be consulted at Kingston Local History Room (KLHR), North Kingston Centre, Richmond Road. There is a useful *Guide to the Borough Archives*, published by Kingston Borough Council, 1971. There is also archival material relevant to Kingston in Surrey Record Office (SRO), which has many parish and schools records, in the Public Record Office (PRO), the British Library (BL), the Bodleian Library, Oxford, and in the House of Lords' Record Office (HLRO). I have detailed my use of these, and other sources mentioned below, in full notes for each chapter, which may be consulted, bound with an expanded version of the text, in special annotated copies of this book deposited with Kingston Local History Room and Surrey Record Office.

To manuscript sources must be added back copies of local newspapers like the *Surrey Comet, (SC)* and *Kingston Borough News, (KBN)*; articles and excavation round-ups in *Surrey Archaeological Collections (SAC)* and the *Surrey Archaeological Society Bulletin*, published by Surrey Archaeological Society (SAS), and in *The London Archaeologist*; the papers and newsletters of the Kingston upon Thames Archaeological Society (KUTAS); Surrey Record Society publications; editions of *Surrey History*; Kingston Museum excavation reports, and reports of the Museum of London Archaeology Service (MOLAS). All these may be consulted in KLHR. The latter and SRO have useful collections of maps, photographs and postcards, and KLHR has an oral history archive, with typescripts. KLHR also contains copies of acts of Parliament relevant to Kingston, and of the Borough Medical Officer's reports; an excellent pamphlet collection; the RBK Archive Packs, such as *Road, Rail and River*, (1974), *Kingston Market Place*, (1979), and *Theatres and Cinemas in Kingston*, (1983), and Joan Wakeford's thesis, and MSS and typescript notes.

June Sampson's books, listed in the Select Bibliography, and her articles in the *Surrey Comet*, form an important printed source. I have used the Bodleian Library for printed editions of the Pipe Rolls, Close Rolls, Patent Rolls, etc; for Records Commission publications; for the Rolls Series and other editions of medieval chronicles, and for the *Letters and Papers of Henry VIII, Calendar of State Papers Domestic*, and *Acts of the Privy Council*.

Kingston Guildhall has copies of the various town plans, such as the *Comprehensive Development Area Plan*, the *Local* and *District* plans of the 1980s, and the current *Unitary Development Plan*, and has statistical information on population, employment and the economy.

Dedication
For Tom, and for Eleanor,
With Love.

In Other Words

'Kingstone, a good Market-Town, but remarkable for little, only that they say, the Antient British and Saxon Kings were usually Crown'd here in former Times, which I will neither assert or deny'.

Daniel Defoe, *A Tour through the Whole Island of Great Britain,* 1724

'Kingston, or Kingston-upon-Thames, . . . is a market and corporate town, and parish . . . most eligibly and pleasantly seated on the southern bank of the noble Thames, which is crossed by an elegant bridge of Portland stone . . . Though in appearance not the most prepossessing, this is a very ancient and respectable place . . .'

Pigot's *Directory,* 1840

'We went to the high-level platform and saw the engine driver, and asked him if he was going to Kingston. He said he couldn't say for certain of course, but that he rather thought he was. Anyhow, if he wasn't the 11.5 for Kingston, he said he was pretty confident he was the 9.32 for Virginia Water, or the 10 am express for the Isle of Wight, or somewhere in that direction, and we should all know when we got there. We slipped half-a-crown into his hand, and begged him to be the 11.5 for Kingston.

"Nobody will ever know, on this line", we said, "what you are, or where you're going. You know the way, you slip off quietly and go to Kingston".

"Well, I don't know, gents", replied the noble fellow, "but I suppose *some* train's got to go to Kingston; and I'll do it. Gimme the half-crown."

Thus we got to Kingston by the London and South Western Railway.

We learnt afterwards that the train we had come by was really the Exeter mail, and that they had spent hours at Waterloo looking for it . . .

Jerome K. Jerome, *Three Men in a Boat,* 1889.

Key to Caption Credits

A	Ed. E. Arber, *An Introductory Sketch to the Martin Marprelate Controversy* (1879) p83
An	A. Anderson, *History and Antiquities of the Ancient Town of Kingston upon Thames* (1818)
B	W. Biden, *The History and Antiquities of the Ancient and Royal Town of Kingston-upon-Thames* (Kingston, 1852)
BAe	British Aerospace, Dunsfold
BL	British Library (Cotton Augustus ii, 20; P.39717,K.Top.XL 15-2.)
C	Mr J. O. Chapman
CB	Clive Birch
H	A. Heales, *The Early History of the Church of Kingston-upon-Thames* (1883)
Ha	J. Hawkey
JW	Jeffrey Wallder
KM	Kingston Museum; pictures taken by Les Kirkin
KM & HS	Kingston Museum and Heritage Service
M&B	O. Manning and W. Bray, *The History and Antiquities of the County of Surrey,* vol I (1804)
PF&S	J. Penn, D. Field, D. Serjeantson, 'Evidence of Neolithic Occupation in Kingston: excavations at Eden Walk, 1965', in *Surrey Archaeological Collections,* vol 75 (1984)
PRO	Public Record Office (E 31/2/1)
R	G. Roots, *The Charters of the Town of Kingston upon Thames* (1797)
RC	The Royal Collection © 1995 Her Majesty the Queen (OM 153)
RR	Rowley W. C. Richardson, *Surbiton: Thirty-Two Years of Local Self-Government, 1855-1887* (Surbiton, 1888)
S	J. Stowe, *The Annales of England* (1601)
SB	Shaan Butters
SC	*Surrey Comet*
TE	Tim Everson
TGA	Tiffin Girls' School Archives

7

Foreword *by The Rt Hon Norman Lamont MP*

It is to me personally somewhat ironic and not a little sad that I should write this foreword to Shaan Butters' admirable book precisely at the time I am severing my long connection with Kingston.

It is now over 20 years since June Sampson's excellent book *The Story of Kingston* was published. Over the years, as the Member of Parliament for the Royal Borough, I have relied heavily on this book for many an anecdote for an after dinner speech, often the Old Tiffinians Association or the Kingston Rowing Club. June Sampson's book is full of such excellent nuggets. Dr Butters' book seems to me very different in its scope and intent. It seeks to give a clear comprehensive and chronological account of the development of Kingston into a town, and its subsequent fortunes. It is very much a social history and each chapter gives an insight into the habits, lives and work of the people of Kingston. The book also goes right back to the Ice Age drawing on archaeological discoveries and evidence that has come to light in recent years.

Dr Butters has done a hugely impressive amount of original research. This may discomfort some readers because it leads her to question some traditional claims made about Kingston and especially its link with Saxon kings. She is right to assert that it is important to present a truthful picture of Kingston, and separate tradition from fact, and to point out what is not proven. This is history at its very best. Sometimes one fears that history would be merely like journalism, written from a point of view based on myths. In my view, that is not what history should be and certainly not what is intended by the scholarly Dr Butters.

Though written with a wealth of detail and indentified sources this is a book for the general reader. I am sure it will be widely read and enjoyed in Kingston as it surely deserves to be.

Preface *by June Sampson*

After 22 years as Features Editor of the *Surrey Comet*, and 30 as an obsessive local history researcher, I've read almost everything that's ever been printed on Kingston's past. So when publisher Clive Birch asked me to suggest possible authors for this proposed *Book of Kingston*, I could reply at once: Shaan Butters.

As a person I knew her hardly at all, having met her only once for a brief newspaper interview. But as a local historian, I knew her to be outstanding — a conviction born of reviewing her history of St Peter's Church, Norbiton. It was meticulously researched, beautifully written, and full of previously unknown facts and informed theories. In short it was everything a local history should be but, alas, so seldom is.

Shaan is one of those rare historians who combines high academic skills and scrupulous integrity with the ability to write interestingly. Thus I, for one, was truly elated when she agreed to undertake *The Book of Kingston*; for what has resulted is the first history of such scale, range and in-depth knowledge ever to be published on the Royal borough.

It fills a long-standing gap and will, I predict, be the definitive work on Kingston for many years to come.

Introduction

Kingston lies on the Surrey bank of the middle stretch of the Thames. It is about 12 miles upstream from London, just above where the river becomes tidal, at Teddington. Kingston's history is bound up with the river, which has given the town a relatively secure site and an artery for access and trade.

Kingston is indeed an 'ancient place'. Though it only became a town in the late 12th century, there has been human activity and settlement in the area since prehistoric times, when the Kingston stretch of the Thames may even have been associated with an ancient river religion. There was a settlement here of some sort under the Romans.

Kingston is best known as the place where Saxon kings were crowned. Patriotic local historians in the 19th and early 20th centuries made much of this. They liked to glorify their town by linking it with major national events, and as monarchists they laid great stress on Kingston's perceived loyalty to the Crown. Thus Biden wrote in 1852 that Kingston was the 'metropolis of the Anglo-Saxon kings' and the 'nursery of England's greatness'. This is exaggerated. It is rooted in a picture of the Anglo-Saxons as a nation of free-born Englishmen, who after 1066 were crushed beneath the tyrannical Norman yoke, and it tells us more about the Victorians than the Saxons.

Saxon kings were sometimes consecrated at Kingston in the 10th century, but it is debateable whether all seven of the kings named on the 'Coronation Stone' were really crowned here. Kingston was a suitable, though not the only suitable, coronation place because by late Saxon times it was of local importance as the administrative centre of a Royal estate (a king's 'tun'), and the site of a major church, but it was not a town.

Even when it gained its first urban charter in 1200, Kingston was of only local importance, and was overshadowed by London. National events impinged upon it, but Kingston rarely influenced them. Maybe the nearest it came to affecting the course of English history was in 1554, when its townsfolk delayed Wyatt's rebels.

From the Middle Ages, Kingston has been a market town for Surrey and a supplier of goods to the capital. Once it gained urban status, its concern was to maintain and extend its privileges, and to protect its trade. For most of the time this was best achieved by obedience to authority. Thus the town usually obeyed Royal orders during the Reformation, and reluctantly supported soldiers of both sides in the Civil War.

Transformed in the 19th century by a population explosion, the coming of the railway and massive building development, the Victorian town saw a great expansion of local government and public services. 20th century Kingston has become a suburb of London, and to an extent a commuter town, though it is still a viable community and economic centre. The Royal Borough of Kingston expanded in 1965 to include Surbiton and New Malden, Kingston's own suburbs; this book is mainly a study of Kingston, but brings in the surrounding areas where relevant.

Today's local historians do not need to justify their interest in a town's past by exaggerating its associations with monarchy or aristocracy, with events of national importance, or with the development of 'modern' ideas or institutions. The life of a town is recognised as important in its own right. Kingston's story is about how a town came to exist and grow, organize itself and flourish, and also the story of those men, women and children who lived, worked and died in it, and of their hopes, fears and dreams. I have tried in this book to tell that story.

9

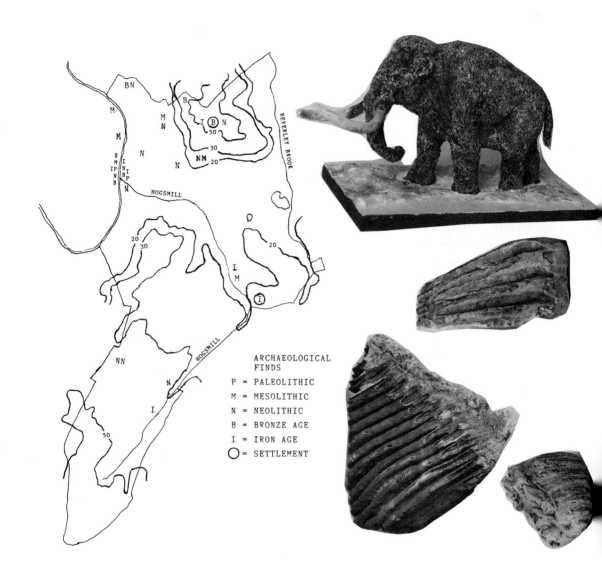

LEFT: Prehistoric finds in the Kingston area. (TE) ABOVE: One of Kingston's first inhabitants: a Woolly Mammoth. (Model in KM) RIGHT: Mammoth teeth found in the Kingston area. (KM)

From Stone to Rome

A time traveller who went back 70 million years, to an era before the dinosaurs died out, and tried to visit what is now Kingston, would have got wet. The area was under water — part of a vast sea that covered the whole country. This left behind the chalk that today underlies the London basin and rises up on its nothern edge as the Chiltern Hills, and on its southern border as the North Downs.

Some 20 million years later, in Eocene times, another sea covered the London area, and laid down the stiff, heavy London clay through which the Thames Valley is now cut, and on which many houses in the Kingston neighbourhood stand. But even when this sea receded, today's Thames and its valley were not yet there. Until about half a million years ago, at the start of the Great Ice Age, the Thames ran to the north of its present course, through the Vale of St Albans.

When the Anglian ice sheet crept down from the north of Britain, reaching north London c450,000 BC, the weight of the ice forced the Thames south into the Thames Valley where it flows today. During the Ice Age of the next few hundred thousand years, the river cut an ever deeper channel, leaving the gravel and sand of its successive floodplains as a series of gravel terraces. Several of these are exposed today as higher ground in the Kingston area, for instance Kingston Hill. After the last glaciation, a silty, sandy material known as 'brickearth' was laid down over the lowest, or Flood Plain, terrace, which stretches along the Thames from Long Ditton to Ham; most of the modern Kingston town centre is built on Kingston brickearth.

During the Ice Age, primitive man walked across the Kingston landscape in search of food. The Ice Age was not a period of continuous cold, but a succession of cold phases, known as glacials, when the ice advanced south, and warm phases, or interglacials, when ice melted, and the climate was as warm as or warmer than that of today. Each phase lasted thousands of years. The landscape changed slowly with the climate, from ice to tundra to forest, and back again. The last glaciation ended about 13,000 BC; we live in what are often called post-glacial times, but may be simply another interglacial before the ice closes in again.

If human beings hunted in the Kingston area before the onset of the Anglian ice sheet, they left no trace. The advent of the ice would probably have made them move south. Though Kingston itself was not covered by this ice sheet, the glacier was at one stage only about 20 kilometres away to the north, so for a long while the ground at Kingston must have been frozen and inhospitable.

However, eventually the ice receded and it grew warmer. Tundra vegetation spread: the ground was still snow-covered in winter, but thawed enough in summer for moss and plants to grow, on which herds of reindeer and woolly rhinoceros could graze. As the Channel and North Sea were dry land for much of the Ice Age, Britain and northern Europe were part of the same large North European Plain. Across this wide, treeless landscape, the herds wandered in search of fresh grazing, and people followed the herds.

One of the oldest known human artefacts from the Kingston area may belong to this period of tundra. It is a primitive Palaeolithic (Old Stone Age) flake cut from a flint core, which looks as if someone had been trying to make it into a hand-axe, but given

11

up half way. It comes from Richmond Park. Another find, from Coombe Hill, is a hand-axe in a slightly more developed style. This could be over 300,000 years old. Other Palaeolithic hand-axes have been found in the Thames at Kingston. They were possibly dropped in temperate conditions, by people who hunted bison and red deer through the grassland and forest near the river. Later Palaeolithic tools have been found in the 18 metre gravel terraces at Surbiton and Old Malden. The tools are probably over 100,000 years old.

These tool makers would not have looked like the human beings we recognize today, who belong to the species *homo sapiens sapiens*. They were an early human species, possibly *homo erectus* or a primitive type of *homo sapiens*. They were nomadic.

During the most recent cold phase, when an ice sheet covered the north of Britain, the Kingston area was inhospitable once more. Fossils of Arctic plants have been found in the Flood Plain gravels of this period, while a number of woolly mammoth teeth and a gigantic mammoth tusk have been discovered. There is no evidence of any Neanderthal presence.

Gradually the climate warmed, and people returned. By c13,000 BC, modern man had replaced the Neanderthals. As the ice melted, the sea level rose, and by about 6,500 BC water filled the English Channel and the North Sea, and England was cut off from Europe. In the warm, damp conditions of Mesolithic (Middle Stone Age) times, there seems to have been more human activity and settlement in the Kingston area. The most important site was by the river at Ham, but there were several others in the Hogsmill valley, on Coombe Hill (*eg* Warren Cutting) and by springs and streams in Richmond Park. In these places, about 7,000 years ago, people worked cores of flint by chipping off different shaped pieces to form axe-heads, scrapers, arrowheads and other blades. They probably moved from camp to camp at different times of year, in search of the best hunting.

It was heavily wooded all around Kingston. Pollen evidence from nearby Putney in about 5,500 BC has shown a mixed forest of oak and alder, with some pine, beech, hazel, lime and willow. This ancient wildwood looked more like a rainforest than today's woods.

The hunters of Mesolithic Kingston used flint-tipped spears and arrows to bring down the red deer and wild cattle of the great forest by the Thames. Kingston Museum has a splendid example of the massive horns of one of the creatures they might have stalked: *bos primigenius*, an early form of undomesticated cattle. Mesolithic people also made axes and adzes fixed to wooden shafts; these were used to cut down trees and grub up roots. Over 20 have been recovered from the Kingston stretch of the Thames. Kingston's early inhabitants probably built boats from hollowed out tree trunks, useful for fishing, fowling and travel.

In about 4,500 BC, farming was introduced to Britain, and the so-called Neolithic period, or New Stone Age began. People began to grow crops and practise animal husbandry. They lived in permanent settlements and made significant inroads into the wildwood. Fields were marked out, and eventually simple ploughs were used. Domestic cattle grazed in the meadows and pigs foraged in the woods. Pottery vessels were used to cook and store food.

Ample evidence of Neolithic activity in the Kingston area is provided by the many flint and stone axes that have been found in the Thames, on its floodplain from Thames Ditton to Ham, and from Chessington, Kingston Hill and Richmond Park.

12

Sherds of Neolithic pottery have been found at the Bittoms. There are also two possible Neolithic long barrows in the Park, on the top of the hill near Ham Gate, and from Neolithic times comes the first firm evidence of settlement or some other form of human activity in what is now Kingston town centre.

Excavations off Eden Street between 1965 and 1977, when the area was developed for the Eden Walk shopping complex, produced sherds of Neolithic pottery, animal bones, burnt flints, and pieces of worked flint and antler. They also yielded information about the lie of the land in central Kingston some 5,000 years ago. Today's town centre was then an island.

In about 3,000 BC, the Thames had an eastern arm, now silted up, a channel which curled from south of the confluence of Hogsmill and Thames, eastwards around a gravel island where church and market place now stand. This channel ran approximately through the modern BHS and Marks and Spencer, and then curved gradually back round to the west to rejoin the main channel of the Thames somewhere near the Electricity Power Station site.

The people who lived when central Kingston was an island knew an environment hard for us to imagine. We have to think away Kingston Bridge, the roads and the buidings, and the tidy, embanked sides of the River Thames. Instead, the river was wider and shallower, fringed on the western side by reeds and marshes where wildfowl nested. Then the gravel island rose from the water, covered with grass, brambles and thistles. Small trees grew there: hazel and cherry, oak scrub, willow and alder. On the eastern (Eden Street) side of the island, the marsh-edged eastern arm of the Thames flowed. It was shallow, and may have dried out in winter. Away from it, the ground rose towards the Fairfield, and streams ran in from the west. Soon, the forest started: massive oak, elm and lime trees, with alder and hazel — though people were already making clearings in it for farming.

People may have lived on the gravel island (or on the channel floor if it ran seasonally dry), or camped there temporarily on fishing or fowling expeditions. It looks as though they ate there, for some of the pot sherds bear traces of what may be burnt food, and the piles of burnt flints have been interpreted as 'potboilers', used to heat water for cooking. Also, the island could have been used by those involved in the Thames axe-trade; Kingston was well situated because the Hogsmill gave access to the southern uplands.

Moreover, the large number of Neolithic axe-heads (at least 35) found in the Kingston stretch of the Thames, and the high quality and good condition of many, suggest that people were making offerings to a river spirit or god. Some of the axes were prestige objects, symbols of individual authority or communal dignity; others were for use. Some could have been lost by accident, but it is likely that some were deliberately deposited in the water. The potboilers found in Eden Street may even represent a ritual meal cooked, or some sort of purification ceremony practised, before an axe was given to the river.

Human activity or settlement (or both) in the Eden Street area continued or recurred through the late Neolithic period and into the Bronze Age. Pieces of late Neolithic and Bronze Age pottery have been found, more potboilers, some animal bones that show signs of butchery, and fragments of saddle querns, used for grinding corn. There are also some interesting pieces of wood, radiocarbon-dated to c2,000-1770 BC. While these could have accumulated naturally or been part of a

13

beaver's dam, they may well be the remains of an artificial platform, maybe a work platform on which people skinned animals and prepared food, or a structure to help people cross the marshy ground. They could even be a funeral platform where human remains were exposed. Part of a late Neolithic/early Bronze Age skull and other, separate, human bones were found nearby. These may have been the result of prehistoric drowning accidents, but one of the bones has marks where the flesh was stripped off after death, which strongly suggests ritual activity.

During the Bronze Age, farming was the dominant economic activity, but by now a wide range of crafts had also become important, including metalworking. Copper and gold were known in Britain from about 2,700 BC, and bronze was introduced some 500 years later. Bronze (a mixture of copper and tin) became fashionable for both weapons and tools, and by 1,500 BC native British smiths were producing a wide range of original designs.

An increasing number of everyday goods were made in bronze. Several different types of weapon, including daggers and swords, were produced, in large numbers, suggesting a more warlike age. Already in the late Neolithic period, the apparently fairly equal society of earlier days seems to have been replaced by a more stratified one organized by an elite, and the quantity and quality of bronze weapons indicates warrior leaders. An increasing population and soil exhaustion put fertile land at a premium, and Bronze Age chiefs probably competed for control.

Control of trade routes was also important. From about 1,500 BC the Thames was a major artery for the distribution of copper and tin, relatively scarce metals which had to be imported from the West Country, Ireland and Britanny. Areas of the middle and lower Thames Valley now flourished as important metal-producing centres, and Kingston was probably one of these.

Besides the early Bronze Age presence in Eden Street, Bronze Age pottery has been found at the Bittoms, and there may have been other riverside settlements. The large number of beautiful bronze weapons found in the Thames near Kingston testifies to the economic importance and prosperity of the area. Maybe some of these were given to the river god, or cast into the water with the bones or ashes of dead warriors as part of their funeral rites.

The weapons may have been made on the top of Kingston Hill, where there was an important late Bronze Age (c1,000-800 BC) settlement. This covered the gravel area between George Road and Warren Road, now the site of Coombe Wood golf course, and a recently discovered Bronze Age ditch at Warren Cutting, probably a field boundary, shows that the site continued round the north-east side of the hill. It may also have extended north and west to the A308, towards Richmond Park. During the 19th century, pits containing Bronze Age pottery were discovered in the George Road gravel quarries. Pieces of urns, bowls, cups and jars were found. Some of the jars were perhaps used for food storage, and it is likely that grain was grown locally. Parts of clay loomweights were also found, so sheep were kept and weaving took place. People may also have buried their dead nearby. Descriptions of a jar half full of ashes found with a possible 'incense' cup, and of an urn found in the 17th century with hair and ashes inside, suggest human cremations. No evidence of buildings was discovered, until an excavation at Renfrew Road in 1986 found post and stake holes of the type associated with dwellings. People would have lived here in wattle and daub round houses with thatched roofs.

Bronze metalsmiths also seem to have worked here. Over 25 pieces of Bronze Age metalwork have been associated with Kingston Hill, including a splendid bronze palstave, a number of socketed axes, a sword-hilt, and several spearhead blades. Cakes of copper and ingots were found there, as were broken pieces of bronze, presumably for recycling, which suggest a metalsmith's hoard of raw materials. A casting mould was also recorded, though it has since disappeared.

The Kingston Hill settlement could have been a major metalworking centre, supplying bronze goods both locally and further afield in the late Bronze Age. It is even possible that the site, like others in the middle and lower Thames Valley, was enclosed by earthworks for defence, though the area has been much too disturbed by ploughing and gravel extraction for any traces to remain. There is no evidence that this settlement continued when, after the 8th century BC, iron grew gradually more popular in the Thames Valley. The hillfort on Wimbledon Common ('Caesar's Camp') might have become the main focus for the local population, or there may be an Iron Age settlement eleswhere on Kingston Hill, waiting to be discovered.

Material evidence of the pre-Roman Iron Age is scarce in the Greater London area as a whole, and in Kingston few iron artefacts have been found in the river. Some Iron Age pottery has been found at Eden Walk, and pottery and a lump of smelted iron presumed to be Iron Age were found at Fairfield West. But the borough is fortunate to have a major Iron Age settlement site near the Hogsmill at Old Malden. Part of this was discovered in the late 1940s, when a local headmaster started excavating on allotments in the Manor Drive area. He found a site surrounded by a ditch with at least five round houses. A study of one hut showed that people lived within wattle and daub walls about four metres in diameter, with a gravel floor and a hearth, and a thatched roof supported by a central post. It had an outside ditch. Pottery finds date the site to the early Iron Age (c500-300 BC), and there was also evidence of Roman occupation. In 1991, when nearby Percy Gardens was excavated, middle and late Iron Age pottery was found in connection with a wide bank and ditch that curved round the hillside, overlooking the Hogsmill river. This seems to be a part of, or a later extension to, the previously discovered site, and suggests a large, defended hilltop settlement, like Caesar's Camp. Another mid-Iron Age settlement has been found not far away, at Alpine Avenue, Tolworth.

There was probably more settlement in the area. Though the Thames Valley was not as prosperous in the Iron Age, because iron ore was in greater supply than copper and tin, and many areas no longer needed to import so much ore *via* the Thames, there was still some trade along the river. By this time local trackways had also developed, linking the Kingston area to nearby settlement along the Thames, to the Downs, and along the ridgeway to the hillfort on Wimbledon Common. It is likely that farmers continued to till the soil and fish the river at Kingston, and that there was some ironworking using ore from the Weald, or from local deposits at Weybridge.

By the time the Romans cast predatory glances at Britain towards the end of the first millennium BC, much of the British landscape was already laid out in fields and settlement. Kingston was not a place of any great importance at the end of the Iron Age — it was not the seat of power of a major Celtic chief, and there is little evidence that it was still a centre of religious ritual. But it already had a long history of human activity and settlement. Even before the Romans came, it was 'on the map'.

15

ABOVE LEFT: A Palaeolithic hand axe found in the Thames at Kingston. CENTRE, RIGHT & LEFT: Mesolithic and early Neolithic tools: a characteristic long 'Thames Pick' from the river at Kingston and other, shorter adzes. BELOW: Neolithic axes in polished flint, three of several from the Thames at Kingston. (All KM) Sometimes prestige objects, some have not been used; one (left) imitates contemporary bronze axes.

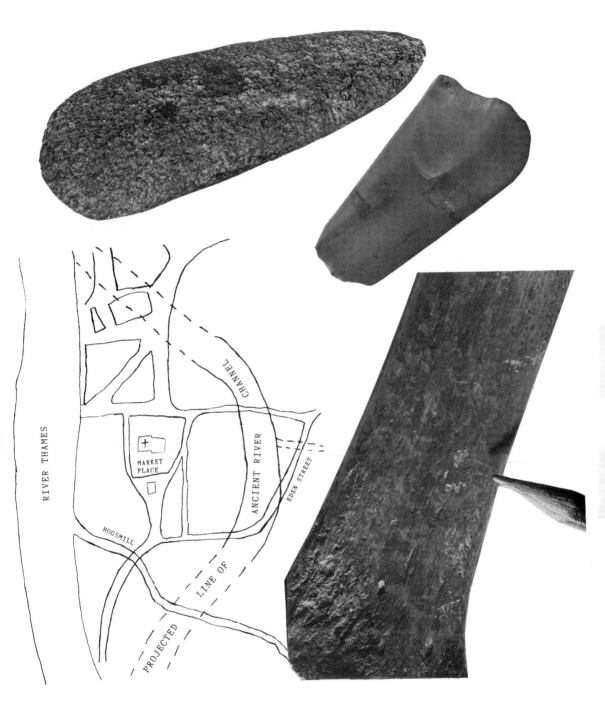

ABOVE: Polished greenstone axes made in the Neolithic 'factory' at Great Langdale, Cumbria, (KM) imported to Kingston *via* the Thames, and higly valued; one (left) badly eroded by water. LEFT: The Eden Walk area, showing suggested line of prehistoric river channel which made today's town centre an island. (TE, after PF&S) RIGHT: A female thigh bone from Eden Walk, c1770 BC, (KM) whose owner was 6ft tall. The cut marks show the flesh was probably hacked off after death, possibly at a riverside holy place.

OPPOSITE ABOVE: Eden Walk: Neolithic pottery; antlers (the cut mark shows the lower antler was intended for a pick), and an early Bronze Age skull, the sides of the head not properly fused together. BELOW: Late Bronze Age remains from Coombe Hill, c900 BC, the cups and bowls flint-tempered from local gravels. The copper cake and bronze awl, axehead, and scraps of a sword and spearhead show that bronze working took place here. RIGHT: These bronze swords and spearhead, also from the Thames at Kingston, may have been battered or twisted to render them unusable, before being 'offered' to the river. (All KM) ABOVE: Bronze Age metalwork from the Thames at Kingston. The sword and rapier have bolts to attach the blades to bone or wood handles. There are also sword chapes, a knife, socketed axehead, spearhead and looped palstave. BELOW: Reconstruction of the Old Malden (Percy Gardens) Iron Age settlement, c400 BC, showing characteristic wattle and daub round houses. (Both KM)

19

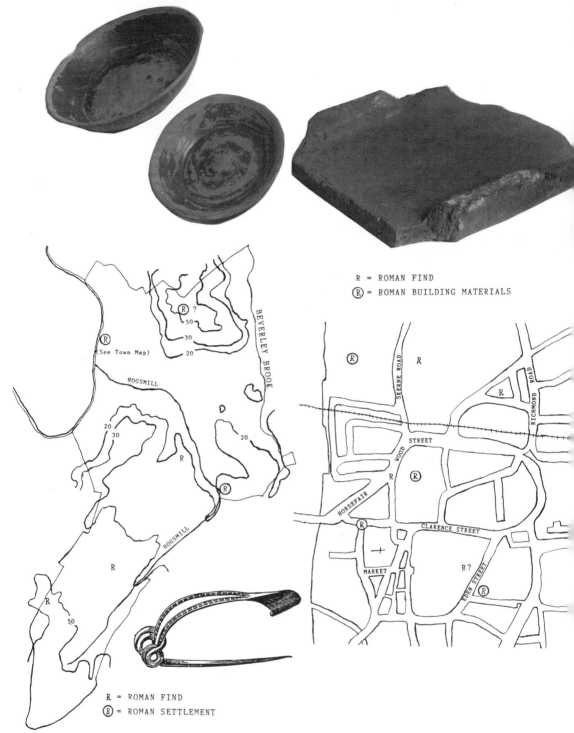

R = ROMAN FIND
Ⓡ = ROMAN BUILDING MATERIALS

BEVERLEY BROOK

(See Town Map)

HOGSMILL

HOGSMILL

SKERNE ROAD

RICHMOND ROAD

WOOD STREET

HORSEFAIR

CLARENCE STREET

MARKET

EDEN STREET

R = ROMAN FIND
Ⓡ = ROMAN SETTLEMENT

ABOVE: A Roman roof tile and pottery from the Electricity Power Station site. (KM) Maps of Kingston's Roman finds, LEFT: Kingston & environs, RIGHT: town map. (TE) CENTRE: 'Biden's brooch' — a brass Roman bow brooch, c50-100 AD, discovered, according to Biden, in Canbury Fields in the early 19th century, near a burial ground. (B)

Coins and Questions

When Julius Caesar first invaded Britain in 55 BC, the country was considered utterly remote. Kingston was certainly settled in Roman times, but little is known about it. However, modern advances in historical scholarship and in archaeology modify some of the more extravagant Victorian notions about Roman Kingston.

The Victorian local historian W. D. Biden claimed that Kingston was the place where Caesar crossed the Thames during his second invasion of Britain in 54 BC. After landing in Kent and defeating a substantial British force under Cassivellaunus, Caesar crossed the Thames against strong opposition and captured Cassivellaunus' base. However, there is really no evidence that Kingston was where the Romans forded the river. All Caesar tells us is that he 'led his army to the Thames in order to enter Cassivellaunus' territory. The river is fordable at one point only, and even there with difficulty'. The bank and river bed had sharp stakes stuck in them to defend the crossing, and Caesar's infantry had only their heads above water. We are also told that Cassivellaunus' territory was about 75 miles from the sea.

This information is simply not enough to allow us to pinpoint Caesar's crossing place. Archaeologists have discovered no certain trace of the defensive stakes; nor is there any conclusive evidence of prehistoric fords. The Thames was probably fordable in several places during the Iron Age, including Kingston, but current opinion now favours somewhere nearer central London, possibly Westminster, as Caesar's crossing place. If the Romans knew that the Thames was the border of Cassivellaunus' territory, they probably marched along beside the river and forded it at the first opportunity. Caesar's apparently erroneous statement that the river was fordable at one point only should be taken in the context of his march, meaning that he crossed the river at the first decent ford he came to on his way upriver from Kent — probably closer than Kingston.

Despite his victories in 54 BC, Caesar did not conquer Britain. It was not until AD 43, when the Emperor Claudius organized another invasion, that the Romans came to stay. During the century between the two invasions, the political situation in Britain was confused. Tribal groups established chiefdoms or kingdoms over quite wide areas, and there was conflict between them. In the south-east, the Thames region appears to have been a border zone; the river was seen as a boundary, the land on either side of it often in dispute. The settlements in the Thames valley were not particularly large or important; the main tribal centres were elsewhere.

Kingston was perhaps originally part of the territory of a local sub-ruler, but fell under the influence of the Atrebates, a major tribal grouping whose power was centred on Silchester. Then in the early 1st century AD the area came under the control of the Catuvellauni, the dominant tribe just north of the Thames, who extended their power south and east during this period. The Roman invasion of AD 43 brought with it more settled conditions. The south east in general seems to have acquiesced in the Roman conquest, and did not have to be strongly fortified. Life on the land in the Kingston area probably went on much as before, but (except during Boudicca's attack on London in AD 61) more peacefully.

21

Kingston was not an important place under the Romans. London soon became the major town in the south east, both as an administrative centre and a commercial port. Good roads were laid down, and London became the hub of a network of communications. No major Roman road passed through Kingston. Stane Street ran a few miles to the east, linking Chichester to London. To the north and west of Kingston ran the road that linked London to Silchester, capital of the Atrebates. This road crossed the Thames at Staines, and from the name of the settlement, Pontibus, it seems that bridges were built there. However, though not on a main through route, Kingston was linked into the Roman road network. There was possibly a Roman road from Putney to Kingston, over Kingston Hill, and perhaps another from Sheen to Ham, running through what today is Richmond Park. It is also possible that a Roman route ran through or near Kingston joining Ewell, on Stane Street, to the Silchester road. If so, it must have crossed the river, either at a ford or a ferry crossing. It is usually assumed that there was a ford at Kingston, but this is only an assumption: we do not know the depth of the water or the configuration of the banks in Roman times.

As far as is known there was never a Roman bridge across the Thames at Kingston. Biden, following the claims of the antiquary Thomas Gale in the early 18th century, says that Claudius built one, but Gale gave no evidence for his assertion. No archaeological trace of a bridge at Kingston earlier than the 12th century has yet been found, and it is doubtful whether the Romans would have deemed the Kingston river crossing important enough to warrant the time and effort, though it cannot be entirely ruled out.

Roman London probably had direct administrative control of its immediate environs and overshadowed a wide surrounding area because of its central importance to the government and economy of the whole British province. The other Roman 'towns' in what is now south-west London and Surrey were mostly small and insignificant. Posting stations were established at intervals along the Roman roads, to provide facilities for those on official business, and settlements often developed around these. There were posting stations at Staines, on the Silchester Road, and possibly at Merton and Dorking on Stane Street. There were also Romano-British settlements at Ewell and Croydon, and at Wandsworth and Putney. Roman burials and a coin hoard have been found at Putney Vale. Staines was a larger settlement, and there might have been a fort there, but even Staines lacked the formal lay-out associated with important Roman towns like St Albans or Bath. No villas have so far been found close to London, though there were several further out in Surrey, such as at Ashtead.

There was certainly settlement in and around what is now Kingston in Roman times. It used to be thought that Romano-British activity was concentrated on Kingston Hill and on the Canbury area, but recent archaeological discoveries show that it was also present in the modern town centre. This probably mainly represents a native population adopting Roman fashions in pottery and sometimes in building, but partly it may represent incoming Roman entrepreneurs or ex-soldiers.

Documentary evidence suggests that there was a Romano-British settlement — or settlements — of some sort on Kingston Hill, though Biden's assertion that it was a town called Thamesa can be discounted. Biden's claim was made on the basis of a mistake made by Thomas Gale, when he was trying to interpret the confusing information in an 8th century book called the *Ravenna Cosmography*. He applied the name probably meant for the river Thames to a place, and identified it with Kingston.

However, we have other evidence that links Kingston Hill with Roman finds. The 16th century topographer, John Leland, wrote in his *Itinerary* (c1545): 'The olde monumentes of the toun of Kingeston be founde yn the declyuing doune from Come parke toward the galoys [gallows]; and there yn ploughyng and digging have very often beene founde fundation of waulles of houses, and diverse coynes of brasse, sylver and gold, with Romaine inscriptions, and paintid yerthen pottes; and yn one in Cardinal Wolsey's tyme was found much Romayne mony of sylver, and plates of silver to coyne, and masses to bete into plates to coyne, and chaynes of sylver'.

Uncertainty as to the extent of Coombe Park and the position of the gallows in the early 16th century makes it impossible to say exactly which part of Kingston Hill these foundations and coins were found on; they could either have belonged to the western side of the hill, between the summit and what is now the Kingsnympton Estate, where the gallows stood by 1637, or to the eastern, or Coombe, side of the hill. Leland's reports are not always accurate but, as he gives us an account of finds made within the last 20 years or so of when he was writing, there is no reason to doubt that ancient coins and foundations were discovered, and the balance of probability is that these were Roman. Unfortunately, no trace remains. Biden's suggestion of a mint, based on Leland's interpretation, is implausible; there was a London mint in the early 3rd century, and its site is still unknown, but it is unlikely to have been 12 miles outside London, off the main road network and away from a military base.

Further antiquities were found locally in the 17th and 18th centuries and, though the 'Roman' urns discovered near the (Kingsnympton) gallows are now usually considered to be Bronze Age, the coins mentioned by Edmund Gibson in his edition of Camden's *Britannia* (1695) sound genuinely Roman. Gibson says that at Coombe Neville 'have been found Medals and Coins of several of the Roman Emperors, especially of Diocletian, the Maximinians, Maximus, Constantine the Great &c'. These coins of the late 3rd and early 4th century AD, which have disappeared since Gibson's day, may come from the same area as the remains described by Leland, or represent a different focus of activity.

Place-name evidence also suggests that there was a Romano-British settlement of some sort on Kingston Hill. On the south-east slope of the hill, near the present day junction of Coombe Road and Galsworthy Road, lies an area which was described in mediaeval documents as 'Waleport', an Old English name meaning 'town of the Britons'. The Anglo-Saxons would have used such a name to denote a native settlement, as distinct from a Saxon one, though whether the settlement described was ruined, or still in existence in the Saxons' own time, is unclear. 'Waleport' may represent Leland's buildings, or a later settlement, either on or near the site of Leland's buildings, or distinct from them. Recent excavations at Kingston Hospital, in the general vicinity of 'Waleport', found no evidence of Romano-British occupation, so the precise site of the 'town of the Britons' remains to be discovered.

Nothing seems to have survived of the remains noted in past centuries, and little Roman material (only a fragment of mosaic from Coombe Hill) has been discovered in modern times. This makes it impossible to say what sort of settlement, or settlements, existed in Roman times on Kingston/Coombe Hill, and when. There could have been a single focus of settlement, based on a complex of romanized buildings. If the coins Gibson mentioned came from this, it would have existed in the late 3rd/early 4th century, though for how long and until when it survived remains a mystery. The

Roman-style buildings may well have been a villa or inn, and a village of wattle and daub huts in the native style could have developed near it. The romanized building could have been the temple of a water deity associated with one of the many springs that rise on the hill. In the latter case, the coins, instead of being hoards buried near someone's home in troubled times, would have been offerings to the local god or goddess, and the silver plate and chains possibly part of the priest's headdress. Alternatively, there could have been more than one focus of settlement such as a romanized villa or temple near the top of the hill, later abandoned, and a British village existing independently on the lower slopes, established in late Roman times. This is speculation; we just do not know.

Nor do we know whether there is any connection between the settlement on the hill and the Romano-British presence that has come to light in the Canbury area. In the early 19th century, human burials, assumed to be Roman, were discovered in Canbury Field, near the old gas works, between Richmond Road and Skerne (previously Lower Ham) Road. An account of the burials written in 1832 mentions 'several layers of bodies' and that the skeletons 'occupied a considerable portion of the fields'. The skeletons, buried with pieces of broken pottery and some ornaments, were apparently those of young males, and it was thought that they were of Romans killed in battle. None of the finds now survives, and Victorian antiquaries, like those of previous centuries, tended to call all ancient discoveries 'Roman', so it is impossible to say for sure to which period the burials belong. However, one brooch, which apparently came from near the bodies, and of which a drawing survives, looks like a mid-late 1st century type, and indicates an early Roman date for some of the burials.

That there was Romano-British occupation near to this possible burial ground is suggested by finds made on the Electricity Power Station site (Downhall Road) of Roman pottery and of a roof tile of the type manufactured (probably not later than the early 2nd century AD) at the Ashtead Villa 'factory'. Roman pottery has also been found in Canbury Passage and in Wood Street. The Canbury Field area was referred to in 14th century documents as 'Walehulle', an Old English name meaning 'hill of the Britons'; this name reinforces the notion of a Romano-British presence in the area.

There was also Romano-British settlement spread quite widely over the modern town centre of Kingston. Pieces of Roman tile were found near the junction of Thames Street and Clarence Street, and bits of Roman tile and brick, including a fragment of flue tile, have been discovered on the site of the new Bentall Centre. The best evidence, however, comes from an excavation at a site on the corner of Eden Street and Lady Booth Road, which took place in 1989. This revealed an ancient water channel, now silted up: perhaps a stream that flowed west from the Fairfield area towards the river, and fed into the prehistoric eastern arm of the Thames previously discovered at Eden Walk.

A large amount of Roman material was found in the water channel: different types of pottery, some coarse ware, some of fine quality; animal bone, including part of the skeleton of a horse or cow; building material; bronze jewellery, including a child's bracelet of braided wire; iron objects such as nails; and about 350 bronze coins, mainly of the 4th century. The building material included a roof tile; a flue tile of the sort associated with underfloor heating systems; brick; fragments of painted wall plaster, and pieces of stone blocks and tiles not native to the Kington area, but imported. There was also a floor tile bearing the marks of a hobnailed boot, where someone had walked across it before it was dry.

No evidence of foundations was discovered, but the lack of abrasion on the bits of tile and pottery suggests that they were thrown or fell into the stream quite close to where they were used, so we may imagine they came from a building or buildings near the bank of the water course. The indications are that the building was substantial, and the possibility of a villa cannot be ruled out. Alternatively, there could have been an inn to service a Thames crossing, and/or a local shrine. The coins deposited in the stream were mostly of low value, and seem to have been dropped over time. Some could have been lost during trading, or paying for services. However, a number were deliberately defaced, which suggests that they were thrown into the water as offerings to a deity. People might have dropped them for good luck for a safe journey before they crossed the old eastern arm of the Thames, either on their way to dwellings on the gravel island, or on their way across the main river. Shrines were often found near a river crossing point. Some rolled and folded strips of lead also discovered at Lady Booth Road could be tablets inscribed with requests or curses for the attention of the presiding deity.

It would be pleasing to make a connection between this site and an altar, now in Kingston Museum, which came from a garden in Eden Street. The inscription on it reads: 'To the goddess Fortune and the spirits of the Emperors'. One can imagine people invoking the goddess, either before crossing the water, or before a gambling game at an inn. But no-one knows which garden the altar came from and because it carries no specifically local reference, no-one knows if it originates from Kingston.

On present evidence there was a Romano-British settlement near the river at Kingston, close to a Thames crossing place. This village boasted some substantial, romanized building, and probably some traditional wattle and daub round houses. Elsewhere within the area defined by the modern borough of Kingston there was certainly continuity of settlement from the pre-Roman Iron Age. In the Hogsmill Valley, the different types of pottery and the coins found at the Old Malden enclosed settlement show that the site was occupied from the Iron Age through Roman times. Most of its villagers probably lived throughout in small thatched huts, though it is possible that someone of higher rank or greater wealth built a more fashionable, Roman-style, house. Nearby, at Barwell Court, Chessington, another Iron Age to Romano-British site has been discovered, possibly a farmstead where iron working took place.

Roman Kingston poses more questions than answers. However, we can think in terms of a Romano-British settlement, involving some substantial Roman-style building, on the slopes of Kingston/Coombe Hill; some substantial Roman-style building in the modern town centre, off Eden Street, possibly associated with a river crossing; and Romano-British occupation in humbler dwellings scattered across a wide area by the Thames, from the town centre to Canbury, where burials probably took place. Then there was the village at Old Malden, and another at Chessington, and perhaps farmsteads elsewhere. Nothing in the area would have looked like a modern town, but the region would have been busy and prosperous. Its inhabitants grew crops and raised cattle, and were visited by the traders, travellers and tax collectors who took advantage of the 'pax romana' to cross the river and follow the roads in a relative security that held good throughout many people's lifetimes.

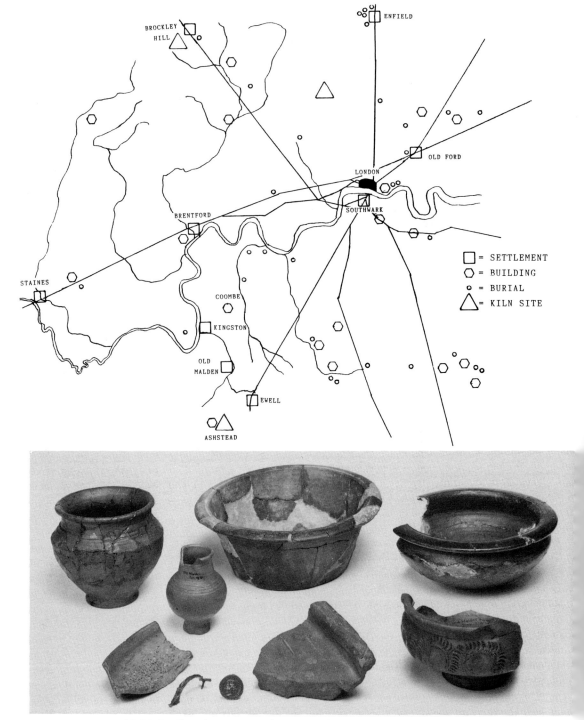

ABOVE: The Kingston area in Roman times. (SB) BELOW: A selection of Roman pottery, a coin and a brooch from the Old Malden settlement. (KM)

26

LEFT: Roman altar from a garden in Eden Street: 'To the Goddess Fortune and the spirits of the Emperors'. RIGHT: An early Roman thistle brooch from Kingston, c43-45 AD. BELOW: Close-up of some of the Lady Booth Road coins: 4th century bronze coins of Constantine the Great and his dynasty, including some barbarous copies. (All KM)

ABOVE: Kingston 'Coronation Stone'. (CB) BELOW: Early Saxon grave goods: urns and cups, shield bosses and spears from the cemetery at Mitcham. (KM) The first Saxons at Kingston would have had similar pots and weapons.

'That Famous Place'?

If Kingston is famous for anything, it is famous as the coronation place of the Anglo-Saxon kings. Outside the Guildhall, surrounded by smart blue railings, stands a hefty lump of sandstone on which, according to tradition, seven Saxon kings were crowned. On the plinth which supports the 'coronation stone' are the names of these rulers and the dates of their coronations. The kings listed are Edward the Elder, who was consecrated in 900; Athelstan, 925; Edmund, 939; Eadred, 946; Eadwig, 956; Edward the Martyr, 975; and Aethelred the Unready, 979.

The tradition that kings were crowned at Kingston was already established among the townsfolk in the 16th century, and reached its highpoint in Victorian and Edwardian times. In 1850, the 'coronation stone' was rescued from obscurity and publicly inaugurated as an historic monument. In 1902, Kingston celebrated with much pageantry both the thousandth anniversary of the coronation of Edward the Elder, and the coronation of King Edward VII. The whole town was decorated, and the coronation stone garlanded with flowers.

But how good is the evidence that seven kings were crowned locally? The sources given by Daniel Lysons in the *Environs of London* (1792), and by Manning and Bray in their *History and Antiquities of the County of Surrey* (1804), and accepted in the early 20th century by the famous local historian, Finny, are the *Anglo-Saxon Chronicle*, the 12th century chronicles of William of Malmesbury, Henry of Huntingdon, Roger of Hovedon, and Ralph de Diceto, the chronicle of Johannes Brompton (*fl* c1436), and the chronicle of Raphael Holinshed (1578). Though at first sight these seem an impressive array of 'ancient authorities', one sees at a closer look that equal importance is given to sources of unequal value. No reliance can be placed on 16th century chronicles like Holinshed's as a source for events that took place 600 years before, nor on an uncritical late 14th or early 15th century compilation like Brompton's *Chronicle*.

The *Anglo-Saxon Chronicle*, which refers to Kingston in early texts dated c1000 and c1050, is a genuinely important source for 10th century events. It only mentions the consecrations of two kings at Kingston, Athelstan and Aethelred the Unready. Of the 12th century sources mentioned by Finny, Malmesbury, Huntingdon and Hovedon follow the *Anglo-Saxon Chronicle*. This, according to Finny's sources, leaves the other five Kingston coronations resting on the word of Ralph de Diceto (*d* c1202), a late 12th century dean of St Paul's. His chronicle for the period before 1154 is based on Sigebert of Gembloux and Henry of Huntingdon, who only gives two Kingston consecrations. There is no suggestion that Ralph used any early manuscripts, and any information found only in his chronicle cannot be relied on. Like most medieval chroniclers, he added his own embellishments, and it is hard to escape the conclusion that he made up some of the Kingston consecrations. He was 'filling in the gaps' — assuming that, because a few kings were crowned there, a whole series was.

However, there is other evidence, more reliable than Ralph, that another king, Eadred, and possibly a further one, Eadwig, were consecrated at Kingston. This comes from the chronicle usually attributed to the monk Florence of Worcester (*d* 1118), though it may have been a later compilation. This chronicle appears to incorporate a version of the *Anglo-Saxon Chronicle* slightly different from those that have survived independently, and which may have given more details than our versions. Florence says that Eadred and Eadwig, as well as Athelstan and Aethelred, were inaugurated 'in Cingestune'. In Eadred's case there is also the evidence of a charter of 946, by which Eadred granted land in Warkton, Northampton, to Wulfric. This says: 'And then he, the king, constantly presented gifts to many in the king's residence which is called Kingston, where also the consecration was performed'. As this charter was preserved at Worcester, where Florence wrote, it is possible that this, rather than any different version of the *Anglo-Saxon Chronicle*, was the source of Florence's statement that Eadred was consecrated at Kingston, and that Florence added Eadwig to the list on his own account. Unfortunately, the charter of 946 has been destroyed, so we do not know whether it is genuine.

This means that there is solid documentary evidence that two Kings, Athelstan and Aethelred, were consecrated at Kingston, plus Eadred if the 946 charter is genuine. That is not to say that others might not have been crowned there. One cannot argue that, because the *Anglo-Saxon Chronicle* does not mention Kingston for the other consecrations, they definitely took place elsewhere. Nor can one say that, because Kingston was named twice as a coronation place, it was always the site used unless otherwise stated. It is possible that the *Anglo-Saxon Chronicle* only mentioned Kingston in connection with Athelstan and Aethelred because it was an unusual place for kings to be consecrated. The only other coronation site named in the *Chronicle* is Bath, where Edgar was crowned (maybe for the second time) in 973 to celebrate the greater degree of 'imperial' control he had recently gained over kings of the north and west, and it has been suggested that Bath was specially chosen for the splendour of its Roman buildings. If so, this also suggests that there was not felt to be any exclusive sacredness about Kingston. There may have been several different places which the Saxon kings, whose style of government was itinerant, considered suitable for consecrations for reasons of holiness, geographical convenience or political expediency.

However, it is still significant that two or three kings were consecrated at Kingston. The reasons for its suitability lie in what happened during the 500 years between the collapse of Roman authority in the early 5th century, and the dominance of the Anglo-Saxon kingdom of Wessex in the 10th.

The earliest Saxon settlement in the Kingston area is likely to have been peaceful. In the early 5th century, after Roman officials and troops had left, local Romano-British nobility organized defence. They adopted official Roman practice, and hired Germanic mercenaries, allowing groups of Saxons to settle with their families in return for providing defence. The 5th and 6th century Anglo-Saxon remains found at Mucking, Essex, and at Mitcham in Surrey could be of settlers brought in by the British authorities to defend London.

Local evidence of Saxon settlement as early as the 5th century is nearby at Ham, where a bowl of 5th century type was found in a Saxon sunken floored hut, apparently one of a group. Early Saxon pottery (possibly 6th century) has been found in Kingston itself, in the Eden Street area. There are indications that the British authorities remained in control in the London region in the early 6th century, and the continuity of settlement at the Saxon sites of Mucking and Mitcham suggests that the earliest Saxons remained friendly. For a while, the native British communities probably co-existed amicably with Kingston's first Saxons.

Later incomers may have taken land by force, or settled by local agreement on land that stood vacant or abandoned. The native population had fallen by the 6th century, partly because of plague, and there was room for new settlement. In Kingston, the Roman style building at Lady Booth Road had given way to a Saxon settlement that produced rough, grass tempered pottery, but the inn or whatever the structure was had ceased to be inhabited before the Saxons arrived. The trappings of Roman civilisation had fallen away during the 5th century: coins no longer circulated, pottery factories ceased production, trade contracted and houses with heating systems could no longer be maintained. At first, the Britons and Saxons formed distinct, separate settlements in the Kingston area yet, as time went on, intermarriage, local trade, and a growing mutual awareness of each other's customs and techniques led to a cultural growing together of native and incomer.

At some point in the 6th century, political control of the area round Kingston passed from British to Saxon hands. From an early stage, the Saxons of the Surrey region either took over existing territorial divisions or laid down boundaries of their own. Provincial territories or 'regiones', equivalent in size to several of the later administrative divisions known as 'hundreds', were established as the units of local government. There were perhaps four such regiones in the area that is now Surrey, each with its own administrative centre to which dues and services from the surrounding settlements were owed. Kingston was the central place of a surrounding 'regio' which probably included the later hundreds of Kingston, Elmbridge, Copthorne and Effingham. This regio might originally have been an independent Saxon chiefdom, but soon it became part of a larger political entity.

Kingston probably became part of Surrey quite early on. Surrey itself was originally the 'Southern Region' of a wider area, possibly of a 6th century kingdom of Middlesex, or of a Thames Valley chiefdom linking land south of the river with the Sonning and Reading areas. In the 7th century, what is now north east Surrey was disputed between several Anglo-Saxon kingdoms as the powerful rulers of Wessex, Kent and Mercia fought for control of the south bank of the Thames. Kingston must have been under Kentish control in 666, when Egbert of Kent founded a monastery at Chertsey, but by the 670s it was probably part of the sub-kingdom of Surrey, ruled by Frithuwald under Mercian overlordship, and by the 680s it seems to have passed to the West Saxons. During the 8th century it was again under Mercian control, but from 825, when Kent, Surrey, Sussex and Essex submitted to Egbert, King of the West Saxons, Kingston was part of Wessex.

What was going on in Kingston itself during these years? Archaeology has revealed surprisingly little evidence for a place where Saxon kings were crowned. There are certainly signs of Anglo-Saxon settlement dotted about here and there. Grass tempered pottery of the 6th to 8th century has been found at 76, Eden Street and at Eden Walk, as well as at Lady Booth Road. A recent excavation in the Bittoms unearthed some 8th to 10th century pottery in what was probably a rubbish pit, and some fragments of clay loomweights were found nearby in what might have been a small sunken building where, presumably, weaving took place. These remains may represent industrial activity on the outskirts of a settlement on nearby (unexcavated) higher ground, where County Hall now stands. A late Saxon boundary ditch has also been found at 29, Thames Street, running at right angles from the road to the river; it

31

· probably delineated a field. The remains of a 10th century pot were found here, and some late Saxon grit and shell tempered pottery was also discovered at Eden Walk. This points to late Saxon settlement on the gravel island in the Thames where the modern town centre stands.

No evidence of dwellings has yet been found, though these would have existed. Saxon structures have so far proved elusive in Surrey generally. They were probably either ploughed out in medieval times, or unwittingly destroyed by 19th century developers. Most Saxon buildings were of wood, and the sunken floors and post holes that remain could easily have been missed by the Victorian builder. Evidence of structures may yet be found, and just a few small huts would transform the meagre archaeological picture.

Apart from the pottery, a few iron artefacts have been discovered locally. A heavy barbed javelin was found at the Kingston end of the Hogsmill: maybe this was carried by a 5th century Saxon mercenary. A beautiful pattern-welded spearhead from the Thames looks like the prized possession of a 7th or 8th century warrior, while a pattern-welded scramasaxe of the same date was someone's all-purpose chopping knife. A wooden canoe, tree-ring dated to the 9th or 10th century, has also been recovered from the Thames at East Molesey. Finally, a fragment of a stone cross, found in the parish church, has been dated on stylistic grounds to the 8th century.

If the material remains disappointing, maybe we expect too much. Because Kingston is now a town, and we know that there was first a place called Kingston in Saxon times, it would be easy to imagine that Saxon Kingston was also a town. One might expect to find evidence from early Saxon times of the continued existence of a nucleated village that grew into a town, which was important enough by the 10th century for kings to be crowned in it. Early writers' anachronistic use of the word 'town' when discussing Kingston's origins reinforce this way of thinking.

Saxon Kingston was not a town, and even in the 10th century it was not necessarily a nucleated village. Throughout the early and mid-Saxon period it was normal for settlement to be scattered widely — a few huts here, a farmstead there, maybe a larger concentration of buildings somewhere else — but all likely to move to a different site if the wooden structures needed replacing, or the stench from the rubbish pits became too great, or if the land was flooded, or attacked. Thus different parts of an area were settled at different times, and it was only from the 10th and 11th centuries that the nucleated village on one site became usual. There were towns in Anglo-Saxon England: survivors of Roman Britain like Canterbury or Bath, ports like London, which revived from about 700 AD, and from the 9th and 10th centuries fortified 'burghs' like Guildford, established for purposes of defence and commerce, and often the site of mints. But there is no evidence that Kingston was ever a burgh, or even a large concentration of people. It was a rural settlement, and in Domesday Book (1086) it is described as a vill with 86 villans and 14 bordars.

However, it was a place of local importance. From the 9th century, it was to the kings of Wessex what it had doubtless been previously to the kings of Mercia: a Royal 'vill', or 'tun', the local administrative centre of a Royal estate. That this was so does not, however, automatically follow from its place-name, even though at first sight it looks as if it might. The name 'Kingston' comes from the Old English words 'cyninges' (later 'cynges') and 'tun', meaning 'king's estate'. The mere fact that a place is called Kingston does not necessarily mean that it was a Royal vill. A recent study of Kingston place-names shows that most modern places called Kingston did not so function, and were remarkable for their lack of significance. Yet Kingston upon Thames does seem to have fulfilled the administrative functions of a king's tun.

The estate owned by Saxon kings at Kingston was extensive: Norbiton and Surbiton mark its north eastern and south eastern boundaries. They were the north and south 'beretuns', or granaries, where the grain from the outlying parts of the estate were stored. In mid-Saxon times, food rent from the estate was paid in kind to the collecting centre, and was used to maintain the Royal household when it visited. If it was not needed for this, it might be sold, and a market develop. Even when food rents ceased to be an obligation in late Saxon times, the vill continued to be important as a centre of local government. The Royal official, the reeve, at Kingston collected the dues owed to the King from all the land in the surrounding hundred. He also supervised justice and the payment of fines at the hundred court.

The King probably had a residence at Kingston. There is as yet no evidence for Finny's assertion that there was a 'royal palace' in the Bittoms, but it is quite likely that somewhere in Kingston there was a large timber hall, a 'palace' in Saxon terms, with outlying buildings, which could be supplemented by tents or other temporary structures if there was a need to accommodate more people for a special occasion. Saxon kings were itinerant: they moved from place to place to show off their power to their subjects, and usually preferred their country estates to towns. While in residence, they might hold a council of leading nobles and churchmen to solve disputes and discuss action. Land grants were often issued from Royal vills, justice done and wrongdoers imprisoned.

We first hear of Kingston as a royal meeting place in 838, when a Council of Kingston was held by King Egbert of Wessex and his son, Aethelwulf, under-king of Kent, and attended by churchmen. In the document which records this council, Kingston is described as 'that famous place which is called Kingston in the region of Surrey', which implies that it was already well-established as a Royal vill, and had probably been the site of previous gatherings. Indeed, as 'tun' place-names are considered a late development, Kingston may have been known earlier by a different name. At this council, Egbert tried to establish good relations with the See of Canterbury by restoring to Christchurch, Canterbury, possession of land at Malling, Sussex, and by promising to allow free elections of abbots and abbesses to the Kentish monastic communities. From then on the West Saxon monarchy enjoyed Canterbury's support.

Some of the priests and deacons who witnessed the 838 agreement at Kingston may have belonged to the staff of the minster church here. Though the first Saxon settlers in Surrey were pagans, they were converted to Christianity in the 7th and 8th centuries. The bishops and kings who took the lead in the process of conversion, established public churches, or minsters, staffed by communities of clergy who organized the religious life of a wide surrounding area. Minsters, often based on Royal vills, acted as the ecclesiastical centres for large parishes. The large size of Kingston's medieval parish suggests that Kingston was the site of an early minster, and the surviving cross fragment indicates an 8th century church, though not necessarily a stone one. It is possible that the stone chapel of St Mary, which once stood alongside the parish church, preserved an originally pre-Conquest stone structure of unknown date. The church in which Athelstan was consecrated in 925 could well have been of wood.

Christian churches were often founded on or near pagan sites, and it is likely that, before its church was consecrated, Kingston was a centre of pagan worship. When the Saxons first arrived, they established the worship of their own gods in places that looked to them holy, and the island site at Kingston, accessible due to the river-crossing place, yet remote because surrounded by water and marshes, must have seemed ideal. It is even possible that the great sandstone boulder now known as the 'coronation stone' was already on the island, having in the past been used as a marker stone for the Thames crossing, and that this added to the appearance of 'sacredness'. The island at Kingston might also have seemed especially hallowed, both to pagan and Christian, because it was near the head of the tide on the river. This apparently was also the case at Scone, where Scottish coronations took place, and may have been one reason why Kingston was considered a suitable place for Royal consecrations.

At a time when pagan Danish armies invaded England, Kingston may have suffered attack in the 880s, when a Danish army came to the Thames and perhaps destroyed the monastery at Chertsey. By the early 10th century, when King Athelstan was consecrated at Kingston, the Danes in the south had been defeated and their colonies annexed to Wessex. Athelstan, the grandson of Alfred the Great, succeeded his father, Edward the Elder, as king of Wessex in 924. He had been brought up at the Mercian court, and was also accepted independently by the Mercian nobles as their king. The *Anglo-Saxon Chronicle* tells us for the year 924 that: 'In this year King Edward died at Farndon in Mercia . . . and Athelstan was chosen by the Mercians as King, and consecrated at Kingston'. His coronation, possibly on 4 September 925, was a splendid occasion that emphasized his authority as king over the peoples of both Wessex and Mercia.

Exactly why Kingston was chosen is unclear. As a Royal vill and the site of a minster, it was obviously suitable, but then so were many other places. Maybe its natural position close to the head of the tide gave it the edge, or perhaps, if the Archbishop of Canterbury performed the ceremony, it was chosen to propitiate Canterbury. Archbishops of Canterbury who, by performing the consecrations bestowed the blessing of the whole southern Church on the new king, might feel it beneath their dignity to travel to the heartlands of Winchester or Lichfield diocese, but be content with somewhere closer to their own sphere of influence. Another possibility is that Athelstan, whose accession in Wessex had not been straightforward, and who had been threatened by a plot at Winchester soon after his accession, wished to be consecrated at a safe distance from any opposition, and Kingston, though in Wessex, was near enough to Mercia to be readily reached by support from there.

Before Athelstan entered the church at Kingston for the religious ceremony, he was ritually acclaimed and enthroned by the nobility in what is now the market place. According to William of Malmesbury, he was slender and of medium height, with flaxen hair 'beautifully mingled with gold threads'. Inside the church, the service began with the petition of the bishops and the response of the King that he would uphold the privileges of the Church and maintain the law and justice. The people acclaimed him; the *Te Deum* was sung; the benedictions given. Then came the sacred ceremony of the anointing, the king's acceptance of the ring and sword, and the crowning. The King next received the sceptre and rod and, after further blessings and prayers, was enthroned and stated his commitment to rule according to three precepts.

After the church ceremony there was a great feast, probably held in the Royal hall close by; this was an important part of the whole inauguration, where the King would extend generous hospitality and eat in comradeship with his followers. In William of Malmesbury's words: 'fire glows among the people with more than wonted festivity . . . the palace seethes and overflows with royal splendour. Wine foams everywhere, the great hall resounds with tumult, pages scurry to and fro, stomachs are filled with delicacies, minds with song. One makes the harp resound, another contends with praises . . . The king drinks in this honour with eager gaze, graciously bestowing due courtesy on all'.

A surviving Old English manumission says that 'immediately after he first became king', Athelstan freed a slave, Eadhelm, and his heirs; this could also have taken place at Kingston. If so, 'Aelfheah the priest and the community', who witnessed the act, could have been the staff at Kingston minster, and 'Aelfric the reeve' might be the local Royal official. It is highly likely that Athelstan visited his vill at Kingston several times during his reign; the two surviving charters that show him there granting land or privileges, in 933 to Chertsey minster, and before 939 to St Buryan's, Cornwall, are no longer thought to be authentic, but that is not to say that Athelstan did not make similar grants from his 'royal vill which in English is called Kingston'.

Athelstan and his brothers, Edmund and Eadred, brought the Danish colonies in England firmly under English control. If the 946 charter is genuine, Eadred was probably crowned at Kingston, and we catch a glimpse of him there, granting lands and presenting gifts to his subjects 'in the king's residence which is called Kingston'. If, as Florence of Worcester suggests, Eadred's young successor, Eadwig, was crowned at Kingston in 956, then that same Royal residence was the scene of a famous quarrel between the King and Abbot Dunstan. An early *Life* of Dunstan tells us that, the day after the consecration, when Eadwig was meant to be attending the coronation feast, 'the lustful man suddenly jumped up and left the happy banquet and the fitting company of his nobles for the . . . caresses of loose women'. These women, a noblewoman and her daughter, were trying to entice Eadwig into marriage. Archbishop Oda sent Dunstan to bring the King back, and he found Eadwig with the women, 'repeatedly wallowing between the two of them as if in a vile sty', while the Royal crown, 'which was bound with wondrous metal, gold and silver and gems, and shone with many-coloured lustre', was 'carelessly thrown down on the floor, far from his head'. Despite the bias of Dunstan's hagiographer, it is clear that Eadwig transgressed against the important conventions of the coronation feast, though he still retained the authority to exile Dunstan for his part in the affair.

Eadwig's successor, Edgar, held a meeting of the Royal council, or Witan, in Kingston in 972. A record of an endowment of St Peter's, Westminster, of lands in Middlesex, has been preserved, and the gift was confirmed in that 'most well known place which is called Kingston'. This well known place was not, apparently, considered grand enough for Edgar's second coronation at Bath in 973, which stressed his 'imperial' authority after the King of Scots submitted to him. Either on this occasion or for his earlier coronation, probably held in 960, the consecration service was changed so that there was a three-fold promise to rule justly at the beginning, instead of a commitment to do so at the end. This coronation oath soon became an important part of the ceremony. However, whether or not the 960 consecration took place at Kingston is not known.

Aethelred, nicknamed 'unready' because he was lacking in 'rede', or good counsel, was the last recorded king crowned at Kingston. The *Anglo-Saxon Chronicle* for 979: 'In this year Aethelred was hallowed king on the Sunday, a fortnight after Easter at Kingston: at his consecration were present two archbishops and ten diocesan bishops'. According to a *Life* of St Dunstan, Aethelred's coronation oath was delivered to him by Archbishop Dunstan at Kingston 'on the day that they hallowed him king, and he forbade him to give any other pledge except this pledge which he laid up on Christ's altar, as the bishop directed him'. This was Aethelred's pledge: 'In the name of the Holy trinity, I promise three things to the Christian people and my subjects: first, that God's Church and all Christian people of my dominions observe true peace; the second is that I forbid all robbery and all unrighteous things to all orders; the third, that I praise and enjoin in all dooms justice and mercy . . .'. He also acknowledged that the duty of a hallowed king was to 'protect widows, orphans and strangers, . . . to extirpate witches and enchanters . . . feed the needy with alms, and have old, wise and sober men for counsellors'.

But the *Chronicle* prepares the reader for disaster with an account of disturbances in the heavens even in the year of the coronation: '. . . this same year a cloud red as blood was seen, frequently with the appearance of fire and it usually appeared about midnight: it took the form of rays of light of various colours, and at the first streak of dawn, it vanished'. Aethelred, unable to cope with a new wave of Danish invasions, could carry out few of his pledged duties while the Danes burnt his villages and slaughtered his subjects. In the end he fled the country, and the Danish kings Swein and Cnut took over.

Cnut apparently visited the vill at Kingston; we find him there before 1020, when a marriage agreement for Godwine to wed the daughter of Brihtric was made in his presence. Finny suggests that Cnut rebuilt Kingston church after previous Danish raids had destroyed it, but there is no evidence for this. In 1042, the West Saxon line was restored and the Royal estate at Kingston reverted to English ownership until the Norman Conquest.

Kingston had been a Royal vill, the centre of a Royal estate, for several hundred years. It is possible that by 1066 it was established as a market, but Domesday Book's reference to 'bedels' at Kingston in 1086 is no evidence that there was a town there then. 'Bedels' at the time were estate officials. When Harold was killed at Hastings and the Anglo-Saxon monarchy came to end, Kingston was a small rural settlement near the minster, with timber buildings from which officials collected taxes, and in which they locked up criminals and supervised the surrounding hundred for the King. It was not a grand place, though it had played host to grand occasions. Over the past 500 years, the Saxons had arrived, had become one people with the native Britons in the Kingston area, had hallowed a church there, had established their language and given Kingston its name. But they ploughed ancient fields, and the huts the ordinary folk lived in, and their way of life on the land, had not changed much in half a millennium.

LEFT: A heavy throwing weapon from Kingston, which may be a Saxon angon, once mounted on a long pole of springy wood. (KM) ABOVE: This stone cross fragment, carved with an interlace pattern, survives in All Saints' Church. It suggests the existence of a church in Kingston in the 8th century. (KM cast) RIGHT: Coins of Athelstan and Aethelred. (KM) CENTRE: The Council of Kingston, 838; this contains the first mention of 'that famous place which is called Cyningestun in the region of Surrey'. (BL) BELOW: Saxon canoe from East Molesey, c900. (KM)

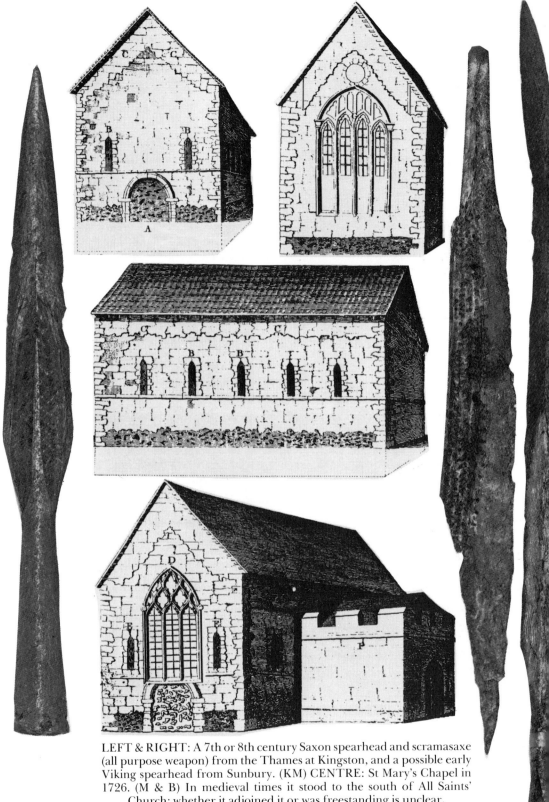

LEFT & RIGHT: A 7th or 8th century Saxon spearhead and scramasaxe (all purpose weapon) from the Thames at Kingston, and a possible early Viking spearhead from Sunbury. (KM) CENTRE: St Mary's Chapel in 1726. (M & B) In medieval times it stood to the south of All Saints' Church; whether it adjoined it or was freestanding is unclear.

Birth of a Town

Some time in the later 12th century, the town of Kingston was born. It stood on an island. The main settlement was within an area bounded by the Thames to the west, the Hogsmill to the south, present day Downhall Road to the north, and to the east, running across what is now Eden Walk, the old silted up eastern arm of the Thames which, though no longer a river channel, was still a stream with damp, marshy ground around it. Like most towns of the time, it was tiny in extent and population. Its island site had much more open space than the same area today, and was surrounded by marsh and mud. Streets were probably unpaved and the single-storey timber and plaster houses could easily be destroyed by gales, fire or flood. Where the marshes stopped, meadowland, pasture and arable fields began, dotted with barns and cottages. To us, Kingston in 1200 would not look like a town at all. Yet by then it saw itself as one, and King John's government, which granted it a charter of privileges in that year, must have felt it was a place capable of managing its own affairs.

An early medieval town was distinguished from a village partly because it felt itself to be different. It was conscious of itself as having an identity and a community of interests; it had leaders to speak for it, and some sort of organisation, and it wanted to have responsibility for its own affairs. Whereas most villagers relied for their livelihood on agriculture (or sometimes on a single industry), a substantial number of town inhabitants earned their livings in a variety of trades, industries and other occupations. A town usually had more people than a village, living closer together, and often it had a physical boundary to demarcate it, such as walls or ditches. However, towns covered a wide spectrum, ranging from the unusually large and impressive city of London at one end to little places hard to distinguish from villages at the other. Some settlements were definitely urban by an early date, and we have archaeological and other evidence of streets, houses, markets and workshops from Saxon or early Norman times. For other settlements, including Kingston, there is less evidence, and such places are harder to categorize.

In 1086, when William the Conqueror's 'Domesday' survey was compiled, Kingston was not ranked as a town. Domesday Book usually called towns 'boroughs' (burgi), and town dwellers 'burgesses' (burgenses), whereas Kingston was a 'vill', inhabited by 'villans'. True, some vills were also described in ways that suggest they were towns, with mention of houses, or of sites called 'closes' (hagae), denoting 'urban' plots. Thus Guildford, where we are told that King William had '75 closes (hagas) in which dwell 175 men'. Though called a vill, Guildford was a town with a population of perhaps 875, the only real town in Surrey after Southwark. But for Kingston, there is no mention of closes, houses or men. The Royal manor of Kingston is described, like most of the economic units in Domesday, in terms of agricultural lands and resources. It had land for 32 ploughs, 40 acres of meadow, woodland for which the tenants paid six pigs, five mills (for grinding corn), and three fisheries.

Domesday was primarily a survey of landholdings, and tells us nothing about the physical arrangement of Kingston's farms, fields, houses or plots. A manor was an estate, an administrative unit, with rights over lands or resources which might not form a physically compact entity, but could be quite widely scattered. Domesday Book tells us, for instance, that Kingston manor had previously held land outside Kingston Hundred, in Mortlake, where Earl Harold had illegally built a fishery on Kingston property, and that Kingston manor had formerly had the right to the tolls paid at a certain riverside enclosure in Southwark.

Domesday does not mention the boundaries of Kingston manor. Nor, later, do we known the extent of the property presumably granted to Merton Priory in the early 12th century, with Gilbert the Sheriff's gift of the living of Kingston, lands which may represent an early endowment of the old minster. Later 12th century Kingston stood mainly on land that belonged to Kingston manor and partly on land belonging to the Priory, but no-one knows exactly where the settlement that grew into Kingston town originally was. Only archaeology can help. Some early settlement was around the church (which is mentioned in Domesday Book) and by the river, and a late 11th/early 12th century structure has been located near Pratt's Passage, but there may have been more than one cluster of population in the area which later formed the nucleus of the town, between the Thames, the Hogsmill, and present-day Eden Walk and Downhall Road.

The 86 villans, 14 bordars and two slaves of the Royal manor of Kingston who, with their families, might represent (approximately) 500 people, did not all live on this island site enclosed by the now defunct eastern arm of the Thames. By contemporary Surrey standards, Kingston manor had a substantial population — Old Malden, for instance, had four villans (maybe 20 people altogether) — and it was probably spread over quite a wide area. There would have been fields, farms, closes and cottages down-river towards Ham, up the Thames past the Bittoms, on the banks of the Hogsmill, where some of the mills may have stood, and towards Norbiton, Surbiton and Kingston Hill. There may also have been some Royal forestland to the north-east of Kingston, in an area referred to in the 12th century as Coombe Park. Domesday Book mentions that Walter Fitzother, Constable of Windsor Castle, who oversaw the king's forests in Berkshire, had put a man 'of the jurisdiction of Kingston' in charge of the king's wild mares, presumably kept for breeding. The mares were not necessarily kept at Kingston rather than Windsor, but they could have been.

Kingston in the second half of the 11th century did have some non-agricultural functions which made it a place local people visited and which helped to stimulate the growth of urban characteristics. Kingston was the administrative centre for an old Royal estate. Domesday Book mentions that land in Kingston Hundred, held in 1086 from Chertsey Abbey by Edric, had before 1064 been held directly from the King by three men who 'could not withdraw without the King's command because they were beadles in Kingston'. These 'bedelli' were probably estate officials, responsible for collecting the rents and dues owed to the King as lord of the manor. Tenants might have brought their dues to Kingston and while there taken the opportunity to visit a blacksmith, or bought something to eat or drink.

Kingston was also the meeting place for Kingston Hundred, and people visited it to attend the Hundred Court and pay local taxes. Humphrey the Chamberlain, who in 1086 held land in Coombe 'of the Queen's holding', had in his charge a villan of the Royal manor of Kingston 'for the collecting of the Queen's wool'; this villan may have had an administrative role in the hundred as a whole.

Moreover, Kingston was a focus of activity as the site of an ancient minster. Local folk came there to attend church and pay their tithes; priests attached to the church of All Saints lived nearby; and the maintenance of worship there must have stimulated a demand for goods and services. The building had to be kept in repair, wine supplied for communion, wax brought in for candles, and rushes or straw for the floor.

Kingston was therefore an obvious place for enterprising local craftsmen to find custom, and for people to bring goods for sale. It had a good natural position by the river and near an ancient crossing place, which facilitated the transport of goods. There was probably already a road from the Sheen area to Kingston and then on towards Guildford, and other lanes from London over Coombe and maybe Kingston hills. Some trade took place at Kingston, and there may have been a market — not recorded until 1242.

None of this made late 11th century Kingston a town. Though some trade and industry existed, there is no archaeological or other evidence to suggest that these involved many people. Domesday Book, though admittedly haphazard in its recording of tolls, does not mention any tolls being collected from Kingston, though they were collected from Southwark, Wandsworth and Putney. If some of the fisheries which belonged to the Royal manor of Kingston were on the Thames and involved weirs, they might have hindered river trade, as the nets or stakes fixed across the river to catch fish often impeded boats. Moreover, Kingston was not yet on a main highway to London. It attracted mainly local traffic, and there is no evidence of a bridge before the late 12th century. If it had a market, this was not necessarily often held, and need not indicate a high level of trade. Also, an infrequent market that was used mainly for selling agricultural produce might not stimulate industry. It seems that late 11th century Kingston was dominated by the mainly agricultural life of a rural manor: by farming, fishing and milling.

Kingston manor sounds quite prosperous at Domesday. It was not on William's direct invasion route from Sussex to London in 1066 and, though many Surrey vills did suffer from the depradations of his army, Kingston was not among them. Nothing in Kingston Hundred is described as 'waste', and the land values are roughly the same in 1086 as in Edward the Confessor's day. Nor, as far as we know, was any part of a settlement there knocked down for the Normans to build a castle.

During the hundred years or so after 1086, Kingston continued to prosper, and came to be recognized as one of the main settlements in Surrey; it had some urban characteristics by the 1190s. In the 12th and 13th centuries many towns developed all over England, as the population increased and trade expanded. Surrey was a poor county, and did not have many big or important towns. Southwark, the main one, was already a suburb of London, which overshadowed them all. But Kingston emerged in the later 12th century as a place of considerable local prosperity and growing self-confidence. Its prosperity can be gauged partly by its payment of taxes.

Both regular rents and occasional taxes called aids or tallages were paid into the Royal Exchequer, and the amounts were recorded in the Pipe Rolls. Before 1167-8, only Southwark and Guildford were considered places worth collecting aids from. But that year, for the first time, Kingston also appears as paying £12 10s, only slightly less than Southwark's £12 13s 4d, and more than Guildford's £9 6s 8d. In 1176-7, the sheriff accounted for 20 marks each for Southwark, Guildford and Kingston with Coombe. Ten years later, Kingston paid a higher tallage than both Guildford and

Southwark; and by the time the men of Kingston offered 30 marks for a charter in 1194, Kingston was one of the richest places in Surrey.

There is also material evidence of Kingston's prosperity. Towards the end of the 12th century, Clattern Bridge was built, in stone, across the Hogsmill, at the southern end of what is now, and probably was then, Kingston market place, thus improving road communications between Kingston and Guildford. Moreover, excavations in the Horsefair area in 1986-7 revealed that the bridge across the Thames was also built (or rebuilt) in the later 12th century with stone foundations and a timber superstructure. This 12th century bridge was further north than the present one, at the end of a street later called Old Bridge Street, which has itself now vanished beneath the John Lewis development. An earlier wooden structure might have existed, either on the same site or further downstream. Whether the late 12th century structure represents the first Kingston Bridge, or a rebuild, it shows by then enough road traffic crossing the Thames at Kingston to make the bridge worthwhile. Once built, it further encouraged traffic and trade. A thriving settlement, probably with a market, now stood by the river.

This settlement also had a large church, built in stone. Though by the early 12th century the church of All Saints, Kingston, (called All Hallows before the Reformation) had ceased to function as a minster, and had become a parish church, it retained widespread influence. It provided the focus for a large surrounding parish, and outlying chapelries at Sheen, Petersham, Thames Ditton and East Molesey came to be dependent upon it. Henry I gave the church to Gilbert the Sheriff, and he in turn granted it before 1130 to Merton Priory. The prior and canons of Merton held the rectory of Kingston until the Dissolution of the Monasteries, and appointed a vicar to serve in Kingston Church. In about 1130 the church of All Saints was built (or rebuilt) in stone on its present site. It was probably cruciform in shape, with a chancel, transepts and a narrow, aisleless nave. The massive piers of the crossing suggest a central tower; the oldest surviving stonework of these piers is 13th century, but this represents a refacing of older columns already in position. A Romanesque doorway discovered in about 1858, during restoration work at the west end, shows that the 12th century nave was as long as that of today. This points to a considerable population at Kingston, and the construction of the Norman church probably boosted local crafts and trade.

Whether or not a majority of Kingston's inhabitants earned their livings from trade and industry by the late 12th century, those who lived there had now developed a sense of communal identity. They realised that they had common interests, and they could organize themselves. They wanted a degree of administrative independence from the sheriff of the county, who collected the Royal dues, and took more than was owed to line his own pockets. Thus Kingston's inhabitants sought the fee farm of their settlement, the right to bypass the sheriff and pay their farm, or rent, directly to the King. They had leaders who could negotiate and in 1194, in a case before the King's court, the men of Kingston claimed they would pay 100s to Richard I for the right to hold their vill until the King's coming, and 30 marks for a charter that allowed them to hold it at the same farm as they had held it in King Henry's day. They also said that they had had a charter from Henry, but that this was burnt by accident.

It is highly unlikely that Kingston actually had a charter before 1194. It is suspicious that the men of Kingston did not specify which King Henry they meant — Henry I or Henry II! Henry II could in theory have granted them the right to hold Kingston at farm for a term of years (he did not grant farms in perpetuity), but in this case there should be evidence in the Pipe Rolls that Kingston accounted for itself, and there is none. Nor does the government seem to have accepted Kingston's claims or granted its requests. In 1199 an apparently non-local man, Joscelin de Gant, was paying the Kingston farm. However, the 1194 court case at least shows that Kingston by then felt it ought to have the right to pay its own rent, and that it deserved a charter, or statement of privileges, to safeguard this and other liberties. Kingston was approaching urban status.

The first recorded charter for Kingston was granted by King John in 1200, though only a record of it survives, not the charter itself. The men of Kingston paid 60 marks for it, and it gave them the right to hold their town at farm (ie to pay their own rent directly to the Exchequer). Their annual rent was £40: £12 above the existing farm of £28. Kingston's first surviving charter (1208) not only confirmed 'to our free men of Kingston our town of Kingston, with all its appurtenances in feefarm . . . to them and their heirs . . . for ever entirely', but also confirmed 'all the liberties and free customs which the same town was accustomed and ought to have at the time in which it was in our hand'. These probably included the right to call its own court (different from the Hundred Court which also met at Kingston); the right of the inhabitants to hold their lands by a freer type of tenure, burgage tenure; freedom from paying tolls; and the right to appoint officials to regulate their own affairs. The rent also went up to £50 per year, because John needed the money.

Once Kingston had a charter, the liberties and privileges involved gave further impetus to urban life. Wine was sold in the town by about 1200, for in 1202 the men of Kingston were fined 20s because William, son of Gervase and William Baret broke the assize of wine, the recent law that set trading standards. This suggests that by then Kingston had taverns or wine shops. However, most of the evidence of trade and industry in Kingston dates from later in the 13th century. It is only from about 1240 that a really convincing picture of urban life emerges.

This is the main entry for Kingston in Domesday book, 1086. (PRO) 'In Kingston Hundred, the king holds in demesne Kingston . . . There is land for 32 ploughs . . . there are 86 villans and 14 bordars . . . There is a church; and 2 serfs; and 5 mills worth 20 shillings, and a third fishery very good but not rented. There are 40 acres of meadow . . .'

ABOVE: All Saints' parish church. The 12th century building lacked side aisles, but probably had a tower, and the nave was as long as the modern one. LEFT: All Saints': the Romanesque west door; discovered during building work in Victorian times, this 12th century arch was destroyed soon after this picture was taken. RIGHT: Excavations at old Kingston Bridge. These late 12th century stone foundations of the wooden bridge over the Thames were discovered in 1986, when the John Lewis store was built. (All KM & HS)

ABOVE: Old Kingston Bridge was so narrow only one cart could cross at a time. BELOW: Clattern Bridge over the Hogsmill has been much widened but its 12th century arches survive. (Both KM & HS)

JOHN, by the grace of God, King of England, Lord of Ireland, Duke of Normandy and Aquitain, Count of Andegavenny. To all Archbifhops, Bifhops, Abbots, Earls, Barons, Juftices, Sheriffs, Provofts, and all Bailiffs and faithful fubjects, greeting. Know ye That we have given, granted, and by this our prefent Charter confirmed to our Freemen of Kyngefton, our town of Kyngefton, with all its appurtenances in feefarm, to have and to hold to them and their heirs of us and our heirs, in their hand for ever entirely,

with all the liberties and free cuftoms which the fame town was accuftomed and ought to have at the time in which it was in our hand, yielding thence to our Exchequer by their hand yearly fifty pounds of filver; that is to fay, half at the Eafter Exchequer, and half at the Michaelmas Exchequer; of which fifty pounds they fhall pay twenty-eight pounds and ten fhillings blank, which was the ancient rent; and the refidue they fhall pay in tale. And we will not that the fheriff or his bailiffs in anywife intermeddle with the aforefaid town or its appurtenances, or with the aforefaid rent, except thofe things which belong to the royal crown: wherefore we will and firmly command, That the aforefaid men of Kingefton, and their heirs, may have and hold in feefarm the aforefaid town of Kingefton, with its appurtenances, for ever, well and peaably, free and quietly, entirely, fully, honourably in all places and things, w all the liberties and free cuftoms belo ing to it, as is above mentioned, as long they fhall well pay the aforefaid rent.

Witnefs Lord P. Bifhop of Winche Lord J. Bifhop of Bath, William Ear Devonfhire, William Brivoerr, Hugo Nevill, Garin, the fon of Gerola, Will Malet, Thomas Baffet, Ralf Gernun, G frey Luterel.

Given under the hand of Hugo de W Archdeacon of Wells, at Tanton, the day of September, in the tenth year of reign.

Translation of the 1208 charter, made in the late 18th century by a Kingston antiquarian, George Roots. (R) INSET: Kingston's first extant charter of privileges, granted by King John in 1208. (KM & HS) The first charter, granted 1200, no longer survives.

Merchants, Market & Manufacture

As Kingston discovered during the 13th century, a charter was no guarantee of prosperity. The new fee farm cost £40 per year in 1200 and then £50 in 1208 and Kingston fell behind with its rent in the late 1220s. Kingston Bridge facilitated trade, but it also needed repair in 1193 after hostilities between Richard I and brother John. Wind and flood damage in the early 1220s rendered it 'bereft of all work, help and skill' in 1223, and flood damage recurred in the 1250s, '60s and '80s; in 1286 the bridge was unusable. Royal taxation was also a burden. In 1227, when Henry III asked for a tallage of £20, he let the town off 10 marks 'so that the poor and more oppressed may feel themselves relieved'.

However, it is also from the 13th century that solid evidence emerges of Kingston's commercial life. There was a market in Kingston by 1242, and it drew traders from Fulham; that year Kingston's bailiffs were accused of charging the Fulham men market toll illegally. Kingston had had a 'guild merchant', a society of tradesmen, for some time already by 1256, for a charter of that year confirms the freemen's right to have it 'as they have hitherto had it'; indeed, it might have been one of the 'liberties and free customs' referred to in vague terms in 1208. A guild merchant was a body which regulated trade, feasted and worshipped together in fellowship, and helped members and their dependants in need. Many of these men doubtless traded locally. But some at least visited more distant parts of the country, for a Kingston charter of 1256 protected its tradesmen from being arrested for debts owed by other merchants, not from Kingston — a provision which implies that Kingston's merchants travelled with traders from other places, to areas where noone could necessarily distinguish a Kingston man from other Surrey traders.

The main trading centre was the market place which, from 1253 if not earlier, stood in part at least where it stands now, between the parish church and the Hogsmill (a document of 1253 speaks of 'the water which is at the end of the market towards Guildford'). It may also have extended further north. The goods brought here included local agricultural produce such as oats, grain and fish, plus livestock, wool and cloth. Some goods were brought by road, some by river. This period left the earliest traces so far of river trade: 13th century timbers from ships, incorporated into wharves of a later date, have been excavated at the Horsefair site, on both sides of the late 12th century Thames bridge. Recent excavations at Charter Quay, at the south end of Thames Street, have revealed medieval timber waterfronts to both north and south of the Hogsmill and, by the late 14th century, there may have been wharves all along the Thames from the Horsefair to the Bittoms.

Kingston was primarily a local market centre, though there was some long distance trade. Kingston was possibly involved in the import of Gascon wine by river: land in the Bittoms known as La Ryole suggests connections with the wine producing region of La Reole, near Bordeaux, from which much wine was shipped *via* London and Southampton. From 1256, Kingston was also allowed to hold an annual autumn fair, 'on the 8 days following the feast of All Souls' (2 November), which probably caused disruption to normal trade while attracting merchants from far and wide.

What of Kingston's own products? The town was manufacturing its own Surrey whiteware pottery by the second half of the 13th century; between 1264 and 1266 Kingston supplied the King with 3,800 pitchers. The clay used was probably imported by river, and some of the finished pottery exported to London. This trade peaked in the late 13th/early 14th centuries, then declined until the early 15th century.

A kiln site possibly dating from the late 13th or 14th century has been found in Kingston behind Eden Street. This area in medieval times was muddy, marshy land on the outskirts of the town, suitable for smokey, messy industry posing fire-risks. Another pottery, dating from the late 14th century, has been discovered in Union Street.

Other messy industries included animal processing. Slaughtering cattle for meat, tanning their hides for leather and carving implements from horns took place from the 13th to the 16th century in the Eden Walk/Union Street area, where excavations have uncovered dumps of animal bones, horn cores, and shallow pits probably for tanning.

Eden Street itself existed, by the name of Heathen Street, by 1315, when there were two shops there, outside the natural boundary of the town. The 'heathens' were probably the countryfolk in the fields and marshes, living in hovels and supplying the labour for 'dirty' industries.

Though most of Kingston's houses were built of wood and plaster, regularly needing extensive repairs or rebuilding, some were being erected in stone, or with stone foundations. A substantial late 13th century building with flint foundations has been found at the south end of Thames Street, and there was contemporary building at Charter Quay. A stone column of c1300, now outside Kingston Library, probably came from a wealthy merchant's house at La Ryole, in the Bittoms area. The Bishop's Palace, built in the 13th century in Thames Street for the Bishop of Winchester when he visited Kingston (then in his diocese), was also made of stone. The 13th century saw repairs and renovation at All Saints' Church; the massive stone piers of the crossing, which held up the tower, were apparently refaced at this time. At some stage the tower was also crowned with a wooden steeple. Such building projects provided work for local craftsmen and labourers. Despite the vicissitudes of flooding and taxation, Kingston looked more built-up and more impressive in 1300 than 100 years before.

Kingston's life then was not much disturbed by local or national politics though the occasional presence of nobles or the King could cause some disruption. There is no evidence that any Norman or Plantaganet king or noble had a permanent home at Kingston. Structures traditionally thought to be part of 'King John's Palace' or 'Warwick's Castle' have now been shown to have been different buildings of later dates. When kings visited Kingston, they probably stayed in the Bishop's Palace, a rich merchant's house, or travelled in for the day, having slept at a local manor house, such as Walter de Merton's at Malden.

In 1217, during the regency of Henry III, the court came to an island in the Thames at Kingston (probably Raven's Ait) to negotiate a peace treaty with Prince Louis of France, who had been helping the English barons who opposed King John. Local ferrymen may have benefitted, but suppliers of food and drink could have found themselves out of pocket, as the King did not always pay promptly or enough. The medieval court was itinerant, but the King had Royal castles at the Tower, Windsor and Guildford, so he did not stay regularly in Kingston. Henry III visited occasionally, for instance in 1261, when he met his baronial opposition there and made peace with Richard of Clare, Earl of Gloucester. Kingston was convenient, because its bridge gave ease of access. Henry III's brother, Richard of Cornwall, had already used Kingston when he rebelled against the King in 1238!

In 1264, during his campaign against Simon de Montfort and Gilbert de Clare in the Barons' War, Henry III made a detour to seize the bridge at Kingston, and captured a castle belonging to Gilbert of Clare. This was possibly a temporary structure, built by Clare during the revolt, to watch the bridge; he had no land of his own nearer than Long Ditton. Possibly Gilbert of Clare or other nobles thereafter used Kingston as a convenient place to hold military tournaments, for in 1274 Edward I forbade Easter jousts, tournaments and military sports at Kingston or elsewhere without permission.

Before the Baron' War, urban life was such that leading townsmen sought more independence from the county officials of the King. Kingston's charter of 13 September 1256 brought the important right of return of writs: the townsmen, not the sheriff, had the right to carry out the King's written orders to summon criminals to court and seize their goods. Royal officials could not enter the town to execute writs unless the townsmen failed to carry them out. Kingston had a local watch in the 13th century, and also a prison — Walter de Braunton, a cattle thief, escaped from it in 1262. Moreover, the charter allowed the men of Kingston to appoint their own coroners, with judicial competence over cases involving townsmen, and gave them the right to have judicial cases concerning lands and property heard within the town. This, taken together with the charter right to hold their own guild merchant, demonstrates local government with locally appointed officials and local courts, long before the town was officially recognized as a corporation. In the next century, Kingston also sent representatives to Parliament, though this was a burden, not a privilege and, at the town's request, it ceased to send MPs after 1373.

Throughout the period, All Saints' was important. Its stone building provided the spiritual focus for the town and district. It also provided a place of sanctuary for criminals fleeing from justice: the thieves Richard le Parmenter and John de Marscall took refuge there in 1262.

However, the size of Kingston parish burdened those in outlying areas. In the 13th century parishioners at Petersham waged a long struggle until Merton Priory agreed to finance a special chaplain to hold services and baptize at Petersham Chapel. Merton Priory was jealous of its rights. Throughout the 13th and 14th centuries vicars of Kingston found their endowment less than generous. Eventually the vicar was allocated oblations (donations at church services), mortuaries (burial fees) and other fees, and most of the tithes. Responsibility was also allocated for repairs to the roof and chancel of Kingston Church and the chapels at Petersham, Sheen, Thames Ditton and East Molesey, and for building and repairing manses.

By the early 14th century, a picture of Kingston emerges: the raised gravel island, bounded to the west by the Thames and to the south by the Hogsmill, enclosed to the east and north by the marshes around the stream and seasonally flooded channel that remained of the old eastern arm of the Thames. In the centre stood the church, its tower overlooking the market place. To the west lay the waterfront; wooden boats plied their trade, and a timber bridge spanned the river. A road ran north-south between river and market place, with plots and houses on its west side. Where the road left the market place to the south, a stone bridge carried it towards Guildford, the county town. On the east of the market, tenements fronted what is now Union Street, and there and in the Heathen Street area stood premises connected with the meat, leather and horn trades, and with pottery making. The most important trades were organized in a guild, and the town enjoyed some independence from central government. Kingston was flourishing.

Outside the town, agriculture dominated. The arable land around Kingston was not all in common fields; by the 13th century some was probably marked off in individual plots, though Kingston did have large common fields nearby, in which individuals owned parcels of land. A 14th century land deed mentions 'two acres in the fields of Kingston: ½ acre is at Elleforlang, adjoining land of Will Moryn; ½ acre is at Brocmed between land of Robert Bronger south and land of the lord of Cumbe north; . . . ½ acre is at Flode between land of James Taylor north and land of the Chapel of St. Mary Magdalene'. Nearly a hundred years later, holdings are mentioned of two acres in Littlefield, two acres in Tenterfield, six acres in Northfield and one acre in The Marsh. Northfield was presumably towards Norbiton, and Littlefield and Tenterfield seem to have been to the south.

There is no evidence of joint cultivation or uniform field systems. Kingston had meadowland by the Thames to the north and south, and was rich in pasture. Kingston's inhabitants could graze animals and gather firewood on the common land at Norbiton and Surbiton. Those townsmen who did not grow food had to buy it; a bad harvest spelt high food prices and hardship. Those who lived in the countryside might depend on selling produce in the town. People with little or no land came there to find work. This relationship of town and country continued for centuries. Market and countryside could not prosper, one without the other.

The burden of the bridge. This 19th century drawing shows how easily sections could be damaged or removed. (KM & HS)

ABOVE: Floods in Kingston High Street, taken in 1895; flooding was a recurrent hazard throughout Kingston's history. BELOW: Kingston Market Place, 1770; the market was already here by the 13th century, without a town hall, and with mainly single storey houses. (KM & HS)

LEFT: A stone pillar from the Bittoms area, c1300, now outside Kingston Library. The Victorians thought it came from a (non-existent) 'King John's Palace', but it was probably part of a rich merchant's house. RIGHT: A medieval tile from All Saints'. BELOW: Pile of oak bark, used in tanning, established in the Union Street area from the 13th century. (KM & HS)

HENRY, by the grace of God, King of England, Lord of Ireland, Duke of Normandy and Aquitain, and Count of Andegavenny. To all Archbiſhops, Biſhops, Abbots, Priors, Earls, Barons, Juſtices, Sheriffs, Provoſts, Miniſters, and all Bailiffs and faithful ſubjects, greeting. Know ye That we have granted, and by this our charter have confirmed to our freemen of Kyngeſton, that they and their heirs for ever may have a Fair every year, to continue during eight days, at Kyngeſton; that is to ſay, on the morrow of All Souls, and during the ſeven following days, unleſs that fair ſhould be to the hurt of the neighbouring fairs. Wherefore we will and firmly command for us and our heirs, that our aforeſaid freemen of Kyngeſton, and their heirs for ever, may have a fair at Kyngeſton every year, to continue during eight days; that is to ſay, on the morrow of All Souls, and during the ſeven following days; with all the liberties and free

cuſ-

Medieval pottery from Kingston (KM) and BELOW: translation of one of Henry III's charters of 1256, granting Kingston a November fair. (R)

53

ABOVE: Kingston Church had a wooden spire from medieval times until 1703, when a storm damaged it so badly that it was taken down. Daniel King's 17th century drawing is the only picture we have. BELOW: Lightning over Kingston. In 1445, All Saints' spire was struck by lightning and nearly destroyed. (KM & HS)

Of Plague and Piety

The 14th and 15th centuries brought their own problems: heavy taxation, disorder and plague. Royal taxes increased alarmingly because of war — against the Scots from the 1290s, and against France (the Hundred Years War) from 1337. Kingston suffered direct taxes on local wealth, and indirectly from the taxes on wool.

Occasionally the town was directly involved in the political conflicts between unpopular or inept kings and those nobles who opposed them. In 1308 Edward II ordered the dismantling of Kingston Bridge in the face of suspected noble disaffection. In the 1320s there was constant tension, and some armed opposition to Edward and his chief advisers, the Despensers. Rebels who had marched up to London from the Welsh marches broke the peace at Kingston in 1323. Hugh Despenser the younger had inherited by marriage the local Clare estates in the Long Ditton area. His moated manor house at Tolworth was confiscated in 1327 and he and his father were both executed by the new government which deposed the King.

At Kingston the townsmen resorted to violence in pursuit of local interests. In 1331 46 Kingston men, including fishermen and tailors, imprisoned the Archdeacon of Surrey and stole his goods, and in 1333 a group, including some of the same men, took 24 horses, 80 cows and 200 sheep (worth £200) belonging to Thomas Roscelyn. In 1339 a gang of criminals plundered and burnt the local village of Hertington Coombe. In 1346 Edward III's government had to appoint a special commission to arrest the 'roberdsmen, wasturs and draghlaches' who were still terrorizing the county of Surrey.

The political uncertainty at the top stimulated crime or settling of old scores at local level. In 1400, Henry IV, the first Lancastrian king, granted the men of Kingston his protection against injury, violence, hindrance or oppression. The Royal letters patent state that the men of Kingston 'have besought us that, since they fear bodily hurt and loss of their goods and property by certain of their foes, and the acquisition of them by force being easily possible, we may graciously desire to provide for their security in this matter'. It points to a high level of local violence, even feuding, which may have had a political element.

In 1415, and again in 1437, Kingston's inhabitants received a Royal pardon. Rent and tax arrears were written off, and even murder and treason forgiven. This suggests an endemic violence and lawlessness even before the so called 'Wars of the Roses' in the second half of the 15th century. However, disorder intensified during the troubled spring of 1471, when the Bastard of Fauconberg's rebels attacked London while Edward IV was crushing revolt elsewhere. Denied entrance to the City, Fauconberg 'went from London westward, as far as Kingston upon Thames', hoping to cross the Thames there, but barges of armed men defending London came up river and forced him to withdraw.

Plague was another recurrent scourge, though the outbreaks decreased in killing power as time went on. The first, most virulent, outbreak of the Black Death may have killed off 30% of the population when it hit England in 1348-9. The urban labour force was suddenly and dramatically reduced. Also Kingston, as a market town, depended on goods brought in from its hinterland, and reduced manpower there reduced town trade. It may have been in an attempt to boost flagging trade that Kingston in 1351 was allowed a second annual fair, to run for eight days from Whit Thursday. Further outbreaks of plague occurred in 1361, 1369, 1390 and throughout the 15th century. Each time, any previous population growth was checked, and Kingston in 1500 probably had no more people than it had had 200 years before.

Some towns flourished in the 14th and 15th centuries. Many did not. Kingston seems to have been in financial difficulties from the later 14th century. In 1381 Richard II granted back to the town, in aid of its annual rent, an estate which had escheated to the Crown (*ie* passed to the Crown on the death without heirs of its owner). This suggests that Kingston was having trouble meeting the rent, which was now £54 8s 6d. By 1413, Henry V slashed the rent to £26, back to the level of the ancient farm of the 12th century. In 1481 Edward IV's charter of incorporation confirmed the £26 rent, and specifically stated that the grant was made because Kingston's inhabitants 'by the payment of the feefarm of that town, and by reason of the great violent inundations and overflow of the waters, lately suffered in that town, and other burdens oppressing the said town, are injured, deteriorated, and so much impoverished, that they cannot pay that rent to us and our heirs, and bear the other burdens which lie heavy on the said town . . .'.

Floods were a specific cause of Kingston's woes. As a riverside town without modern technology to control water levels, it was particularly dependent on weather. Kingston suffered from bad flooding in 1382 and 1435, as well as in 1481. In 1445 the church spire was struck by lightning and burnt down, and the fire ran out of control and destroyed much of the town.

Damage from wind, fire and flood not only affected goods and houses. If it affected the bridge, it placed a burden on the whole town, because of the weight of the common repair bill, and because the bridge brought trade. Natural wear and tear had to be made good; the town paid for repairs by levying tolls on the goods travelling over or under the bridge. In the 14th century the government granted the right (known as pontage) for specified periods. Three grants of pontage were made in the period 1376-1400, and the major rebuilding programme, while it doubtless boosted timber imports and gave work to local carpenters and labourers, must have caused traders considerable nuisance. In 1449, Henry VI gave the bailiffs and freemen pontage for 51 years: tolls became a permanent and much resented fact of life.

From a list of goods paying tolls in 1449, we have an idea of what was brought to Kingston then, either by river or across the bridge: wine, salmon, sea fish, wool, cloth, woad, hides, skins, iron bars, nails, malt, hogs for bacon, draught animals (like horses and oxen), arrows, salt, cheese, butter, oil, hemp, suet, tallow, bark, boards, timber, coals, firewood, millstones and grindstones.

Some goods were sold in Kingston market. Others were directly imported and redistributed wholesale by merchants, up or down river, (especially to London,) or inland. Some goods supplied local shops and industries. Documents mention a street called the Butchery, near the Market Place, and refer to a meat market in the early 14th century. Butchers and tanners owned land in Heathen Street. Some leather was sold in the Leather Market, and some bought by the local shoemakers of Souters Row. Kingston had its own fishing industry — the Thames in those days was full of salmon — and much of the fish caught locally, like much of the meat from the slaughterhouses, was salted to preserve it. Kingston had a Salterers Lane near the Market Place. Some fresh meat or fish was probably made into pies baked, along with bread, in Cook Row, where townsfolk paid to use the ovens to cook their own. Bakers, barbers, smiths, masons and carpenters are also mentioned in land deeds.

Malt was imported for the brewing industry. In the 14th century maltsters and brewers were mentioned separately alongside merchants and artificers as paying personal tithes. Ale, and also wine, were sold in Kingston's taverns and inns. There were several of these by the early 15th century, including the Saracens Head, which stood between the Thames and the High Street, and the Chequer, in what is now Church Street and was then King Street. Kingston was also on the way to the south coast. In 1415 Sir Thomas Grey 'lay at Kingston' overnight before setting off for Southampton *via* Guildford.

Kingston had a wool market, and the prominence in local worship of St Blaise, the patron saint of wool combers, highlights the woollen industry. The parish church had an early 15th century wall painting of the saint, holding his wool comb, and a light dedicated to him, and the feast of St Blaise was marked by special services. Hosiers are mentioned in land deeds and a Tenterfield in the Bittoms area in the 15th century suggests a local cloth industry, for tenter grounds were places where cloth was hung to dry after fulling.

Some pottery was perhaps still made in Kingston in the early 15th century, but by then the town's export trade in Surrey whiteware to London had all but collapsed, and clay is not mentioned in the 1440s as an import on which toll was charged. However, from the late 15th or early 16th century a new red ware industry was producing pottery: excavation has discovered waste material from a kiln south of the Hogsmill and roughly behind no 17, High Street. Jugs, pitchers, cooking pots, bowls, dishes and jars were made there.

Despite — or perhaps because of — its struggles to pay its yearly rent, Kingston in the late 15th century was granted more specific and more comprehensive privileges. The vague wording of previous charters was causing disputes between Royal officials and townsmen. The townsmen claimed that by virtue of King John's charter they 'were accustomed to have and enjoy within the said town . . . a certain court on every Saturday, before the bailiffs and steward', with the power 'of hearing and determining all pleas of debt, covenant, account, trespass, and other contracts and personal matters . . .'. Moreover, they claimed for the town all escheats and forfeitures of land and goods, and all judicial fines within Kingston Hundred. However, Kingston's officials 'were hindered and interrupted' by some of the Royal officers of the county, to Kingston's 'no small loss and prejudice'.

Kingston had probably held its own court since John's charter; there was certainly one in existence by the 1230s. From early times the town may also have had the right to take for itself judicial fines imposed within the hundred. However, it is debateable whether it ever had the right to escheats. It had also had a long dispute with the Crown over its perceived right to have charge of the assize of bread and ale, and only in 1441 was this privilege conceded. Thereafter the town, not the Royal clerk of the market, was responsible for setting and checking the weights and measures used in Kingston's shops and market, and could take fines from any vendors who gave short measure.

Edward IV's charter of 1481 clarified the situation, and allowed Kingston the rights it claimed in order to help it recover. Kingston was also granted the privilege of incorporation. Its citizens became: 'one body in deed and name, and one perpetual corporation of two bailiffs of that town, and the freemen of the same town', with a 'perpetual succession'. This meant that the town was now a permanent corporate body with an identity at law; the corporation as a whole, not the town's leaders as individuals, would bring or defend actions in the law courts, own property, pay or receive fines. The liability of Kingston's leaders was thus limited: they had more freedom and more security to act on the town's behalf. The corporation was also able to 'make and ordain within the town ordinances and statutes' for the town's 'wholesome regulation and government', and was allowed a common seal. The charter specifically permitted Kingston corporation to take 'escheats, forfeitures, goods, chattels and fines' within the town, demesne and hundred, even if these had previously been taken by the Crown's officers. It was permitted to hold its Saturday court, and to appoint one or two Serjeants at Mace to carry out its commands.

The town would still look small to modern eyes. The main settlement was along the High Street between the market and the Thames, and in the streets east of the Market Place. Thames Bridge Street or Thames Street, which continued High Street towards the bridge, was now also lined with houses. Near Clattern Bridge, houses and wharves continued along High Street south of the Hogsmill. In the Heathen Street area, some of the marshy land was being reclaimed. The stream that remained of the old eastern arm of the Thames, which ran across what is now Clarence Street, a little to the west of Pratt's Passage, was now crossed by a bridge called Bow Bridge or Stony Bridge, carrying a road from London into the heart of the town. The stream was also called the Town Ditch, and had doubtless long been used as a sewer. It ran north west, and to the west of it the King's highway went north and crossed the ditch at another bridge called Bar Bridge before continuing on to Ham. (Later, this main road was called Lower Ham Road.) The ditch, meanwhile, turned west towards the Thames at Downhall. East of the King's highway was land called Bar Field.

Between the town ditch and the King's highway, occupying roughly the area of the modern Bentall Centre, stood the 14th century vicarage. The vicar of Kingston was involved in a long-running dispute with Merton Priory over their division of income, and the priory had to 'provide a competent manse for the residence of the vicar'. The house was to be 'a hall with two rooms, one at one end of the hall, and the other at the other end, with a drain to each, and a suitable kitchen with fireplace and oven, and a stable for six horses; [all] covered with tiles'. By 1366 this had 'fallen into ruin'. The vicar was allowed to pull it down and use the materials for a new vicarage.

Kingston was an important church. The vicar was allowed to appoint parish clerks and church officers, and to establish in the parish 'schools for teaching children to read, chant &c'. The fabric of All Saints' Church had to be kept in repair, and the building was enlarged in the late 14th century when the side aisles were added on either side of the nave. The nave itself was probably widened at about the same time; the chancel may have been widened earlier. Two other chancels, or chapels, that of Holy Trinity to the north of the main chancel and that of St James to the south, were remodelled in the 15th century. By this time, anyone entering the church would have been struck by its rich splendour. The floor was bright with coloured tiles, the walls painted with pictures of saints and holy stories, and the windows glowed with stained glass. There were crosses on the altars, carved and coloured images of the Virgin and saints, and probably an elaborate rood screen between chancel and nave. There were holy relics which people came to venerate, pyxes where the holy bread was kept, and a certain number of books. Special vestments were provided, which the vicar wore when he celebrated high mass on a Sunday before the High Altar.

All parishioners were meant to pay tithes for the upkeep of the vicar. Among the special services held at Kingston Church were those on All Saints' Day (the day of the dedication of the church), on the day of the Purification of The Blessed Mary, and on her Assumption and Nativity, and the Assumption and Nativity of St Blaise.

Lay participation in the services was limited, but many ordinary people gave money for masses to be said for their souls, or those of their loved ones. Often they contributed towards the upkeep of lamps and candles, in memory of the souls of those departed. Thus Roger Adam of Kingston granted 4d a year to the common lamp of Kingston Church for the souls of Aveline Harding and his wife Johanna.

Special chantry chapels were sometimes endowed, where chaplains were employed permanently to pray for the souls of the dead. In 1459, William Skerne, member of a leading Kingston family which owned land near the Bittoms and at Downhall, founded a chantry in Kingston Church, at the already existing altar of St James. The chantry chaplain was to pray for the King and the Bishop of Winchester, and the souls of members of the Skerne family. Later, in 1477, Robert Bardsey endowed a fraternity of the Holy Trinity, a religious society of both clerks and lay people, organized by two wardens. Its aim was to augment the worship in Kingston Church. Bardsey left money to pay the salary of a priest, who was to celebrate divine service at the altar of the Holy Trinity in Trinity Chapel.

The most striking monument to lay piety in Kingston was the Lovekyn Chapel. The building still stands opposite Kingston Grammar School. It was originally endowed by Edward Lovekyn of Kingston in 1309, and dedicated to the Blessed Mary Magdalene. However, Edward's successor, Robert Lovekyn, neglected the project, and in the 1340s we hear that divine service had virtually ceased. The chantry was rescued in 1352 by John Lovekyn, citizen of London, who refounded it and rebuilt the chapel. Its chaplains were to pray for Edward III and the Royal family during their lifetime, for their souls and the souls of John Lovekyn and family 'when we are withdrawn from this light', and for the souls 'of all faithful departed'. There was a warden in charge of the other chaplains; they lived together in a manse next to the chapel.

A grammar school associated with the Lovekyn Chapel may also have been established during the 14th century. In 1364, a grammar school had already existed for some time in Kingston, for a letter written in that year by the Bishop of Winchester mentions that one Hugh of Kingston, a master of the Canterbury monastic school, had recently gone to Kingston to teach its boys and scholars and 'preside over the public school there'. Hugh was apparently moved partly by local patriotism, because Kingston's parishioners were 'to their grief' without a 'teacher or master of their boys and others coming to the said town, where a school has been accustomed to be kept'.

There is abundant evidence of conventional popular piety in 14th and 15th century Kingston. But in 1393 the Bishop of Winchester complained 'that certain persons, both cleric and lay, frequented the churchyard to play at ball and cast stones (whereby the church windows were often broken and other damage done), and for singing, dancing, shows and other dishonest sports'. Such antics were forbidden on Sundays and festivals, on pain of excommunication. There were also many who neglected to

LEFT: All Saints': piscina in north east pier of the tower, where the altar
of St Katherine's Chapel probably stood in the 15th century. RIGHT:
This 15th century wall painting from the parish church shows St Blaise,
patron saint of wool combers, holding his carding comb. (KM & HS)

pay their tithes, resented the exactions of the Church, or criticized churchmen. Only
a few challenged conventional religion and were caught up in the heretical movement
known as Lollardy.

Lollards believed that current religious practices got in the way of a direct, personal
relationship between man and God, and that it was important to cultivate such a
relationship by reading the Bible. There was some Lollardy in the Malden area in the
early 16th century. In 1513, four Lollards were examined at Kingston, and one of
them, Thomas Denys, was burnt in the market place. However, he does not seem to
have inspired further martyrs. The life of All Saints' Church, and of the town, went on
as normal. For most people, most of the time, business weighed heavier than belief.

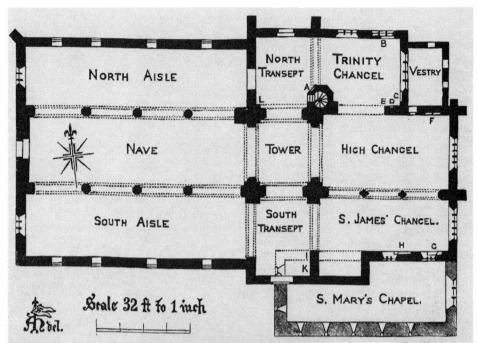

ABOVE: Plan of All Saints' Church. (H) By the 15th century, the north and south aisles and the side chapels had been added. BELOW: Interior of All Saints', showing the late 14th century arches of the nave. (KM & HS)

ABOVE: Mass manufactured medieval fish net weights, found in the Thames at Kingston. (KM) BELOW: A wealthy inhabitant of 15th century Kingston — a brass commemorates Robert Skerne (d1437) and his wife is in the parish church. His descendant William founded St James' Chantry. (M & B)

ABOVE: Kingston's Charter of Incorporation, granted by Edward IV, 1481. BELOW: 14th century cellar from a house (probably of a wealthy merchant) at the corner of Thames Street and Old Bridge Street. It was discovered beneath the 'Rose & Crown' pub, and excavated 1985-6. (KM & HS)

LEFT: The 14th century Lovekyn Chapel, pictured in 1799. RIGHT: Detail of a bracket from the base of the east window. The carved head of a king was probably that of Edward III; there used to be a second head beside it, probably of his wife, Queen Philippa. BELOW: Interior, looking towards the Decorated east window. (KM & HS)

Populous and of Great Trade

In about 1540, John Leland called Kingston 'the best market town in the whole of Surrey'. Nearly a century later, the introduction to its charter of 1628 describes Kingston as: 'a very ancient and populous town, and situated on the banks of the celebrated and navigable river the Thames, . . . from which town, by means of that river, different goods and merchandizes laden in wherries and boats, are daily transported backwards and forwards to our city of London, and the adjacent parts'. Contemporary opinion in the 16th and 17th centuries saw Kingston as a flourishing, prosperous place, though by modern standards it was still small. By 1603 it had perhaps 1,260, and by 1676 2,250 people.

That bustling prosperity was based partly on the established market, and partly on new economic conditions. England's population was increasing, and this stimulated demand for food, raw materials and other goods. Rising prices also gave people an incentive to produce for the market. Kingston was granted a third annual fair in 1556, and its dominance of local trade was assured when its charter of 1628 gave it the right to be the only market within a radius of seven miles. But there were two other important influences: Hampton Court Palace, and the growth of London.

Henry's VIII's chief minister, Cardinal Wolsey, built Hampton Court in the decade after 1515, and prudently gave it to the King in 1525. Thereafter, work continued on the buildings and grounds through the 1530s, and the Royal court, which was still itinerant, often resided there. This brought good business to Kingston. Some of the materials needed for the construction of the palace were supplied by Kingston tradesmen — for instance, William Morer of Kingston was paid 10s for 500 floor tiles for the Great Hall — and some Kingston craftsmen and labourers were employed there, like Edmund More, who carved the Royal arms on stone tablets over the gateways in Base Court. Kingston also provided supplies for the maintenance of the Royal establishment at the Palace: on one occasion, '4 bushels of wheat, at 14d the bushel, and 4 bushels of oats at 4d the bushel, and 3 bushels of barley at 9½d the bushel' were bought in Kingston market for the King's pheasants.

The proximity of Kingston to Hampton Court and other Royal palaces, such as Sheen (Richmond), Nonsuch, and Oatlands, brought court traffic and custom. In August 1526, the Burgundian embassy stayed for a week at the Crane, an inn at the south end of the market place, then called High Row. The town was already a recognized meeting place for county officials connected with the local law courts, or with Royal commissions such as those for the sewers. Several alehouses flourished in the 16th and 17th centuries, including the Chequer (later the Old Crown), in Church Street, and the Red Lion (formerly the Swan), the Castle, the Golden Griffin and the Sun, all in High Row.

Ale brewing, using malt and water, was already an established local industry by 1500, and the brewing of beer, using hops, became increasingly important during the 16th century. Ale or beer was often brewed in premises attached to an inn; the barley (for the malt) and hops were often grown locally, and were readily available in Kingston market. By the 17th century there were several wealthy brewers, such as the Tiffin family, who left a charitable bequest now remembered in the names of the Tiffin schools. Malt production was profitable and 'foreigners' *ie* traders from outside Kingston, tried to cash in. Kingston Corporation passed an ordinance in 1580 forbidding 'foreigners' to sell malt retail except on market day.

London's population increased dramatically, from perhaps 50,000 in the 1520s to about 200,000 in 1600 and 400,000 by 1650. Kingston became an important centre for cattle trading, supplying the metropolis with meat: in 1603, James I granted Kingston a Saturday cattle market. It is likely that drovers brought in cattle and sold them in Kingston to dealers who fattened them, using local farms and grazing land, to sell them on to London butchers. By the 1670s, John Aubrey mentioned 'fat cattle out of Wales' as a notable feature of Kingston's November fair. Kingston was granted an extra general produce market on Wednesdays in 1662.

Increasingly, malt, grain and other foodstuffs and raw materials were shipped by barge from Kingston to London, as were the fruit and vegetables that Surrey market gardeners were starting to produce. Marshy land was drained — in the Heathen Street area, for instance — by the 16th century, for gardens and orchards. The slaughter houses and tanyards associated with Heathen Street moved to Thames Street. In the 17th century, the medieval Bishop's Hall site became a tanyard, occupied in 1664 by tanner Obadiah Wicks, who played a prominent part in local politics just after the Civil War.

The Thames remained central to the life of the town. Roads — even the Royal highways, and despite the time and money Kingston Corporation spent maintaining them — were poorly surfaced and muddy in wet weather. They were slow, unsatisfactory and unsafe. The main road over Kingston Hill was a notorious spot for robbers. River transport was often easier, safer and cheaper. The Thames was the main thoroughfare. The churchwardens of All Saints' hired a boat to go to Walton for the local games known as the Kingham in 1510, and to take the church organs to London to be repaired in 1514-5. The church bells rang, not just when the King or Queen rode through the town but when the Royal barge passed on the water.

From time to time Royal commissioners for the sewers cracked down on illegal fish weirs that impeded river traffic, and this made local passions run high. In 1532, Erasmus Ford of Norbiton Hall, a Royal commissioner, complained that, when he tried to proceed against the weirs of a Mr Dean of Kingston, this 'taker of timber and board for Hampton Court', came to Norbiton Hall and maliciously 'dug up by the roots 35 of my purest and fairest elms', trees which were 'the chief pleasure of all my house'. Nevertheless, fishing was still important and profitable; the town's coat of arms shows three salmon on a blue background. In 1556 a Royal charter gave Kingston Corporation the right to establish a fish weir in the Thames, and use the income for the upkeep of the bridge. The Thames was still well stocked with salmon, pike and barbel in the 17th century.

If the Thames itself was one major artery, the great bridge was the other. It was made toll-free in 1565, when Robert Hammond gave lands worth £40 for its upkeep. The Bridgewarden's accounts, which survive from the early 16th century, show the constant expenditure on timber, bricks, stone, gravel and iron. Major repairs were needed between 1585 and 1600, when the stone foundations were rebuilt. The superstructure was still of timber, and sections were still removed in times of revolt or civil war. In the later 17th century, it had two seats for pedestrians to avoid carts.

Kingston trades by 1580 were organized into four companies, or guilds: the Woollen Drapers, for dyeing, weaving and tailoring; the Mercers, for barbers as well as grocers and haberdashers; the Butchers for trades related to the supply of food and drink, like baking, brewing and fishing; and the Shoemakers (Cordwainers), for the leather, metal and wood working trades and for glaziers and bricklayers.

Men (and occasionally women) who wished to practise their trades within the town on a daily basis had to be 'free' of one of these companies. A person became a full member, or freeman, of a company usually by being a freeman's eldest surviving son or by serving an apprenticeship with a freeman. Apprenticeships were often for seven years, and it was usual for the apprentice to live in his master's house as one of the family while he learnt his trade. Then, on payment of 3s 4d to the guild's wardens, he could set up in business in Kingston.

Restricting the free practice of trade within the town to guild members safeguarded the livelihood of Kingston's inhabitants. 'Foreigners' were not forbidden to trade in the town, but they had to pay for the privilege. Not that this was always sufficient. In 1637, Kingston's bailiffs claimed that the town's two bakers were scarcely able to maintain themselves, because on market day so many bakers came from elsewhere to sell their wares that they supplied people with enough bread to last all week. However, Kingston Corporation was normally prepared, for a fee, to grant 'tolerations', or permissions to trade, especially if the trade concerned benefitted the town, or was one that few freemen practised.

Individual and corporate prosperity was still precarious. The economy depended on the weather and the harvest. 1586 seems to have been a particularly bad year for famine in Kingston. It was referred to as 'the time of the dearth', and led to Kingston, along with other parts of Surrey, being counted for tax purposes as a 'poor town'.

Food shortages led to malnutrition, and a run of bad harvests left a weakened population susceptible to plague or influenza. The great plague of 1665 is well remembered; less well known but also devastating was the 'flu epidemic of 1558, when up to a fifth of the population died. The parish registers of Kingston Church show that 'plague deaths' reached double figures roughly once a decade. The years 1593 and 1603 saw particularly severe outbreaks. In 1593 Kingston's authorities contained the infection by building an isolation hospital. Queen Elizabeth noted approvingly that: 'They presently . . . caused an house to be made in the fields distant from the town, where the infected might be kept apart and provided for all things convenient for their sustenance and care'. Even so, 85 people died that year of plague.

In 1603, when there were 71 deaths, Kingston's churchwardens paid people to attend the sick and take food to them. Sometimes the central government, concerned to protect Hampton Court, ordered the bailiffs to build plague houses. This happened in 1636, when Kingston was ordered to put up 'sheds or hulks' in the fields for the sick. However, the bailiffs on this occasion did not rush to comply. Maybe they did not think the situation warranted such action, and maybe they were right: only 13 people succumbed to plague that year.

Plague could seriously disrupt the economic life of the whole town. In 1625, when Thomas Locke wrote that 'the sickness is very much about Kingston and its neighbourhood', and was also 'violent in London', river trade was stopped to prevent the spread of infection, and 'those that go to London must not return into the country'.

William Goldstone, who in 1625 had contracted to buy 600 loads of timber to supply the navy, had to leave part of it at Kingston, and in 1629 lamented that 'the same still lies on the waterside' because he was unable to afford its carriage to Deptford.

People in 16th and 17th century Kingston lived close to death and natural disaster and many were poor. Between a third and a half of the population was below the poverty line. Poor and vagrants were apparently increasing; wages did not keep pace with prices. When the monasteries, traditional dispensers of charity, were dissolved 1536-41, parish churches, town councils and private charity had to fill the gap.

Kingston did not have a monastery, though the Carthusian houses at Richmond and Merton Priory were both close, and gave some relief. When these religious houses were dissolved, Kingston felt the impact. Kingston itself had some sort of charitable institution associated with the chantry chapel of St Mary Magdalene (the Lovekyn Chapel). Leland says: 'There was and is a chapel called Magdalene's, and attached to it is a hospital which had a master, two priests and some pauper men'. Presumably this refuge, possibly for the aged poor, was closed either when Henry VIII seized the Lovekyn Chapel's lands for the Crown in 1540, or when Edward VI finally dissolved the chantries in 1547.

Charity in Kingston was organized partly by the Corporation, and partly by the churchwardens of All Saints' and, after 1601, by the parish overseers of the poor. The four trading companies also helped their own members. Various private charitable bequests for the poor were vested in Kingston Corporation, for instance those of John Price (1524), Robert Norton (1599), John Hartopp (1608), and Henry Smith (1624). Edward Buckland, by his will of 1618, left a wharf, the profits from which were to be used to buy coal as cheaply as possible and sell it cheaply to the poor. John and Thomas Tiffin, in 1638 and 1639, left money to educate poor boys and apprentice them to learn trades. It fell to the Corporation to administer these charities. Kingston Corporation Chamberlains' accounts show payments for 'faggots for the poor' at Christmas.

The charitable bequest that is probably best remembered today is that of William Cleave, who by his will of 1665 left all his property in Kingston 'for the maintenance of twelve poor people of the said parish, for ever'. These were to be single people over 60 years old: 'six poor men and six poor women of honest life and reputation'. Married couples were admitted in 1889. Cleave also left £500 to build an almshouse for the old people to live in, and this was finished by 1670. Cleaves Almshouses still stand today, at the Kingston end of the London Road, one of the oldest surviving brick buildings in Kingston.

Kingston seems to have had almshouses much earlier than this, in the 16th century, but it is not clear who ran them. Money for the relief of the poor was often collected in church and distributed by the churchwardens; churchwardens' accounts for 1594-5 show that 12d was given to a poor Irishman, 8d to John Hawkins, a blind man, 12d to Agnes Wells of Kingston, another shilling to 'a very poor maid', 6d to a poor soldier, and several shillings to two traders who had lost their goods at sea.

Many who received charity were not natives of Kingston. However, only those considered deserving cases were treated kindly. In 1572, a number of people considered to be rogues and vagabonds were 'whipped about the market place and burnt in the ears'. Even vagrants who received help were likely to die in winter of cold and hunger, like the 'walking woman' found dead in Mr Hillier's barn in 1595.

The organization of a regular sysem for coping with poverty was theoretically placed, by the great Tudor poor law of 1601, in the hands of parish officials called the overseers of the poor. They were meant to collect a 'poor rate' from those who could afford it, and use the money to relieve the old and sick, to apprentice pauper children, and to buy materials to 'set the poor on work'. Kingston's earliest surviving poor rate assessment books and overseers' accounts date from the late 1680s, but it is clear that long before this the parish collected a poor rate. Kingston had overseers for the poor by 1603, and by 1610 there seem to have been four of them. From then on we hear of the overseers, along with the churchwardens, apprenticing poor children to learn trades: in 1610 they bound Elizabeth Allison to a cooper. In 1608, Kingston Corporation's ordinances governing the trading companies mentioned that people living in the town paid duties for the poor, and the churchwardens' accounts for 1613-4 mention the 'table and form where the collectors for the poor sit'. In 1662 the churchwardens distributed the money 'as they saw occasion and necessity required'.

In practice, looking after the poor in Kingston was a communal effort. But whatever efforts were made by guild, church or Corporation, individual acts of charity still counted. Sometime before 1570, 'Ward the smith' took in a young beggar called John, and looked after him. Had he not done so, John Smith might have met the fate of another child whose burial appears that year in the Parish register: 'a child of 6 years old, that came from Windsor and died in the street', without anyone knowing his name.

The town also began to take some responsibility for education. If there was a school connected with the Lovekyn chantry chapel, this would have been lost when the chantry was dissolved. At the beginning of Elizabeth's reign, Kingston petitioned the Queen, and Kingston Grammar School was established in 1561. It was endowed with lands for its maintenance, and by the 17th century children born in the town were taught free of charge. The bailiffs of Kingston acted as its governors, and special schoolwardens kept its accounts and presented them to the town council.

Kingston's ruling body, the equivalent of today's town council, was called the Court of Assembly. It was responsible for the regulation of trade, the town's bridges, including the Thames bridge, and the upkeep of local roads. It also supervised Kingston's finances and the administration of Corporation property. The Court of Assembly was headed by two bailiffs, instead of a mayor. The bailiffs were the leaders of Kingston Corporation and were also Justices of the Peace. There were various different Corporation officials who were either members of or responsible to the Court of Assembly; these included the aletasters, who maintained standard weights and measures in Kingston market. The town also had several different courts. The most serious criminal cases were reserved for the Assize courts, when a Royal judge visited the county. The Surrey Assizes were sometimes held in Kingston.

The town council met, and the local courts sat, in the Guildhall or Court Hall which stood in the market place, near the pillory. The Chamberlains' accounts show that constant work was needed to keep it in repair. In particular, the windows kept getting broken. Sometimes, at the Assizes, when rowdy behaviour was expected, the glass was removed first, or boarded over, before the stone throwing started. People in the 16th and 17th century were volatile and violent, and the authorities were both more tolerant of disorder, and more afraid of it, for there were no police. High prices, heavy taxes and religious changes could start a riot, and there were enough of all three to give Kingston's leaders headaches.

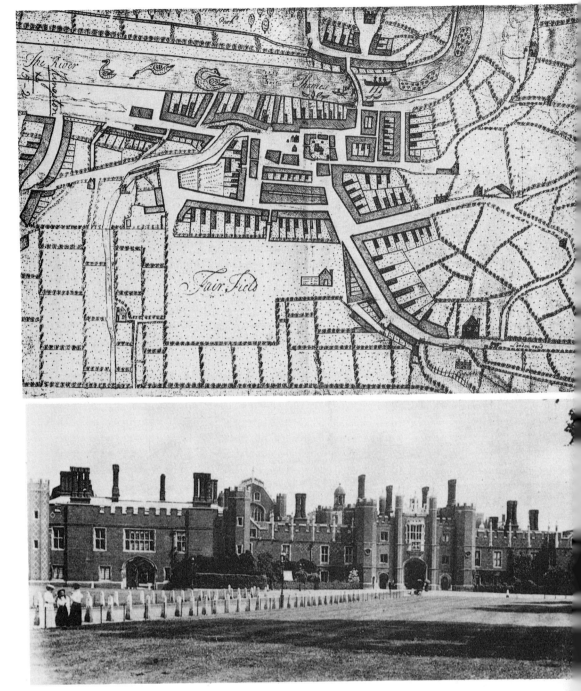

ABOVE: Copy of the 17th century earliest known 'street map' of the town. (BL) BELOW: Hampton Court Palace, an important influence on Kingston's trade and prosperity. (KM & HS) OPPOSITE: Coombe Conduit House. Wolsey built several conduit houses in the early 16th century to tap the natural springs on Coombe Hill. Lead pipes carried the water underground to Hampton Court. BELOW: The site in Kingston Market Place of the Castle Inn, later Hide's department store. RIGHT: A 17th century staircase survives in the building. (KM & HS)

ABOVE: The Griffin, a famous inn for several hundred years, stood on the same spot in Kingston Market Place in the 16th century, when it was called the 'Golden Griffin'. BELOW: Kingston Grammar School, founded (or refounded) by Elizabeth I in 1561, was originally housed in the Lovekyn Chapel. (KM & HS)

ABOVE: 'Fat cattle out of Wales': cattle on the Fairfield, c1925, but Kingston's November fair was already famous for cattle by the later 17th century. BELOW: Cleave's Almshouses, founded 1665, built in local brick c1668-70, stand in London Road and are still inhabited. (KM & HS)

73

LEFT: Old Harrow Passage; parts date from the 16th century. RIGHT: A 17th century trader's token. Some Kingston traders issued their own tokens, for use instead of coins, because of a shortage of small change. This rare square token was issued in 1668 by Stephen Feilder, who made his money from candle-making in the 1650s; by 1668 he was a wealthy dealer in general merchandise. BELOW: Kingston Tannery, Thames Street, photographed in the 1930s. There was a tanyard here from the 17th century. (KM & HS)

A Town Divided

Most of the time, local concerns were more important than the policies of central government. But occasionally Royal policy changed the very fabric of local life. This happened from the 1530s with the Protestant Reformation, and in the mid-17th century with the English Civil War and its aftermath.

Until the 1530s religious life still centred on All Saints' Church. The churchwardens, who were substantial citizens and officers of Kingston Corporation, were in charge of maintaining the church buildings and the ornaments of worship. The steeple was a particular expense, and the bells often needed mending. Then the candlesticks on the high altar had to be regularly cleaned, the vestments washed, the rood light re-made.

Worship was carried out with considerable visual display: extra candles at Christmas, a special Paschal candle at Easter, the priest robed in a blue velvet cope on holy days, a gilded cross and chalice and silver candlesticks upon the altar at high mass. But it was also a mystery, whose central ceremony was performed on the people's behalf behind the great carved rood screen that separated the nave, where the laity stood, from the chancel, where the priest celebrated.

Vicars at this time were often absentees. Nicholas West, who was vicar of Kingston from 1502 probably until 1515, was frequently at court or abroad on diplomatic business. The day-to-day religious life of All Saints' was in the hands of a succession of parish priests, and this continued under the vicars of the 1520s. However, Laurence Stubbs, who was buried at All Saints', did live here from 1531 until his death in 1536. Even if a vicar was non-resident, this did not necessarily mean a lack of care. Parish priests may not have been well educated, but they could baptise and bury, take services, hear confession, comfort the sick, and bless the crops. They could say prayers for rain, and dispense holy water to ward off fire or plague. Every year, Kingston parish collected 53s 4d to pay the priest's wages, and his services were valued.

Sometimes a clergyman was unpopular. Nicholas West provoked local anger by charging too much for burials. William Cox, curate in 1536, was so disliked that the churchwardens did not pay his wages. Maybe this was because the plague struck Kingston that year, and his prayers and rituals were ineffective. He complained that: 'I am thought no more worthy of men's company than the mouth of the hangman of Calais is of any man's cup'. But dissatisfaction with individual clergymen was not the same as dissatisfaction with the beliefs or ceremonies of the Catholic Church. Payments to the churchwardens kept up in the 1520s. 'Honest men of the parish' were willing to contribute £4 12s — enough money for a person to live on for a year — towards a new rood loft in 1526 and, as late as 1537-8, £2 was spent 'for gilting of our Lady in the High Rood Loft'.

By this time, however, the Reformation had already started. Throughout the 1530s, Kingston's inhabitants would have heard rumours of religious change. Visiting preachers made them aware, if they were not so already, of Henry VIII's 'great matter', his attempts, despite papal opposition, to divorce his wife, Catherine of Aragon, and of the religious implications. The offcial line — which Friar John Laurence preached at Kingston in 1532 — was that it was the duty of people to obey their princes. This they mainly did, but many in their hearts may have been as outraged at Henry's actions as were Friar Laurence's superiors at the Carthusian Friary at Richmond, who protested that 'all our religion should be slandered thereby'.

Protestant doctrines of salvation by faith alone, and of the authority of the Bible were openly discussed. A witness called Stephen Kempe says that in 1534 (the year Henry VIII denied papal supremacy), 'he heard the parson of Hanworth preach at Kingston . . . that whoever came to church to seek God would not find Him, unless he brought Him with him; and that men ought to put their trust in God's word, and have better regard to good sermons and preaching than to the Sacrament of the Altar, mass, matins or evensong'.

The conflict between the Protestant teachings of Luther and Calvin and the traditional ways of the Catholic Church raged for about 30 years. It is unfortunate that the churchwardens' accounts for the vital period 1539-61 no longer survive, so we have few details about how Kingston reacted to the frequent religious changes imposed by the government. But the impression gained from existing evidence is one of only reluctant conformity. There seems to have been no particular enthusiasm for Protestantism in the 1530s, and no image-breaking up to 1539. The churchwardens did not dash out to buy an English version of the Bible though, according to the Royal injunctions of 1538, they were supposed to. Moreover, Henry VIII's confiscation of the lands of the Lovekyn Chantry Chapel in 1540 can have done little to promote reform.

In Edward VI's reign, the government officially endorsed Protestantism. Traditional ritual and ceremony in church services were condemned. In 1552-3, the plate and vestments of Kingston church, carefully maintained and a focus of local pride, were confiscated for the Crown. All Saints' was left with its bells, two communion chalices, two hangings of red and white silk for the communion table, and a black satin hearse cloth embroidered with the name of Jesus. Gone were the other chalices, the crosses, candlesticks, two pairs of organs, and the vestments and altar hangings in embroidered silk and velvet.

Perhaps the bailiffs and churchwardens tried to save some precious items. An inventory of Kingston's church goods made in 1549 does not appear to list the best (silver or gilt) altar cross or the silver candlesticks which the church still had in 1539, nor does it specifically mention the double gilt chalice bought in 1535. Moreover, in a second inventory made in 1552, two of the four chalices mentioned in 1549, the organs, and the lion's share of the silk, velvet and damask vestments and altar hangings were no longer listed, though a number of vestments reappeared to be sold off for the Crown in 1553. As to the unlisted items, it is possible that the wardens did what the parishioners of St Nicholas', Guildford did — sold them to pay for church repairs. But it is more likely that they were hidden to avoid confiscation. In 1553, the Privy Council demanded of Kingston Corporation plate which the town 'pretended to be theirs by way of escheat', and it is tempting to think that this represents church treasures which the bailiffs 'rescued'.

When Queen Mary restored Catholicism, Kingston did not object. No martyrs were burnt in its market place. Protestantism had by now won over some hearts and minds, but no one was prepared to suffer for it. Many people probably welcomed the return to the old ways. The churchwardens either invested in new altar hangings and vestments, or brought out ones they had previously put away; they were still selling these off in the mid-1560s. When Thomas Wyatt tried to cross the Thames at Kingston in 1554, during his rebellion against Mary's marriage to Catholic Philip of Spain, no one from Kingston appears to have joined him. Instead, the town held up his crossing by removing the middle section of Kingston bridge.

Protestantism really took root in Kingston during Elizabeth's long reign. In the 1550s, the churchwardens of All Saints' sold off their vestments, took down the high altar and replaced it with a communion table, and finally sold the rood screen and other pieces of carving. A Bible was placed in the chancel. A lot of old and broken (presumably coloured) glass in the windows was also replaced by new, presumably clear, glass. However, the church was not at this stage in Puritan, or 'hot Protestant', hands. Its priests wore surplices, which Protestant extremists disliked, and the church still had a choir, an organ, and a painted cross, and staged an Easter play in 1563.

From the later 1570s there are signs that a more enthusiastic Protestantism gained ground, one which eschewed church ceremony and music, and concentrated on preaching the Word. Apparently, Kingston church no longer had a choir or organ. In 1583, the wardens' accounts mention an hourglass (used to time sermons), so sermons were obviously important. It was about then that Kingston came under the influence of a leading Puritan preacher, John Udall, who ministered there because the vicar, Stephen Chatfield, did not then reside; Udall was preaching in the church by 1584.

Udall was a Presbyterian extremist. He believed in the abolition of bishops and the establishment of a system of church organization based on synods of godly lay 'elders' working with their minister, along the lines of Calvin's Geneva. Elizabeth's government frowned on such views, and it was probably as a godly preacher, not as a Presbyterian, that Udall was invited to Kingston. However, once there, he seems to have had some success in establishing a local synod based on All Saints'. The names of those who joined Udall in the public meeting he held in the church in December 1585 show that by then he had on his side one of the bailiffs of Kingston, George Snelling, as well as two important local gentlemen, John Evelyn and Thomas Vincent, and both churchwardens. At this meeting, they agreed to move the pulpit to a central position, and to alter the seats so that the parishioners should be 'placed in order in their degrees and callings'. They also decided to hold another meeting in January to discuss church matters.

To the government, this might well seem an illegal attempt to introduce Presbyterianism by the back door. Udall's sermons also contained views that were unorthodox. In 1586, he was called before Elizabeth's religious watchdog, the Court of High Commission, and nearly banned from his ministry. Influential friends saved him. Undeterred, Udall held clandestine meetings at Kingston with John Penry, and later with the Puritan printer, Robert Waldegrave, and they set up a secret press at East Molesey to print anti-episcopal tracts. Udall's (anonymous) pamphlet was a reasonably sober exposition of Presbyterianism; Penry's (on which Udall may have collaborated) was the much ruder 'Martin Mar-prelate' attack on the bishops.

However, by the time these were in circulation, in 1588, Udall's sermons in Kingston church again offended High Commission, and he was forbidden to preach in the town. He left Kingston by the end of the year. He had not made Kingston a Puritan town — that would have required more years, and successors with similar views — but he had shown that, if a minister of fire and zeal could gain the support of a few leading men, he could briefly transform the official worship of a whole community.

His ministry also marks the coming of age of Kingston as a Protestant town. Thirty years on from the Elizabethan settlement, Catholicism had become a persecuted minority religion. There may still have been a few practising Catholics in the town, though none are known; if so, they would have attended mass secretly and been served, either by the private chaplains of local Catholic gentry families, or by visiting priests trained abroad and often prepared for martyrdom. One such priest, William Way, was executed at Kingston in 1588. He was probably dragged on a hurdle up Kingston Hill to the gallows, where he was disembowelled alive before being hanged. He suffered 'with great constancy'; his head was stuck on a pike on Kingston bridge. Way, though active in south London, may have had no contact with Kingston's inhabitants, but a Catholic execution in the year of Udall's expulsion was good politics. It underlined both the government's commitment to Protestantism, and its willingness to take severe action against those whose religious views challenged the establishment.

After Udall, there remained some support for his brand of extreme and enthusiastic Protestantism in Kingston. But the clergy at All Saints' from 1590 to 1630 were mainstream Anglicans. They showed a genuine commitment to Protestantism, but they felt comfortable conforming to the government's 'official' version. Preaching was still important, and the ministers saw it as their duty to teach the young the rudiments of the Protestant faith — in 1623 the church had a 'form that the children stand upon to answer the minister'. But services were according to the Book of Common Prayer, and it was considered legitimate to care about the dignity and beauty of their surroundings. This moderate Protestantism had widespread support.

From the early 17th century, the vestry from time to time set a church rate, collected by the wardens, which raised large amounts of money for church repairs and alterations. Coloured glass was reintroduced. In the 1620s there was a major programme of church 'beautification', which included 'blueing the 8 upper windows in the middle aisle' and new glass in the other windows. It also involved 'blueing the Arches of the Church and Chancel', 'colouring the three church doors in oil', painting the north and south porches (the latter in red), and 'colouring the screen in the walk'. Scriptural verses were also painted upon the same screen and on the walls, to educate the congregation. Such decorations fell short of the full-blown 'beauty of holiness' promoted by William Laud's High Church party, but they would have been enough to raise Puritan hackles.

By 1630, Kingston presented a challenge to 'godly' reformers. But the next year, the town's dissatisfied but determined minority found a redoubtable ally in a Puritan minister called Edmund Staunton. He preferred Kingston to his previous benefice 'because his opportunities of service would be there the greater', and because 'he was of his mind, who was wont to say, his opportunities were his greatest riches'. Those townsmen who supported Staunton made life so uncomfortable for the vicar, Dr Seaton, 'that in a short time he resigned', and in 1632 the church bells were rung to welcome Staunton to Kingston.

For the next three years, Staunton was zealous in preaching and teaching, and made many converts. His protegé, Richard Mayo, says that he 'preached twice on the Lord's day, and catechized the younger and ignorant sort of people; and he did not satisfy himself in teaching them publicly; he taught them also from house to house. Then also he set up a weekly lecture, which was supplied . . . by as eminent Preachers, as that part of England did afford, and within a little time, partly by his powerful preaching, partly by his holy and exemplary life . . . he wrought a general reformation throughout the Town . . .'.

Staunton made a considerable impact on Kingston, though he was not resident there for half of the 27 years he held the vicarage. In 1635 he was suspended for refusing to read out of the Book of Sports in church, and spent the next 3½ years studying in Oxford. Back in Kingston presumably from about 1639, he was a member of the Westminster Assembly of divines from 1643, and must have been often in London during the Civil War. From 1648 he was absent altogether, because he became President of Corpus Christi College, Oxford, and lived there. Yet Mayo tells us that in 1648, when he left, 30 Kingston people wrote him a farewell testimonial acknowledging him as their spiritual father.

However, it is clear even from Mayo's hagiography that Kingston opinion about Staunton was divided. Mayo says that he was loved by the godly but feared by the wicked, and quotes Staunton's own double-edged remark about the people of Kingston that 'were it not for some wrangling persons, a minister might live as comfortable a life among them, as amongst any people in the land'. Presumably, while some saw their zealous minister as an inspiration, others thought him a pain.

After 1642, controversies over religion were bound up with the political divisions of the English Civil War. This, the unlooked for result of the conflict between Charles I and his Parliament, was seen by virtually everyone as a tragic disaster. Staunton and other Puritan enthusiasts supported Parliament, while moderate Anglicans tended to support the King, but there was little enthusiasm for the war in Kingston. The town merely became the unwilling host to both Royalist and Parliamentarian soldiers, whose presence was imposed upon it largely because of its geographical position and strategic importance.

Even before the 'official' start of the war, there was trouble in the town caused by visiting soldiers. In January 1642, when Charles I fled the City for Hampton Court, some of the armed soldiers and courtiers who accompanied him stayed in Kingston. According to one report, the Royalist supporter, Colonel Lunsford, marched into Kingston with about 300 troopers, and 'about the middle of the town they went in to drink, and continued there part of that day swaggering, and swearing blasphemous oaths (which filled the town with fears) and some amongst the rest, to frighten the town, swore bitter oaths that they should see bloody times ere long; which words raised jealousies and suspicions in the town, and presently word was brought from Kingston to London . . . that Colonel Lunsford was risen up in rebellion at Kingston on Thames'. However, Lunsford was soon arrested, and order restored.

When the Civil War proper started, Kingston was an obvious target for military occupation by one side or the other. It was the site of the first bridge upstream from London, and also of one of the military storehouses for Surrey. The Southwark trained bands, part of the Surrey local defence force, occupied Kingston first, on behalf of Parliament, because Sir Richard Onslow, the man in charge of Surrey's defences, was a Parliamentarian. Worried by this turn of events, many of Kingston's inhabitants tried to remove their goods to a safer place; the Southwark men's captain prevented them, and relations became strained. Townsmen were reluctant to give their unwelcome visitors food or accommodation — they probably feared shortages, or that they would not be paid — and eventually the trained bands withdrew.

79

However, the town was not left alone. The trained bands were replaced by Parliamentarian troops, led by Sir James Ramsey under the overall command of the Earl of Essex. There was considerable excitement in November 1642 when the Royalists, encouraged by their success at the battle of Edgehill, attacked Brentford, and supplies were sent by river from Kingston to relieve it. Ramsey then led his troops to help defend London, and met the King's army at Turnham Green. While he did so, Kingston was momentarily free of occupying soldiers. But when the King's army retreated from Turnham Green, part of it marched through Kingston and occupied the town for a few days before withdrawing to Oxford.

Royalist supporters in Kingston welcomed the Cavaliers 'with ringing bells for joy', and 'laid the bridge for their entrance'. According to a Parliamentarian pamphleteer, 5,000 troops entered the town on 13 November: 600 horsemen, and 4,000 Welsh and Irish foot soldiers. The writer of the pamphlet may well have exaggerated both the numbers of soldiers and the havoc they wrought — he claimed they 'made such spoil that it is impossible that any foreign enemy had the heart to do the like', and that they plundered, burnt, and used the church as a stables — but it does sound as if their visit was a frightening and unpleasant experience. When the King's army had gone, Parliamentary troops reoccupied Kingston, and for much of 1643 soldiers were billeted there. For the rest of the first civil war, Parliament kept control of Surrey.

During the Civil War, some of Kingston's inhabitants were sympathetic to the King's cause, and some to Parliament. Charles had made himself unpopular in some quarters by his forced enclosure of Richmond Park in the 1630s, and by the suspension of Staunton. In 1636, those in charge at Kingston Church had specifically paid the bell ringers NOT to ring the bells when the King came to Hampton Court. By the 1640s, some felt that taking up arms against the King was justified, including Staunton and a group of 'godly' followers, who also favoured religious change. It may have been this pro-Parliament faction that told the authorities about Lunsford's brawl. However, there was obviously a Royalist faction, perhaps led by the Mr (George?) Snelling who made the arrangements for the King's army to enter the town in November 1642, and the pamphleteer who recorded this thought that most of Kingston's inhabitants supported the Cavaliers, for he wrote that 'this town for the most part are all Malignants'.

How Royalist the majority of townsmen, or of those on Kingston Corporation, really were, is hard to say. Personal and local interests often overrode wider political or religious principles, and many people probably tried not to take sides, or conceived their greatest dislike for whichever set of soldiers was occupying the town and making life miserable. As to the divisions of opinion upon Kingston Corporation, we know that men later identified as Royalists as well as those who later supported Cromwell served on it. Kingston bridge was apparently partially dismantled after the Parliamentary troops left to go to London, otherwise it would not have needed laying again when the King's army approached. Even if Mr Snelling acted with full Corporation backing when he laid the bridge for the Royalists, this does not necessarily show general enthusiasm for the King's cause. It was no doubt partly prudence, and considered preferable to risking the town being taken by force. When the Royalists had gone, the Corporation did not try to stop Parliamentary soldiers entering the town. It seems to have taken the line of least resistance.

Certainly, whatever individual views, Kingston Corporation as a whole seems to have been mainly concerned to limit the damage done. In 1643, it presented a united front to complain about the quartering of Parliamentary troops on the town, and pressed Parliament for payment. The bailiffs and inhabitants petitioned Parliament several times. They claimed that over £289 was owing for the food and lodging of Colonel Sir Henry Cholmeley's 460 soldiers, for four weeks between 13 March and 10 April 1643, that sick and wounded soldiers of Lord Robert's regiment had cost £529 since early April, and that another £156 was owing for other soldiers' accommodation and food. All this was besides 'the great damage, spoil and losses sustained by soldiers quartered here', which had cost the town 'many thousands of pounds'. Heavy Parliamentary taxation was another cause for complaint. Town officials also travelled to Farnham in 1643 to ask the Parliamentary commander there to reduce demands.

By the end of the first civil war, the divisions of 1642 had become further complicated by the rise to power of the New Model Army as an independent force in politics. In 1647, the army which occupied Kingston under Sir Thomas Fairfax (he lodged at the Crane) was itself to use force against Parliament, which now wished to disband it. The whole country was sick of war and sick of soldiers. But there was nothing Kingston could do except complain.

In 1648, the Earl of Holland tried to drum up support for the King in Surrey. His small Royalist army passed through Kingston — apparently without the excesses of 1642 — and was defeated on common land near Surbiton. According to tradition, Lord Francis Villiers, who was killed in the battle, fought with particular bravery. Knocked off his horse, he fought on with his back against a tree until, considerably outnumbered, he received his death blow. Villiers Road, Surbiton, is named after him. But the inhabitants of Kingston played little part. The town was occupied by Holland's ally, the Duke of Buckingham, and later by their opponents under Sir Miles Livesey, but Kingston Corporation itself did not take sides.

Once the King was executed and the Commonwealth proclaimed, a group of Presbyterian and republican supporters in Kingston started to exert their influence against those members of the Corporation who appeared to them to be 'Royalists' — which might have meant genuine sympathy for the ex-monarch or for monarchy, or a preference for traditional Anglicanism in religion, or simply a lack of enthusiasm for the new republican government led by Oliver Cromwell. Some of Kingston's 'Cromwellian' group may have been sincere men of principle, but one of its leaders, Theophilus Colcocke, bailiff 1653-4, appeared to opponents as a blatant trouble-maker: 'the most proud, malicious, insolent, perfidious, and turbulent and shameless hypocrite that ever came into any Corporation'. Associated with Colcocke were his fellow bailiff Obadiah Wickes (1653-4 and 1657); Sackford Gonson, bailiff four times between 1648 and 1659, and Kingston's new minister, Richard Mayo, who held services while Staunton was at Oxford, and finally replaced him in charge in 1659. Wickes, Colcocke and Mayo petitioned Cromwell's Council of State in 1654 against the Surrey MP, Robert Wood of Kingston, whom they obviously felt was not sufficiently 'godly'.

Colcocke's faction tried to establish control over Kingston Corporation by illegally debarring their opponents from office, and packing the Corporation with their own supporters. In September 1653, Sackford Gonson refused to admit Edward Beale to the town council because, though he had been properly elected, Beale was a man 'ill affected to the present government', having refused to serve as a soldier against Charles II at the battle of Worcester (1651). Instead, one of Colcocke's followers was elected. In 1654, another of Colcocke's faction, Thomas Hancock, became an attorney of the town court, even though he had not served the necessary apprenticeship. At a meeting of the Court of Assembly, the freeman and apprentices of the town petitioned against this breach, and demanded an explanation. When the bailiffs refused to answer and tried to dissolve the meeting, the other members of the Corporation banned them from holding office. But Mayo enlisted Protector Cromwell's help in getting the bailiffs' candidate appointed Town Clerk, and Colcocke then called an illegal Assembly without the knowledge of his six leading opponents, and discorporated them in their absence. His own candidates replaced them, so he then had majority support on the town council.

After a court case, the judges in 1655 found in favour of the men Colcoke had discorporated, but they were not fully reinstated. Despite the opposition to them, Colcocke's determined malpractices had paid off. At Charles II's restoration in 1660, when Colcocke and Gonson were again bailiffs, they secured the illegal election of their preferred candidate as Kingston's High Steward, but this time they ran into trouble. The whole past history of political malpractice in Kingston was re-examined. Finally, the illegally elected members of the Corporation were expelled, and proper elections held.

Throughout the Protectorate, the Presbyterian minister, Richard Mayo, remained at Kingston, aided after 1657 by Richard Byfield. These men were active in preaching and teaching and, with the backing of Colcocke's party, and of Cromwell, their positions were secure. However, they were not unopposed. Mayo's theological views were challenged by the members of a new religious sect, the Quakers, who held meetings openly in the town. Quakers believed in the 'inner light', and were often seen as dangerous radicals in the 1650s, because their stress on the individual conscience was deemed socially subversive. Mayo saw it as his duty to convert them but, when in 1658 a leading Kingston Quaker, Edward Burrough, criticized and probably misrepresented his views, Mayo accused him of slander and he was imprisoned. When the case came to court, the judges were the bailiffs, Sackford Gonson and Henry Wilcox, supporters of Mayo. It is not surprising that Burrough was not allowed to speak and was found guilty; on this occasion few townsmen objected.

Mayo was also resented by those who preferred the traditional Anglican church, with its bishops, its ceremonies and its Book of Common Prayer, officially swept away in 1646 but still supported by many. A pamphlet in 1661 tells how one of Mayo's main opponents in Kingston was Thomas Butler, and a petition of 1657 tells how those from Kingston who were 'potent against the power of godliness' made common cause with similarly disaffected worshippers in Thames Ditton, and probably attended services held by 'a prelatical minister', Sir Thomas Evelyn's household chaplain. Byfield complained that the 'prelatical party is the most numerous, dissatisfied, closely working', and when in 1660 the Anglican Church was restored, the majority returned to its fold.

However, a significant number did not. Religious dissent was an enduring legacy of the upheavals of the mid-17th century, and in 1676 non-conformists accounted for over 15% of Kingston's population. In 1662, Mayo refused to conform and take the Anglican sacraments, and was deprived of his living. However, he continued to preach from time to time to those Protestant dissenters in Kingston who, like him, could not accept Anglicanism as restored by Charles II, but who were not members of radical sects like the Quakers. After 1664, it was illegal for any group of religious dissenters to meet together to worship, but nevertheless they did. An inquiry of 1669 into dissenting assemblies discovered that about 100 non-conformists met regularly in Kingston, at the mansion of Downhall, and that Mayo was one of their ministers. In 1672, a Royal declaration of indulgence briefly suspended the laws against dissenters, and some groups received licences for public worship. John Pigot of Kingston was licensed to let a dissenting congregation gather at his house, and Mayo was allowed to preach there. From 1673, dissenting meetings were again illegal, but Kingston's Presbyterians continued to hold them. In 1677, they had their own meeting house, which was apparently owned by Mayo, for Mayo was fined that year because he 'wittingly and willingly did suffer a Conventicle . . . to be held in his house called the Barn Meeting or Presbyterian Meeting House in Kingston'.

Kingston's Presbyterian dissenters suffered some persecution 1664-89, for the members of Kingston Corporation, whose bailiffs were the town's JPs, were officially Anglican after 1662 and not meant to tolerate conventicles. Thus Presbyterian meetings were sometimes broken up, and those who attended them or preached at them fined. However, there was influential local support and protection for them. Their congregation included several leading citizens (like James Levitt, Obadiah Wickes and Henry Wilcox) who had previously been on the Corporation, and some Corporation officials were still sympathetic, or even dissenters themselves. In 1677 Joseph Hammond, one of the headboroughs, was convicted of attending a Presbyterian meeting about which he had not told the JPs, and Thomas Burt, another Presbyterian headborough, refused to deliver the warrants against Richard Mayo. Mayo himself, who died in 1695, was much respected, and was buried in All Saints' Church with a plaque describing him as 'the excellent Mr. Richard Mayo, Gentleman'.

Things were different for the Quakers, initially a more extreme and exclusive sect who, in the 1660s, in 1670, and from 1675 were persecuted by the Kingston authorities for their illegal meetings. Many Quakers, including leaders such as John Feilder, Stephen Hubbard and Francis Holden, were beaten up, fined and imprisoned. Nevertheless, they persevered. In 1673 they built their first meeting house, probably on the corner of present day Union Street and Eden Street, and already had their own burial ground in London Road. From 1689, William and Mary's Toleration Act granted freedom of worship to all Protestant dissenters, and persecution of the Quakers ceased. Soon, they even began to appear 'respectable'. Religious divisions still existed in Kingston in 1700, but they were accepted, and the different Protestant worshippers lived fairly amicably together.

Political troubles in Kingston, like religious divisions, did not end with the Restoration, though any republican sentiment was soon denied a platform. In 1662, members of Kingston Corporation who refused to pledge support to Charles II and the Anglican Church were dismissed. Altogether about 20 people lost their positions, nearly half the Corporation, and for a while there must have been quite an undercurrent of discontent. Thereafter, the Corporation itself was officially supportive of Charles II and, after the discovery of the Rye House Plot against him in

1683, it sent him a loyal address thanking God for delivering the King from this 'most horrid and traiterous conspiracy'. However, though loyal, not all Corporation members shared the same religious perspective. Some, like John Hollis, seem to have been dissenters or sympathized with dissenters, and often would not have agreed with Royal religious policy.

Eventually, Charles grew worried enough about political opposition to interfere in local government in order to ensure its obedience. In the 1680s, Kingston fell victim to the Royal campaign to gain more control over urban corporations by remodelling them. On the pretext of investigating 'by what warrant' (quo warranto) towns held their privileges, Charles challenged and called in borough charters and issued new ones which gave the Crown powers to approve local government appointments. The King could then ensure the obedience of urban officials and, in Parliamentary boroughs, make sure that 'Tory' candidates, who supported the right of Charles' Catholic brother, James, to succeed to the throne, were returned to Parliament.

Kingston seems to have been threatened with a recall of its charter in 1682, but nothing happened. Kingston was not a Parliamentary borough, and remodelling its charter could not have been a priority. However, it seems that in 1683 there was a quarrel between Kingston Corporation and the county Sheriff over infringements of the town's liberties, and in 1684 Charles threatened to bring a writ of Quo Warranto against the Corporation. The government was obviously now taking a close interest in Kingston's affairs, and was concerned that its officials should be loyal and tractable, for the Attorney General expressed pleasure at the choice of Francis Browne as Kingston's new Recorder. The Corporation, frightened it might lose its privileges, was concerned as to what best to do. The Bailiffs and others conferred with their Recorder, and with the Lord Chief Justice, Judge Jeffreys. They went to Whitehall to ask the advice of Kingston's High Steward, Lord Arlington: when they heard he was sick, they spoke instead to his secretary, whom they gave a guinea 'that they might keep him their friend'. In November, Kingston Corporation decided to surrender its charter without waiting to fight a writ of Quo Warranto in the courts. It was rewarded in December with the news that such a 'voluntary' surrender of its charter meant that it should only be charged half fees for a new one.

However, matters were complicated by Charles II's death in February 1685, before the surrender could be enrolled. Although Kingston Corporation had already proved its obedience and, despite the loyal address it delivered to the new king, James II, in March, the government went ahead with a writ of Quo Warranto against it. This put the Corporation in a quandary. It gave further proof of loyalty by granting a trade toleration to a baker favoured by Lord Arlington. Soon afterwards, the Bailiffs visited Judge Jeffreys and begged him to 'be pleased to take the matter upon him'. He agreed, and directed the Attorney General to prepare a new surrender: 'an absolute surrender of every person in the Corporation, their respective offices and places therein'. Kingston Corporation accepted this with great reluctance. They surrendered all their liberties, charters, lands and manors, and the Quo Warranto proceedings were stayed. Kingston then received a remodelled constitution, granted in August 1685, which gave it a mayor, aldermen and common councilmen. The new charter was delivered to the town in October, when Kingston's newly appointed Corporation laid on 'a splendid Dinner, with great Demonstrations and Expressions of their Loyalty to His Majesty' to entertain their High Steward and Recorder, and the principal Surrey gentry.

The King could now remove any officers of whom he did not approve. From the start, Royal influence was exercised over Kingston, for the members of the new Corporation were nominated in the charter, and the aldermen in office 1685-8 included a few local gentry who had not previously been Corporation members. One of these, Sir Edward Evelyn, was well known as an ultra-Tory. Moreover, the previous bailiffs, Edmonds and Cooke, were off the Court of Assembly completely during this period. However, most of the members of the new Court of Assembly had served before, so at first there was no wholesale purge. But in the spring of 1688, as James realised his support was dwindling, he dismissed several members of the Corporation, including the Recorder, and appointed new ones in a desperate attempt to buy loyalty. By the summer, however, he was forced to admit defeat. In an attempt to stave off the threatened invasion of William of Orange, James restored old borough charters. In October 1688, Kingston was given back its 'ancient charters, liberties, rights and franchises'. Its old form of government was revived, and 'by the unanimous consent of this Corporation', Thomas Edmonds and John Cooke were brought back as Bailiffs and JPs. The previous Crown nominees, including Sir Edward Evelyn, did not return to office.

William III's reign put an end to the political manipulation of urban corporations. From now until the end of the 17th century, Kingston enjoyed harmonious relations with the central government, and an era of great political calm began. If the Tudor dream of religious uniformity had been permanently shattered by 1700, the dream of political unity and of religious peace had largely been achieved.

Bout ij° years synce [*i.e.* in 1587] being in Master VDALLS studie, after priuate conference had betwixt him and mee, hee shewed me certen written papers, which when I had seen, I clapt them vp together agayne and told him I would not proceed to reade any furder of them, demaunding of him where he had them: He aunswered they were sent him from a frend of his. I told him, if he Loued his owne quietnesse, he should retourne them where he had them [from]: forsomuche as in deed, by the tytles of the bookes I perceaued they did importe suche matter as is conteyned in this scandalouse Libell

2. About a ffortenight before Michaellmasse[1588] last Master VDALL and I hauing conference together in a field called "the little ffield" nere Kingeston, after certen speeches vsed in choller touching his putting [*being put*] to silence by Doctor HONE, he sayed that it was best for them not to stopp his mouth: ffor yf they did, he would then sett himself to writing, and geue the Bishoppes suche a blowe as they neuer had the lyke in their lyues. STEPHEN CHATFILD.

Let DODDESON bee examined whether he did not offer one of the libelles to ROGER WATSON of Kingeston for vjd.

The Martin Marprelate controversy, 1588-9. Kingston's vicar, Stephen Chatfield, gives evidence against John Udall, the town's 'godly' minister.
(A)

The labels in the window read:

The Fool. The Moor. The Spaniard.

A MERY MAY

The Franklin. The May-pole. The Minstrel.

The Peasant. The King of May. The Lover.

The Queen of May.

The Disard. The Friar.

THIS WINDOW (FOUNDED ON A 16TH CENTURY WINDOW) WAS UNVEILED BY ALDERMAN GEORGE HUCKLE, J.P., MAYOR, TO COMMEMORATE THE CORONATION ON THE 22ND JUNE 1911 OF KING GEORGE V. AND QUEEN MARY AND THE REVIVAL ON THAT OCCASION OF THE OLD KINGSTON-UPON-THAMES MAY-POLE AND MORRIS DANCES.

The 'May Window'. (KM) This early 20th century stained glass shows characters from the local pre-Reformation May Games. From the Churchwardens' accounts, it seems the main games took place at Whitsuntide. They were known as the 'Kingham' or 'Robin Hood Games', and involved feasting, morris dancing, and dressing up as Robin Hood and his merry men.

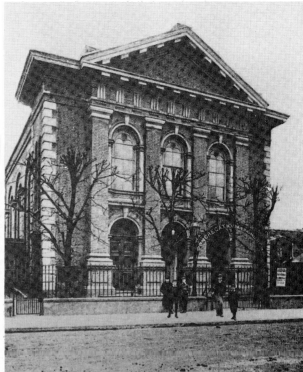
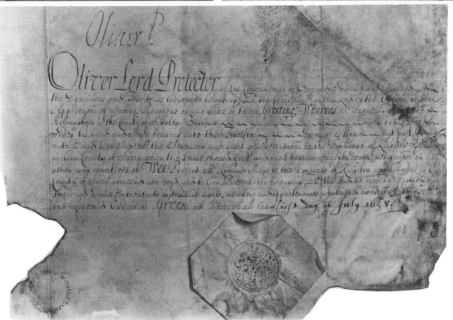

LEFT: George, 2nd Duke of Buckingham, and his brother, Lord Francis Villiers, as children. (RC) Francis was killed at the Battle of Surbiton; George escaped. RIGHT: Kingston Congregational Church, Eden Street was a 19th century descendant of Mayo's post-1660 Presbyterian dissenting church. BELOW: Oliver Cromwell's presentation of Richard Mayo to the benefice of Kingston, 1658. (Both KM & HS)

A LETTER

Of a great Victory obtained by Sir _Miles Livesey_, neer _Kingstone_, on Friday _July_ 7. 1648. _The Duke of Buckingham Routed, where was slain, the Lord_ Francis Villers, the Duke of Bucking-hams Brother, Col. Tho. Howard, The Earle of Berkshires Son, 20 Officers and Soldiers, The Earle of Holland hurt, 200 wounded, 200 Horse taken, 100 taken prisoners, &c.

Right Honourable,

THE Lord Duke of _Buckingham_, the Duke of _Richmond_, the Earl of _Holland_ the Lord _Francis_, the Lord _Andover_, with the rest of the Lords, and chief of the Gentlemen at _Kingstone_, and hereabouts, had a consultation about removing the Horse quarters, and it was concluded to goe to _Rigate_, and accordingly they went this day intending to possesse themselves of it.

Sir _Miles Livesey_ who had before taken _Horsem_, with twenty prisoners, and defeated the Cavaliers in _Sussex_) being come up, possessed himselfe of _Rigate_, before them, which caused the Lords to retreat back towards _Kingstone_.

Major _Gibbons_ comming to joyn with Sir _Miles Livesey_ against the Duke of _Buckinghams_ party (who were about 700 horse) they pursued after them and discovered them neer _Nonsuch_.

The Duke of _Buckingham_ with some of the Horse was then (it being almost night) got into _Kingston_, And a man of Collonell _Hammonds_, that was sent to view, was comming backe taken by six of their Scouts, and his Horse worth 20l. taken from him, (Colonell _Hammond_ Lieut. Col. of the Ordnance himself being neer to joyn with Sir _Miles Livesey_ but could not find him, and other parties were comming with better strength.

Upon the approach of Sir _Miles Livesey_ there was an Alarme in _Kingstone_, whereupon the guards were doubled, and all to horse, whereby Colonell _Hammonds_ man made an escape into a Corne-field.

Sir _Miles Livesey_, Propounded in the head of his Souldiers, whither they would stay untill more assistance came to them, or fall on that night

They all cried (as one man) Fall on, fall on, which accordingly they did, And fought with them between _Nonsuch_ and _Kingston_, and both the Kentish men and the rest fell on with such valour that the Lords stood not out the first Charge, But fled towards _Kingston_, Sir _Miles Livesey_ pursuing them, doing execution many being killed and taken.

When Sir _Miles Livesey_, came to the Turnepike at _Kingstone_ townsend, he had some opposition by some foot placed there, but after some dispute gained it.

The Cavaliers plundered Sir _Gilbert Gerrards_, and divers other horses, and fled towards _Harrow_.

Sir _Miles Livesey_, with his Forces is marching over _Kingstone_ bridge against them, it is said they are some 400 horse that are gone thither, which is all that is left of them of whom it is hoped there will suddenly be given a very good account,

Sir I am

Nonsuch the 7 of July 1648

Your Honours humble servant,
Hen. Frierson.

A LIST of the particulars of this great victory obtained by Sir _Miles Livesey_ against the Duke of _Buckingham_ and the rest of the Lords neere Kingston on Friday night _the 7 of July 1648._

Slaine of the Duke of Buckinghams part.

The Lord Francis Villers.	300. _Armes_, besides good store of pillage.
The Duke of Buckinghams brother Col. Thomas Howard.	3. Of Sir Miles Liveses men slain.
The Earle of Berkshires son.	20. wounded.
20. Officers and Souldiers.	The Duke of Buckingham.
The Earle of Holland hurt.	The Duke of Richmond.
200. wounded.	The Earle of Holland.
200. Horse taken.	The Lord Andover.
100. taken prisoners.	And the rest fled towards Harrow, and are pursued by Sir Miles Livesey. Some others being expected to joyne with him.
Taken also,	
9. Boats full of Pistols & Saddles	

LONDON Printed by _Robert Ibbitson_ in Smithfield neere to the Queens-Head Taverne.

Newsheet reporting the Parliamentary victory at the Battle of Surbiton, 1648. (KM & HS)

The Peaceful Century

In many ways, Kingston did not change much during the 18th century. From 1700 until the coming of the railway in 1838, Kingston continued to thrive as a small riverside market town. Its built-up area was still fairly compact, centred around the church and market place, though some ribbon development of shops, inns and houses increasingly lined the roads to Norbiton and Surbiton. The Kingston shown in John Roque's map of 1745 does not look significantly larger than that of 100 years before and, even in the 1830s, fields surrounded the town. Merryweather, in the 1880s, remembered from his boyhood 'the quiet country by-ways, with their high hedges glittering in spring time with hawthorn bloom, and their banks bestrewed with primroses, celandines and violets'. But already one important change was taking place: the population was increasing. The 2,250 or so people of 1676 had become 3,295 by 1725, and 4,438 by the time of the first census in 1801. This would soon cause problems.

The fields around 18th century Kingston were dotted with the small wooden cottages of agricultural labourers, and here and there with the elegant mansions and 'pleasure parks' of the wealthy. The Rowlls family, who owned a large brewery in Brook Street, lived at Kingston Hall, surrounded by their pleasure grounds, Rowlls' Park, only a stone's throw from Kingston Market Place, on the site of today's St James' Road. A few big houses near Kingston were owned by London gentlemen. Daniel Defoe described 'houses of retreat . . . gentlemen's mere summer houses . . . whither they retire from the hurries of business, and from getting money, to draw their breath in a clear air and to direct themselves and their families in the hot weather.' Here they 'live deliciously all the summer', and then shut the houses up in the winter, when they returned to the 'smoke and dirt, sin and seacoal' of the busy city. Some came for the 'sin': *Woodward's Miscellany*, 1731, mentions that Surbiton had long been recognized as a place to 'entertain kept mistresses', who could be seen of an evening taking the air with their lovers.

Agriculture continued to be significant to Kingston's economy. Food produced locally fed the growing population, both of Kingston itself, and of London. The Thames aits grew osiers, which supplied the local basket-making trade. By the late 18th century, many improvements in agricultural practice had been adopted.

Most of the land was already enclosed by local agreement; Roque's map shows the hedges that surrounded individual holdings. However, the common land remained 'open'. Surbiton Common, stretching over the Ewell Road/Southborough/Hook area, consisted of 430 acres of furze and bramble, while Norbiton Common, between Norbiton and what is now New Malden, contained 320 acres. The furze was useful for fuel, but improvers felt the land was not being efficiently used. A report drawn up in 1794 suggested that 'As the soil is a good loam, upon gravel and clay, it is very deserving of being enclosed' for arable husbandry. In 1808, the Kingston-upon-Thames Enclosure Act enclosed all the commons and waste land within Kingston manor, and divided them among the freeholders and established occupiers of the land. Arable farming then expanded.

Kingston was still important for livestock sold on to London but, as the 18th century faded, calves, lambs and hogs reared for the London market were in decline, though more oxen were bought at Kingston's November fair and fattened for the capital. This business was concentrated in the hands of large-scale malt distillers like Hodgson of Battersea, who fattened the oxen on the grains used in the production of malt. Hodgson's firm bought about 500 animals a year at Kingston, at £8 per head, and sold them on to London butchers at £16 each. Kingstonians also kept cows to sell their milk. Local 'milk people' could then make 75% profit by buying milk from the farmers at 14d per gallon, and selling it on to the householders at the equivalent of 24d per gallon — and that was if they sold it pure! 'But when it is understood, that a large proportion of water and other ingredients are mixed with this milk, their profit must be immense.'

Many Kingstonians made money from farming and market gardening. Some, like Thomas Jackson, who had a nursery in London Road and one on Kingston Hill, owned or rented their land. There were a few large farms and estates, like Lord Liverpool's on Kingston Hill, but most were smallholders or cottagers. Many were employed as agricultural labourers or hired gardeners. They earned maybe 12s a week, and for this they worked in winter from dawn to dusk and in summer from 6am to 6pm, with half an hour off for breakfast and one hour off for lunch. Sometimes, instead of a weekly wage, workers were paid by the job: 4s an acre plus beer for mowing grass, or 8s for hoeing turnips. Other seasonal jobs were paid by the day: women received 1s per day, plus beer, for haymaking. But seasonal work brought locals no advantage if 'gang' labour from outside was used. Reaping, said a commentator, was 'generally performed by the itinerant Irishmen, who at this season are found traversing the country in large bodies.'

Despite the importance of agriculture to local people, Kingston's function in the 18th century was still that of a 'good Market-Town', with an excellent position on the Thames. It had three annual fairs and two weekly markets, mainly for livestock, corn and malt, and was a centre of fishing, coaching, malting and brewing. Its wooden bridge was still the only one upstream from London until Putney bridge was built in 1729, and in 1828 it was replaced with a new, wider stone structure a little to the south. Kingston maintained its position as a market centre because of its bridge, the continued importance of the River Thames for commercial transport, and because of improved roads. All sorts of products were still shipped by water to and from Kingston, including barley and timber from Surrey, malt, wheat and vegetables from Kingston to London, and coal and manure from London to Kingston.

Before the 18th century, public roads were notoriously badly maintained. The parish was meant to repair them, but road surfacing was poor. From the late 17th century, turnpike trusts provided a partial solution. Trusts, run by local landowners, were established by act of Parliament and allowed to build and repair roads, and levy tolls. Turnpike gates and toll houses were built to collect the money. Local agricultural traffic was usually exempt.

By the mid-18th century, Kingston was at the hub of four major turnpike routes. Firstly, there was the ten mile stretch of road from London to Kingston, which ran across the new Putney bridge, and over Putney Heath, Wimbledon Common and Kingston Hill to Manningate Lane (Park Road). Secondly, the Portsmouth road was the continuation of this route from the other side of Kingston, starting at Surbiton Street, at the south end of High Street. It ran to Esher, Cobham, Ripley and Guildford, and eventually on to Sheetbridge, near Petersfield, from which another stretch of turnpike road carried on to Portsmouth. Special arrangements were made for the linking section of road, running from Manningate Lane through Norbiton and past the Lovekyn Chapel to what is now Clarence Street, where the pavement of Kingston town began, and then through Kingston to the end of its pavement at the town's south end. This, the road running through Kingston itself, was maintained by a separate trust, but the trustees were not allowed to erect a turnpike; instead, they received an annual income from the trustees of the Kingston to Sheetbridge route. A third turnpike route ran from Kingston to Ewell, while the last was the Kingston to Leatherhead road.

The turnpikes themselves were unpopular with travellers, who sometimes attacked them. Accordingly, toll barriers were not usually erected too close to towns. Thus an act of 1748 said no turnpike on the Portsmouth Road could be placed nearer to Kingston than Cobham. Tolls were, however, levied at Kingston bridge after 1828. These maintained the improvement of the thoroughfare between Kingston and Hampton Wick, but were still unpopular, and there was jubilation when they were abandoned in 1870.

Turnpikes were a good way of raising money, but they did not guarantee good roads. Those in charge of the trusts were town officials and local gentry, among whom, unfortunately, 'a knowledge of the fundamental principles of making roads is not deemed at all necessary'. However, eventually engineering and road construction improved and, whereas in the 1780s the fastest London to Portsmouth run took 14 hours, this was down to nine or ten hours by the 1820s.

This was of immense benefit to the coaching trade — a major activity in 18th and early 19th century Kingston. Mail coaches carried letters and passengers, and stage coaches with names like the *Rocket* conveyed people between Kingston and London, and Kingston and Portsmouth or Southampton. Other local coaches took Kingstonians to Reigate, Windsor or Brighton. Early coach travel was not comfortable. Among the miseries were draughts, suffocation; extremes of heat and cold; crowding into a confined space with several other 'companions morally or physically obnoxious'; and 'being politely requested, at the foot of a tremendous hill', to get out to ease the horses.

Coaching, and the general increase in horse-drawn commercial traffic, brought prosperity to Kingston's inns. George Ayliffe mentions the Jolly Sailors in Norbiton Street in the 1830s, whose 'extensive stabling' was 'much used by the Portsmouth coaches and trade vans, which were then very numerous and travelled all night'. At the Jolly Butchers, near Clattern bridge, it was normal 'to see 3 or 4 sets of post-horses waiting there, with travelling carriages, post-chaises and pairs standing in a long row, and fish vans laden with Worthing mackerel.'

The famous Griffin inn, the Lion and Lamb (later the Druid's Head) and the Castle, all in the Market Place, flourished. Between the Lion and Lamb and the Castle was Kingston's post office, kept by Thomas Baker; the Portsmouth mail coach left from there at 10pm every night, and Ayliffe describes how it galloped into the market place, with its driver dressed in scarlet and gold livery. 'The sounding of a horn by the guard set the town alive for a few minutes, the people crowding round to see the coach loaded with passengers'. The mail from Portsmouth to London reached Kingston at about 5am, and then the Wandsworth mail arrived, its driver resplendent in a scarlet coat with blue facings and gold lace.

Flourishing inns helped stimulate Kingston's two major industries of the 18th and early 19th centuries, malting and brewing. In 1834, a government commission declared that: 'The trade of the town consists chiefly in malting'. In 1839, Pigot's *Directory* listed 15 maltsters, many of whom had premises at Town's End, near riverside wharves where barley could conveniently be unloaded and malt exported. 'In the carriage of barley and malt from Kingston to the metropolis many barges are generally employed'. Alderman Gould remembered that 'the old maltmen, many of whom were wealthy men, were to be seen about the streets in their skullcaps, knee breeches and worsted stockings, and every day they did their full share of hard work by the side of their men'.

Brewing, Kingston's other staple industry, was already well established. The town had a number of breweries in the 18th century, but the most famous was the one in Brook Street, which was bought by John Rowlls in 1745. Rowlls' Brewery stayed in the family until it was sold to William Hodgson in 1854 and became Hodgson's Brewery. In the early 19th century, other well-known breweries included Salter & Forster, at Town End, John Skyran's Original Brewery, and Flint & Shaw in Church Street.

Other industries included tanning and milling, fishing and boat-building, brick-making, candle-making and, from the late 18th century, linseed oil production. Tanning was long established in the town, and the Kingston Tannery, by the river in Thames Street, on the old Bishop's Hall site, manufactured leather from the late 17th century until 1963. The hides were tanned with oak bark, and the leather produced was advertised as 'the best in the world'. The production of leather in Kingston was part of a major Surrey industry: in 1850 it was reckoned that one third of all the leather in Britain was dressed in Surrey.

Corn milling, originally the occupation of all Kingston's mills, survived as a prosperous commerical activity into the 19th century. Chapel Mill, on the Hogsmill river, switched from flour to linseed oil production in the 1770s, but Middle Mill was a corn mill till the mid-19th century, and Hog's Mill for even longer. In the 1830s and '40s, it was known as Mercer's Mill after its owner, William Mercer. Linseed oil was produced from the late 18th century at Chapel Mill, which in the 19th century was known as Oil Mill, and the road past it, now Villiers Road, as Oil Mill Lane. Linseed was imported up the Thames, and pressed into oil by noisy steam machinery. Cattle cake was a useful by-product, made from the waste linseed. W. C. Bryan remembered the constant noise, from which there was relief only on Sunday.

There were several activities associated with the river. Kingston's fishermen continued to supply the fish market, the Thames watermen carried goods and passengers and there were several boat builders. One of these, Turk's, established in 1777, still operates passenger boats. Kingston had several bricklayers, and also some brick and tile makers. There were brickfields along the road between Kingston and Malden, and also by the Ewell Road in Surbiton. One of the best-known brick makers was Benjamin Looker senior who, in the early 19th century, owned a pottery and brick works on the lower slopes of Kingston Hill, near its junction with what is now Queen's

Road. Kingston was also a centre for candle-making which, by the late 18th century, was dominated by Ranyard's works in the Market Place, near Kingston Tannery. This family firm was established by Robert Ranyard in 1762, and produced tallow candles from melted animal fat, with cotton wicks, and rushlights from rushes dipped in hot fat. When Samuel Ranyard retired in 1857, his manager, James Smith, took over.

Kingston was never the centre of large-scale heavy industry but it was still an industrial town. It had all the small-scale craftsmen needed to supply people's daily needs: tailors, dressmakers, hat manufacturers, boot and shoe makers and watch makers. It had blacksmiths, small-scale iron foundries, coach-makers and repairers, saddle and harness makers, wheelwrights and coopers. It had plasterers, painters, plumbers, glaziers and carpenters. There were also businesses which provided financial services like banks (Knight, Haydon and Shrubsole existed by 1808), local agencies for insurance companies, and auctioneers.

Retailing also became increasingly important during the 18th century. Shrubsole's, which set up as a draper's in the Market Place in 1760, was still there as a department store in the 1860s. By 1837 Thames Street alone boasted several tailors, drapers and shoe shops, fish shops, a bakery, a grocery and tobacco shop, a leather seller, pawnbroker, chemist, straw bonnet shop, a cutler and a toy shop. There was Jackson's fruit shop, Reed's china shop (appropriately invaded by a bull during a cattle fair), Nuthall's confectioner's, and a basket shop run by an eccentric called Mr Parkhurst, who liked to march up and down the road dressed in military uniform.

Daniel Defoe said of 18th century Kingston that it was 'remarkable for little', and its inhabitants were probably pleased that this should be so. After the political and religious tensions of the preceding period, people were glad to get on with their lives undisturbed. In 1694, Kingston Corporation had sent a loyal address to William III expressing the hope that: 'Now may we like the Jews of old sit down every man under his own Fig tree in peace and safety reaping the Fruits of his own labours through your Majesty's most gracious protection'. This set the tone for the next century. Kingston Corporation was untroubled by political or religious controversy, and was on good terms with the central government. There was no support in the town for the political radicalism that toppled continental monarchs during the French Revolution. In 1809, despite years of war against Napoleonic France, Kingston thanked George III for the 'perfect tranquillity' and prosperity maintained by his rule.

Kingston Corporation's main concerns were to preserve its own liberties, to maintain law and order, and to protect the trading privileges of its freemen. Its liberties were not under threat in the 18th century. The Corporation did not bother to apply for parliamentary representation either. Maintaining law and order was the duty of Kingston's JPs (the Bailiffs and Recorder) and the parish constables, who arrested those who broke the law. The local JPs presided over the twice yearly Kingston Sessions of the Peace, but more serious crimes were reserved for the Surrey Assizes. Kingston suffered no serious riots, and few murders, but minor breaches of the peace, such as drunken brawls, were frequent, especially among the fishermen and watermen of the Back Lanes. The Corporation was also vigilant in preserving restrictive trading practices — those who did business in Kingston either belonged to a trading company or bought a special 'trade toleration' or permission to trade. Kingston's Court of Assembly was much occupied with granting these tolerations, and with serving notice on those who were trading illegally.

Kingston Corporation also had to manage its own property and the town's financial affairs. The Chamberlain collected rents from Corporation lands, and used the receipts to keep Corporation property, including the Thames embankments and the borough fire engines, in good repair. Major projects, however, such as the rebuilding of the old Guildhall in 1706-7, were a financial headache. The Bailiffs received the market tolls and manorial rents, and also judicial fines. They were responsible for keeping the Market Place clean, and for paying the Paving Wardens to keep the town's paved streets (only the ones used by market traffic) in repair.

Then the Corporation was responsible for managing trusts: the Bridge Trust, which maintained the Thames bridge; the School Trust, for Kingston Grammar School; the Almshouse Trust, which ran Cleave's Almshouses, and various other trusts to deal with charitable gifts. All this was carried out honestly and efficiently, especially after a reorganization in the early 18th century. Though there was a lot of work involved, everything was still small scale. The inmates of the Almshouses (the 'respectable poor') were chosen personally by the Court of Assembly, which kept a humane eye on them. In 1702, the Court of Assembly ordered that 'the widow Seamor' who was now almost blind, was in danger on her own in the Almshouse, and ordered 'that the widow Horne be put into the said house to look after her'. The names of the six poor boys and six poor girls who were educated and clothed on the Tiffins', Brown's and Smith's charities, and probably taught in the charity school set up in the Horsefair 1713-4, were also approved by the Court of Assembly, which sometimes examined the children on their learning.

Kingston's poor were helped by other Corporation initiatives or by the vestry of Kingston parish church (or by both together), funded by the parish poor rates. This was necessary, for the problem of poverty was becoming greater as the population grew. Already in 1696, Kingston's leading citizens protested to Parliament 'that the poor of the said town daily increase and are becoming very burdensome to the inhabitants'. In 1697 seven acres of Norbiton Common were enclosed to grow flax to 'set the poor on work', and the old Pest House was re-erected in the Horsefair as a Workhouse for them. It had six inhabitants in 1711, and other poor folk were maintained in private houses. In 1725 an initiative was launched for a more comprehensive scheme, whereby the Workhouse was to house the elderly and children as well as adults in need of work. However, even with this new Workhouse scheme in operation, much poor relief was handed out in the form of monthly pensions to poor families in their own homes.

By the early 19th century, poverty and the weight of the poor rate were seen as significant problems. It was as an increase in the number of poor cottages that the population rise was first noticed. Kingston Corporation was ill-equipped to deal with the difficulties. It had no proper salaried officers or staff, no general budget or unified accounting system, and no power to levy a general rate to finance local government. Overcoming these handicaps, and developing a new type of local government to cope with the greater scale and complexity of problems in the railway age was to prove the challenge of the next hundred years.

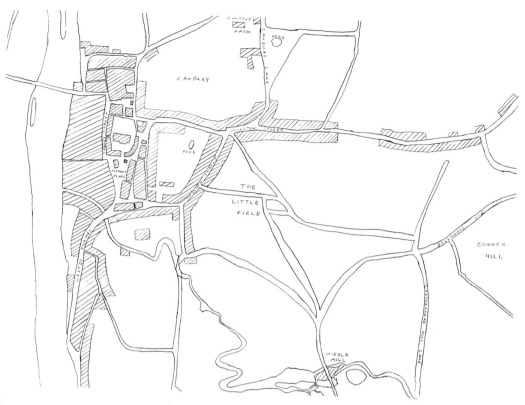

ABOVE: Map of Kingston c1745, after John Roque. (TE) BELOW: One
of the area's great mansions: Norbiton Place, remodelled in the early
19th century by Charles Pallmer, MP for Surrey. (KM & HS)

An Act for inclosing Lands in the several Manors of Kingston-upon-Thames, and Imworth, otherwise Imbercourt, in the County of Surrey, and for selling Part of such Lands for the Purpose of providing a Court House and Market House for the said Town. [18th June 1808.]

WHEREAS there are certain Commons and Waste Lands within and belonging to the several Manors of Kingston-upon-Thames, ... otherwise Imbercourt, in the Parishes of Kingston-... the said County of Surrey, contain-

upon-Thames ... ... or thereabouts, and
ing in the W ... ... in the
also certain ... ... res or
Pastures w ... ... longing
said Parish ... open to
thereabout
to the said
each othe
ß...

July 26, 1737.

TOLLS ... Suffex, as follows,

			Newington, Lambeth, Vaux Hall, Kingston, and Croydon.			Blue Anchor, and East Grinstead.		
			l.	s.	d.	l.	s.	d.
FOR every Horse, Mule, or Ass,	Laden or Unladen		0	0	1	0	0	2
For every Chaise, Cart, Dray, or Carriage,	Drawn by One Horse only		0	0	2	0	0	3
For every Coach, Chariot, or Calash,	Drawn by Two or more Horses		0	0	6	0	1	0
For every Waggon not laden with Hay or Straw			0	0	6	0	1	0
For every Waggon laden with Hay or Straw			0	0	3	0	0	6
For every Cart, Dray, or Carriage,	Laden with Hay or Straw, or other Goods,		0	0	2	0	0	4
For every Drove of Oxen, or Neat Cattle, after the Rate per Score			0	0	2	0	0	10
For every Drove of Calves, Hoggs, Sheep, and Lambs, after the Rate per Score			0	0	1	0	0	5

To be paid before passing.

ABOVE: The Kingston Enclosure Act, 1808. CENTRE: Farming continued important — this farm still flourished in the Surbiton area in the late 19th century. BELOW: Tolls payable by through traffic on Kingston's turnpike roads, 1737. (All KM & HS)

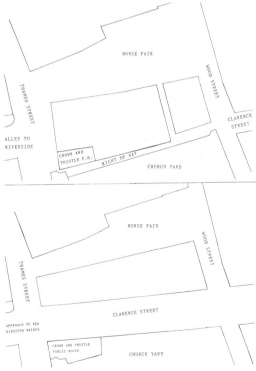

ABOVE: Toll house and gate at the entrance to new Kingston Bridge. LEFT: Celebrations in 1871, when the Bridge was freed from toll. (Both KM & HS) RIGHT: Map of the Horsefair area, showing it before and after the new bridge was built. (TE) Clarence Street, named after the Duchess of Clarence, who opened the bridge in 1870, was the new approach road.

OPPOSITE ABOVE: A coach in Kingston Market Place, late 18th century; stocks and pillory were kept at the central oat market. CENTRE: Kingston Town Hall, c1800; the Tudor building was remodelled in 1706, and a gilt statue of Queen Anne, the then monarch, installed in a niche at the south front. This now graces the Market House. BELOW: Brewery and malthouse on the Brook Street site of the 18th century Rowlls' Brewery, (Hodgson's after 1854). ABOVE: The Fighting Cocks in London Road. BELOW: Oil Mill (formerly Chapel Mill), on the Hogsmill River, produced flour until the late 18th century, then linseed oil. (All KM & HS)

You are hereby required to take Notice, That by the Ancient Usage and Custom Time out of Mind, used and approved of within the TOWN OF KINGSTON-UPON-THAMES, in the COUNTY OF SURREY, no Person, not being free of the said Town, may or ought to keep a Shop, or utter or offer to utter or sell by Retail, any Wares or Merchandizes whatsoever within the said Town, or to use or set up any Trade, Mystery, Science, or Occupation, whatsoever within the said Town: And that at a Court of Assembly of the Bailiffs and Freemen of the said Town, holden in the Guildhall of the said Town, the Twenty-eighth Day of March, in the Year of our Lord One Thousand Six Hundred and Thirty-five, IN PURSUANCE, and by Virtue of divers Powers, Liberties, and Privileges, in that behalf given and granted to the said Bailiffs and Freemen of the said Town of Kingston-upon-Thames, in and by divers Letters Patent, made and granted by divers of the late Kings and Queens of this Realm, to the said Bailiffs and Freemen of the said Town of Kingston-upon-Thames, and by them the said Bailiffs and Freemen for the Time being, held, used, and enjoyed, by virtue of the said Letters Patent or otherwise, it was amongst divers other Orders and Constitutions, then made and agreed upon by and between the said then Bailiffs and Freemen of the said Town, ORDERED AND CONSTITUTED, That if any Person or Persons should keep any Shop or Shops, or utter or offer to utter or sell by Retail, any Wares or Merchandizes whatsoever within the said Town, or should use or set up any Trade, Mystery,

not being first made or allowed a Freeman
on the Fair Days] that then every such Person
for every such Offence, six Shillings and eight
ry Market Day within the said Town, on
llings and eight Pence, to the Use of the
Successors, PROVIDED always, that it
ell Victuals upon the Market Days of the
re to sell and utter the same in open Market,
upon the like Penalty of six Shillings and
he use aforesaid: If therefore you do or
ntioned Order or Constitution, after this
ommenced against you by and in the Name
the recovery of the Penalty or Penalties to
t such Order or Constitution.

" On *Monday* last, our sexton, with his son and daughter being employed in digging a grave, part of the ancient chapel called St. *Mary's*, fell in upon them, killed the sexton and one other man (*Richard Mills*) on the spot; bruised and wounded several others; and buried in the grave both the son and daughter for above seven hours; during which time many were employed in digging out the rubbish, in order to get at the bodies that were buried. Mr. *Belcher* and Mr. *Sigings*, the Bailiffs of the Town, with the Officers, were so good as to attend the workmen and give proper directions. After the removal of the timbers and several loads of rubbish, they heard very plainly some loud groans and cries in the grave. Soon after they came to the heads of two persons; the Man was speechless and almost dead, having his head closely confined between two stones; the Woman was not so much pressed: but being immediately taken care of by Dr. *Cranmer*, they are both in a fair way of recovery. The Bailiffs and Churchwardens, by their great humanity and diligence on this occasion, had a great share, in preserving the lives of the two perpersons abovementioned, by the speedy removal of the rubbish, and by keeping off the crowd, who pressed in upon the labourers in great numbers. The damage, besides the lives already lost, is computed to amount to above 1000*l.* "

ABOVE: Warning given to Daniel Hall, who was not a freeman of the town, that he must pay for permission to trade in Kingston (KM & HS) LEFT: Letter of March 1730, recording the collapse of St Mary's Chapel, undermined by careless grave-digging. (An) RIGHT: Esther Hammerton, daughter of the sexton killed in the chapel's collapse, was dug out alive and succeeded her father (KM & HS)

A Town Transformed

The two most potent forces for change in the 19th century were the population explosion and the coming of the railway. By 1900, these had transformed Kingston from a small rural market town into a much more built-up population centre, with housing radiating from the new railway stations at Surbiton, New Malden, Kingston itself, and Norbiton. The local economic structure altered as agriculture became less important, and malting and long-distance coaching declined. Some of the resident population began to work in London, and became daily commuters, but at the same time Kingston developed as the economic focus of Surrey and its own suburbs. Surbiton and New Malden themselves became both London commuter areas and local economic centres, but they also came within the orbit of Kingston as a regional centre of employment, business and services. Kingston thus gained that dual function — London commuter town and regional economic centre — which it has maintained ever since.

Even before the railway, Kingstonians noticed their town was growing, and remarked upon the greater concentration of cottages in the Canbury area, at Norbiton and at Surbiton. Kingston's population, in line with a national trend, had already increased significantly during the 18th century. It grew dramatically during the 19th. By 1811, the parish population was nearly 5,000; it had nearly doubled by 1841, and was over 12,000 a decade later. It then doubled again, and by 1901 the borough population for Kingston was 34,375. Moreover, by the later 19th century, Surbiton and New Malden, which developed because of the railway, were weighing in with substantial populations of their own. Surbiton had about 15,000 people in 1901, and New Malden over 6,000.

The initial increase was probably due to the rising birth rate of surrounding areas, which prompted an influx, boosting the native population. This was due partly to improvements in diet through agricultural prosperity, and partly due to the decrease in deaths from smallpox, following new methods of innoculation in the 1760s. In Kingston itself, mortality remained high. During the early 19th century, baptisms began to outweigh burials more frequently, but in years of cholera this was reversed. Not till the later 19th century, when improvements in medical science and urban living conditions led to fewer epidemics, did the town's death rate consistently fall. Increasing numbers were also, from the mid-19th century, a product of the railway, which attracted new residents like a magnet.

The railway came to the Kingston area in 1838, when the London and Southampton Railway Company opened its line from Nine Elms (London Vauxhall) to Woking. This had a station called Kingston, though it was actually at Surbiton. A trial run was made on 12 May. Crowds gathered at the gaily decorated station on Surbiton Hill to cheer as the first steam train passed. The coaches were full, 'with the more venturesome travellers on the roof, holding their hats and flying madly along at the perilous rate of twenty miles an hour'. The line opened on 21 May. The journey between Surbiton and Nine Elms, stopping at all stations, took 31 minutes, and there were five trains a day each way.

Early rail travel was not comfortable. Second-class carriages had bare seats and open windows which let in rain, and third-class, though these only ran once a day, were mere open trucks until 1844. Even the first-class compartments were filthy. Nevertheless, the railway prospered. By 1855, there were 12 daily trains each way between London and Surbiton, and in 1887 there were 57 trains to and 49 from London. The London and Southampton Railway Company became the London and South Western in 1839, and in 1840 the line was extended to Southampton; Waterloo replaced Vauxhall as the London terminus in 1848. Meanwhile, the first 'Kingston Station' at Surbiton, which was a tiny building in a cutting near today's Ewell Road bridge, moved to its present site, and much improved accommodation, in 1840.

Traditional wisdom has always had it that Kingston was anti-railway in the 1830s, fought off the idea of a station in, or nearer to, Kingston itself, and thereby missed an opportunity for prosperity and expansion which went instead to Surbiton. The idea that Kingston was against the railway was established by Biden as early as 1852. He said that the directors of the railway company, 'compelled by the opposition of the town of Kingston, diverged their road from its intended route near the town, and cut through the hill at Surbiton'. This became the accepted version; in 1860 John Guy had heard that, when the railway first came to Kingston, the Corporation drove it away.

This is plausible. Coaching interests in particular might be expected to oppose any competitive form of travel which threatened them. Unfortunately, we lack local contemporary evidence from the 1830s. The Court of Assembly minutes are missing for the crucial period October 1831 to December 1834, when the railway company's plans were drawn and discussed, and the *Surrey Comet* was not in existence to record local opinion. However, there is material on the passing of the London and Southampton Railway Bill in the House of Lords' Record Office, which suggests that this tradition of Kingston's opposition is much exaggerated.

The idea of a railway line from Southampton to London was first conceived, by Southampton interests, in the late 1820s, and the London and Southampton Railway Company was established in 1831. Francis Giles was appointed its engineer. He surveyed the land, and deposited the earliest railway plan with the Surrey JPs at the end of November. The line as planned in 1831 went from Vauxhall to Wimbledon, and then crossed Worple Lane (now Worple Road) to the north. It crossed Coombe Lane, skirted the eastern slopes of Coombe Hill, cut across Norbiton Common, and entered the Kingston area north of the junction between the road to Malden (now Kingston Road), and Dickerage Lane (now Dickerage Road). Then it crossed the Hogsmill, and skirted Surbiton Hill to the north before curving away south in the direction of Ditton Marsh. The line did not come in to Kingston town centre; at its closest point it was still in Surbiton, about three quarters of a mile south of Kingston Market Place. Giles tried hard to avoid interfering with residential property, especially the estates of major landowners, and a series of meetings was held in the autumn of 1831 to test local opinion at various places along the projected line.

One of these meetings was at Kingston. It was held 'a day or two after' the Basingstoke meeting, which took place on 9 November, and it was said to have been 'numerously attended'. John Briscoe, one of the MPs for Surrey, took the chair, and the railway company's resolutions for the line were 'unanimously adopted'. We do not know precisely who attended the meeting, but the other meetings drew local landowners and townspeople, and this is likely to have been the case in Kingston. Even allowing for exaggeration, and for the possibility that some leading Kingstonians may not have attended the meeting, or may have changed their minds afterwards, it sounds as if in 1831, contrary to accepted tradition, much Kingston opinion was actually in favour of the railway.

An act of Parliament was needed before the line could go ahead, but as yet the promoters made no application, because they needed time to attract money. The delay also gave objectors time, and Charles Pepys, later Lord Cottenham, who owned land in Wimbledon, opposed the line because it ran through his estates. He was an influential man (appointed Solicitor-General in 1834), and the railway company must have thought there was no point introducing its bill into Parliament while he disliked its route. Instead, Giles resurveyed the land in 1833 and drew up new plans. The line now kept south of Worple Lane and thus avoided Cottenham's park. By 1834, when the bill for the London and Southampton railway finally came before Parliament, Cottenham found the route acceptable. Giles said in June 'I have arranged the plan with him'; his opposition was withdrawn, and the bill passed.

Tradition says Kingston Corporation joined forces with Lord Cottenham to drive the railway further from Kingston town, but there is no hint of this in the Parliamentary evidence. Cottenham's opposition alone would have been enough to persuade the railway company to alter its route and, once the line ran to the south, rather than the north, of Worple Lane to appease him, this naturally moved the whole line further south, and thus further from Kingston. The railway in the 1834 plan followed more or less the line it does now, crossing the Kingston Road south of the Dickerage Lane junction, and crossing Lower Marsh Lane and the Ewell Road before cutting through Surbiton Hill. It was now well over a mile from Kingston Market Place. However, the line was still seen as one which served Kingston, and as a facility its people wanted. When questioned by a House of Lords' committee which implied it was inconvenient for the town's inhabitants not to have the railway running through it, a railway spokesman said he thought some 'mode of conveyance' would be found to take people from the railway to the town.

It is, of course, quite possible that coaching interests in Kingston were unhappy with the original plan, and tried to influence the railway company, but there is no evidence and it is unlikely that Cottenham needed any help. They may have been pleased with an out-of-town station which gave them the opportunity to carry passengers between station and town, but the coaching interest in general was insufficiently organized or influential in 1831-4 to mount a determined campaign. Local opinion was divided: some people were pro-railway, some anti-railway, and some either indifferent or undecided.

Those who owned land on the projected line were the most closely affected. We know that some local landowners, like Christopher Terry and Alexander Wyllie of Surbiton, did not want to sell their land to the railway in 1834. Others, including market gardener Alexander Mitchelson, and Kingston bailiff Thomas Fricker, were happy to do so. Another Kingston bailiff, John King, was so convinced of the railway's potential that he bought land near its line in the Kingston Road area in 1835 which he later sold at a handsome profit. Some landowners, including Kingston's vicar, Samuel Gandy, were neutral about selling. Kingston Corporation itself, in its capacity as trustees for the Almshouses, remained neutral, and in 1835 it was concerned merely to get the best price for the Almshouse land. Kingstonians do not appear particularly enthusiastic about the railway by 1834, though this might have been because it was inconveniently far from the town centre. Only one townsman, William Ranyard, had bought shares in the London and Southampton railway company, and Kingston did not petition Parliament in favour of the line. But it did not petition against it either and more landowners sold land willingly than not for the railway.

Whatever the feelings of Kingstonians in 1834, the growth of a new, flourishing suburb near the station at Surbiton soon made the benefits of the railway obvious. By the time it finally came to central Kingston, in 1863, Kingston opinion was solidly in favour of having its own station, though there was a diversity of views as to where it should be built and what route the new line should take. From about 1856, individuals and companies had put forward several different railway schemes. By late 1858, the most popular proposal, backed by a packed public meeting of Kingston ratepayers held on 24 October, was that of William Bull, for a line linking Isleworth and New Malden, with stations at Teddington, Hampton Wick, Kingston central, and Norbiton. However, Bull's scheme was opposed by the London & South Western Railway (LSWR), which did not want any competition to its Surbiton to Waterloo *via* New Malden line.

The LSWR therefore introduced its own scheme for extending railway provision. At first it planned only a branch line from Twickenham to Hampton Wick, with the new 'Kingston' station on the Hampton side of the Thames at Hampton Wick. This would have meant that visitors to Kingston using the station would have to pay tolls to cross Kingston bridge. Not surprisingly, this had little support in Kingston but, rather than back Bull's line, Kingston Corporation preferred to negotiate with the LSWR and tried to persuade it to adopt a line similar to Bull's. Council deputations of 1858 and 1859 pressed the directors of the LSWR to bring their projected new line from Twickenham over the river into central Kingston, and on through Norbiton to New Malden. In 1859, a compromise was reached. The LSWR agreed to give Kingston its central station, if Kingston backed its line rather than Bull's, and the Council agreed. The LSWR bill to build a line from Twickenham to Hampton Wick was then approved in Parliament, on the understanding that an amendment would be introduced as soon as possible, extending the line to Kingston.

This amendment went before Parliament in 1860. But it was not for the whole Twickenham to New Malden extension which most Kingston people wanted, and which the Council had officially urged. Instead, it was for a line from Twickenham which ended in a central Kingston terminus, and which did not guarantee a station at Hampton Wick. Local opinion then diverged sharply. Hampton Wick, seeing only disadvantages for itself in the new proposals, petitioned Parliament against the amendment. Kingston petitioned in favour for, though most people did not want the line to end there, they did want a central station, and they thought (rightly) that an extension to New Malden would soon follow. The argument was taken before a House of Commons committee in May and June 1860, and was decided in Kingston's favour, though a House of Lords committee secured a station for Hampton Wick as well as Kingston. The Kingston Extension Bill was passed, and work on the line started in 1861.

On 1 July 1863, Kingston station quietly opened on its present site. There was no ceremony: shortly before 7am, the trains just started to run. The line from Hampton

Wick crossed the Thames on a bridge designed by John Errington, and was described by Kingston's mayor as a 'beautiful specimen of engineering ability'. However, the line as it stood was not really what was needed, for the journey to Waterloo *via* Richmond took about an hour — twice as long as on the main line from Surbiton. Kingston did not get anything like a proper service until after 1869, when the line was extended to Norbiton and on to New Malden, thus joining with the main line from Surbiton to Waterloo. Even in 1869, the extension did not at first give travellers the hoped-for direct journey to Waterloo. The direct trains took passengers from Kingston to Ludgate Hill, *via* Streatham (53 minutes); only if people changed at Wimbledon could they catch a train through to Waterloo. In this case, their journey time was reduced to about 37 minutes, and this ultimately proved the more popular route.

The coming of the railway brought great changes. Surbiton expanded dramatically. Since early times there had been a hamlet called Surbiton to the south of Kingston, but this was mainly to the north of Surbiton Hill, nearer to Kingston than the heart of the modern suburb. By the early 19th century, according to Biden, more houses were being built on Surbiton Hill, 'and already a hamlet promised to arise on its summit', but the number of inhabitants was still small — perhaps 200. However, when the railway came to Surbiton Hill, speculators began to build near the station. Thomas Pooley, a Kingston maltster, bought the Maple Farm estate in 1838, and started to lay out streets and put up houses. He had a vision of a wonderful new town, 'Kingston-upon-Railway', which he hoped would have its own church and market, well designed avenues and crescents, and elegant villas.

His dream quickly took shape. As early as 1840 the *Observer* remarked that 'a completely new town is in the course of formation between the old corporation of Kingston-upon-Thames and the South Western railway', and referred to the many 'snug and aristocratic villas' that were being constructed. In 1841 *The Times* reported that the 100 acre site of this new town 'exceeds the site of the old town of Kingston nearly fourfold', and that 'on the spot where, last harvest two years, a large crop of oats was reaped, now stand rows of handsome houses . . . a splendid hotel and tavern.' In 1841, there were 69 inhabited houses in Surbiton and a population of 387; by 1852, some 300 houses and about 2,800 people. Pooley himself, who borrowed heavily to finance his building, was ruined 1842-6 by his bankers, Coutts, and by Kingston Corporation, who were jealous of the 'town' of 'New Kingston' and mounted a successful campaign against the proposed market there. But Surbiton, even without a market, grew and flourished as land prices rose and more estates were sold off for development. In 1845, the first new 'parish' of the area, the ecclesiastical district of St Mark's, was established, a church built, and other churches followed.

In 1853 and 1854, Kingston Corporation, though it had done little to give Surbiton proper streets, drainage or lighting, tried to extend the limits of Kingston Borough, as defined in 1835, to include the new town by the railway, but already Surbiton's inhabitants had their own leaders and had developed a new sense of community, and Kingston's attempts were successfully resisted. In 1855, Surbiton obtained its own Improvement Commission by act of Parliament. From then on it was in charge of its own paving, lighting, and sewage disposal, and often introduced improvements more quickly than Kingston itself.

Surbiton developed as a comfortable middle-class residential area for well-off London commuters: in 1859, John Guy said that Surbiton station was surrounded by 'hundreds of villas, in which dwellt gentlemen of wealth which was earned in London and spent in Kingston'. Such development, in the course of which good quality houses were built and new wealth came to the area, was viewed by contemporaries as highly desirable — much more desirable than the recent 'blind persistence in cottage building in Kingston' deplored by Biden, but necessary if the poorer sections of the increasing population were to be accommodated. Indeed, one reason why many of the inhabitants of Norbiton, Kingston and Hampton Wick wanted their own station was because of the improvements in local prosperity and to the local environment which might follow. John Guy said in 1860 that Hampton Wick would be a proper suburb of Kingston if it had a station, otherwise it would just be a collection of wooden houses. 'If there is a station, proper houses will be built, and much cottage property that is a nuisance will be cleared out.'

New Malden grew more slowly than Surbiton, and was less fashionable. Malden itself, now called Old Malden, was a village by the Hogsmill, to the south-east of the modern A3 road. The area to the north of it, now New Malden, was virtually uninhabited until the 1840s, with just a few farms and cottages scattered over its extensive fields which, with Norbiton Common, stretched between Malden, Coombe and Kingston. The railway ran across this area on its way from Wimbledon to Kingston, and a station was built at what is now New Malden in 1846. According to Merryweather, the station was meant 'to accomodate the few wealthy inhabitants of Coombe', but they did not welcome the 'village in the valley' which began to develop around it. A small house near the railway embankment became the Railway Tavern in 1852, and new houses were built to the north of the line (in the Groves area) by the National Freehold Land Society, and to the south of it by private speculators.

However, as yet there was no proper lighting or mains water supply, and an open sewer ran down Coombe Road. The station was in a dreadful state: 'no better than a cattle station' in 1857, and still only a 'collection of wooden shanties' in 1883. So bad was the drainage that the fields near the railway often flooded, and people used to ask disparagingly if the inhabitants were web-footed. Kingston Council neglected the area, but by 1860 New Malden had a church, a school and about 900 inhabitants, who now began to take their own road and drainage improvements in hand. A Local Government Board was established in 1866, and New Malden then managed its own affairs. The High Street, local shops and community life developed, and the new suburb grew. It did not at first have the impact on Kingston that Surbiton had had, but by the later 19th century the train service, the station, and local facilities had improved.

Two other parts of the Kingston area which became much more built-up after the railway came were Canbury (the area north of present day Clarence Street, Wood Street and Cromwell Road) and Norbiton. In Canbury before 1863, Mr Fitt's market garden covered the Fife Road area, and a great tithe barn stood where Kingston station now stands. There were meadows up the Lower Ham Road from Downhall to Bank Lane, where white violets grew in the hedgerows. On Richmond Road, apart from some building at the south end and a few mansions and gardens, it was mainly fields all the way north to Ham and east to the slopes of Kingston Hill. Lord Liverpool's farm covered much of the land around the area now the site of Kingston Barracks in King's Road. Although houses and inns lined the road between Kingston and Norbiton, there were fields behind them, and fields behind the cottages of Norbiton which straggled a little way up Kingston Hill. Norbiton's cottage population had increased enough by the 1830s for a new church and parish, St Peter's, to be established to serve the area in 1842. Yet as late as 1864, when William Hardman bought John Guy's mansion, Norbiton Hall, Norbiton was considered rural, and Hardman called the house his country residence.

However, after Kingston station opened in 1863, Canbury began to be developed. In 1868 Lord Liverpool's farm was sold off, much of it to the British Land Company, which built streets of brick houses in the Elm Road and Acre Road area. By 1871 Elm Road, which in 1861 had had two dwellings and five inhabitants, had 37 houses and 210 inhabitants. By the 1890s, several residential streets ran east from Richmond Road, and Canbury's population was about 4,350. The area had its own parish church, St Luke's, and its own residents' association.

Norbiton gradually became built-up in brick after the opening of its station in 1869, though much of the land near the station itself remained part of the pleasure grounds of the mansion of Norbiton Park till these were sold off for building in 1900. Already from 1868 Hardman had begun to sell off parts of his Norbiton Hall estate, and he moved out in 1873. Birkenhead Avenue was laid out in 1882 across what had been his gardens, and houses were built there. Meanwhile the lower slopes of Kingston Hill were being developed by private speculators like James Goulter, and by the National Freehold Land Society, which laid out Queen's, Liverpool and Crescent Roads. In 1870 an iron church was built to serve the new population, and in 1881 the parish of St Paul's Kingston Hill was established.

Though the Cambridge Road (previously the Malden Road) between Norbiton and New Malden stayed rural till after 1900, the Hawks Road/Wanderings area to the south of it and the fields near Bonner hill were being built on from the 1860s, as was the area between Fairfield South and Surbiton Hill. Already by 1860, it was said that there was an almost continuous line of building linking Norbiton and Surbiton, and then the fields between the two suburbs were gradually filled in during the later 19th century.

The railway brought town expansion, and new suburbs, planned streets of brick-built 'villa' housing and plenty of work for local bricklayers, plumbers, tilers and glaziers. The overall impact is harder to assess. Over the next 50 years it destroyed one of Kingston's main trades, malting, changed significantly the face of another, coaching, and helped to cause the decline of local agriculture.

Malting seems to have been an early casualty. Malt and barley could now be transported more cheaply by rail from inland towns direct to London, and Kingston's malt was undercut. Merryweather describes an immediate and catastrophic effect: 'The diminution of trade was so great that in the spring of 1840 there were 17 large malthouses vacant in the town.' This sounds like an exaggeration, for Pigot's *Directory* of 1839 only lists 15 maltsters for the whole area, and malting did not disappear completely. However, the number of firms was greatly reduced by the 1880s, when there were four maltsters in Kingston, and by 1899 only one independent maltster remained.

The railways also sounded the death-knell for long-distance coaching and for long-distance horse-drawn commercial carrying. The journey from Southampton to

London by rail took just over three hours, instead of between eight and eleven by road, and it was an obvious advantage for passengers to travel by train, and for firms of carriers to use rail transport for deliveries, especially for perishable goods like fish, meat and fruit and vegetables. The Royal Mail switched quickly from coach to rail for its letters and parcels — the last mail coach ran in 1845 — so the Portsmouth Mail no longer stopped in Kingston Market Place on its way to London. The London-Southampton stage coaches also ceased to run in the 1840s, and by 1845 Southampton carriers sent their goods to London by rail.

However, the coaching trade as a whole adapted, survived and flourished in the later 19th century. Many people still preferred coach to rail travel, and coaching over medium distances remained popular. A number of new coach services started up, such as the *New Times*, established in 1874, which stopped each day at Kingston on its way from Guildford to London. There was also a Kingston-London coach service, and a Brighton-London coach with stops at Kingston and Surbiton. Short-distance coaching, or horse-drawn omnibus travel, expanded as a result of the railway. In the 1840s and '50s omnibuses took passengers between Surbiton station and Kingston: one omnibus service was run by John Williams and Joseph Linton of the Griffin Hotel in the Market Place. Short-distance coaches or omnibuses increasingly tied in with railway timetables, and ran to places not linked by rail. They continued to be well used until superseded in the 20th century by trams and motor 'buses. Firms of carriers similarly continued to use horse-drawn waggons and vans for local deliveries, and to and from railway stations, until the advent of motor transport.

Most of Kingston's other trades continued throughout the second half of the 19th century and, though several had declined by 1900, the railway was not the only influence upon their fortunes. The decline of long-distance coaching led in some cases to the decline of the inns that had served the coaches, but many continued to flourish as pubs, of which Kingston still had large numbers in 1900. Brewing continued to flourish, and was dominated by four main firms: Hodgson's; Fricker's, near Eagle Wharf in High Street; Nightingale's, established in 1830 in Pheasant Lane; and East's. Joseph East, a nonconformist who became Mayor of Kingston, took over Flint and Shaw in the 1850s, and moved his brewery to Villiers Road in 1867. However, Nightingale's and East's breweries had ceased production by 1891, and Fricker's was taken over by Hodgson's in 1903. By the 20th century, despite the continued success of Hodgson's, brewing was no longer such an important occupation.

Corn milling in Kingston had also ceased by 1900. It was still a going concern in the later 19th century in the hands of the Marsh brothers, who from 1865 produced high-quality flour in their modern, steam-driven Downhall Mill in Vicarage Road, and who in the 1870s took over Hog's Mill, which then became known as Marsh's Mill. When the Marshes retired, the firm declined. In 1896, Johnston & Company bought Marsh's Mill, and made 'Yewsabit' metal polish there until about 1910. Middle Mill, at the end of what is now Mill Street, stopped producing flour in the 1870s. For a while it was a coconut fibre works, making mats and brushes, before it was bought by Kelly's publishing company in 1880 and became a printing works.

Linseed oil production was more directly a casualty of the railways: it ceased in the 1880s, when a railway company bought Oil Mill for a line which never materialized. However, other Kingston industries survived into the 20th century. Tanning and candle-making continued. Indeed, William Smith took over the old oil mill as a candle factory in 1895, and also made a special kind of soap there, 'Kingston Volvolutum'. When he died in 1922, Price's Candles bought the factory and continued production. Distilling, one of Kingston's 18th century occupations, still flourished. The Kingston Distillery in High Street, which made 'Kingston Gin' according to a secret recipe, survived till 1925. Another industry which became established during the later 19th century was soft drinks manufacture, and Raynsford's mineral water was in production from the 1850s until 1893. Service industries also flourished. Laundries were the largest employers of female labour in late Victorian Kingston.

It does not seem, therefore, that Kingston's economy collapsed when the railway came to Surbiton. The *Surrey Comet* felt in 1858 that Kingston was still 'keeping up its name and business in these stirring railway times', and that the town was still alive with interest and wealth, 'such is the flourishing state of our Royal Town'. People wanted Kingston to have its own central station because they felt this would bring yet more wealth, rather than to reverse an overall decline. However, by 1900 significant economic changes had taken place. Kingston still had its industries, but the important pre-railway concerns of malting, milling, brewing and long-distance coaching either no longer existed or no longer dominated.

The local economic structure also changed because the railway brought with it London commuting: Surbiton in particular was a place where from the 1840s onwards many residents travelled to London to work, but by 1900 the same was happening in Norbiton, Kingston and New Malden. This meant that Kingston and its suburbs were required more than ever to provide a pleasant residential environment, which was not always compatible with the needs of industry. Moreover, as the Kingston area and the whole of Surrey became more built-up, local agriculture became far less important, and Kingston Market, primarily a centre for agricultural produce, ceased to be vital to the local economy. Shops began to take its place and Kingston's retailers tried harder to attract customers from the suburbs.

John Guy mentioned in 1860 that the new, wealthy inhabitants of Surbiton were spending their money in Kingston. But as a more sophisticated consumerism developed in the later 19th century, Kingston's shops could not hope to keep their custom unless they also kept pace with their expectations. In the 1870s and '80s, strong competition from the London department stores galvanized Kingston's shopkeepers into improving premises and often into offering a greater variety of goods at better prices. Some Kingston retailers now reorganized themselves as department stores. Shrubsole's, for instance, whose drapery shop had been in the Market Place since the 18th century, enlarged their premises and opened as a department store in 1866. The shop was bought by Joseph Hide in 1873, and continued as a department store until the 1980s. Bentall's, Kingston's most famous department store, was also expanding from a drapery shop to a department store in the 1880s and '90s. By 1900, Kingston's shops were quite successful. Some rich people preferred to shop in London, and shops in Surbiton, Norbiton and New Malden catered for some local needs, but Kingston's town centre drew shoppers, not only from Kingston itself and its suburbs, but also from elsewhere in Surrey. Though not necessarily obvious at the time, it was in its shops that Kingston's economic future lay.

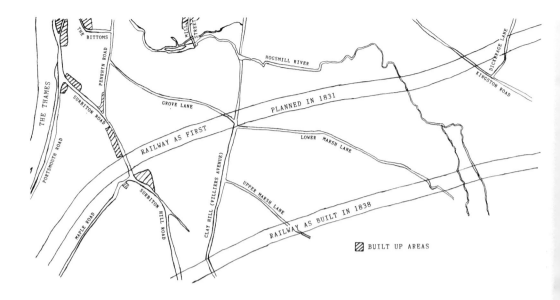

In the sixty years between the advent of the railway and the end of the 19th century, Kingston had changed beyond recognition. The small, compact town of the 1830s, with fields only a short walk away from its centre, had expanded tremendously by 1900, and residential streets were beginning to cover the fields towards Ham, Norbiton and Surbiton. Kingston's traditional identity as a market town was less relevant to the new reality of an increasingly urban Surrey, but it was not this alone with which Kingston had to come to terms. The huge increase in population during the railway age also caused serious problems of public health, public order, poor relief and social well-being, and eventually necessitated a radical new acceptance by Kingston Corporation of responsibility towards the people of its town.

LONDON & SOUTHAMPTON RAILWAY.

The London and Southampton Railway IS NOW OPEN for the conveyance of Passengers and Parcels from London to Woking Common (near Guildford), and the intermediate places.

The times at which the Trains will start are as follow:

FROM LONDON.		FROM WOKING COMMON.	
Morning	8	Morning	half-past 7
Ditto	10	Ditto	10
Afternoon	1	Afternoon	1
Ditto	half-past 3	Ditto	half-past 3
Ditto	6	Ditto	7

EXCEPT ON SUNDAYS,

When the Trains will start

FROM LONDON.		FROM WOKING COMMON.	
Morning	7	Morning	7
Ditto	9	Ditto	9
Afternoon	5	Afternoon	5
Ditto	7	Ditto	7

The Fares will be charged as under, viz.

From the Terminus at Nine Elms,
NEAR VAUXHALL,

	FIRST CLASS	SECOND CLASS
	£ s. d.	£ s. d.
To WOKING COMMON	0 5 0	0 3 6
To WEYBRIDGE	0 4 0	0 2 6
To WALTON	0 3 6	0 2 3
To DITTON MARSH	0 3 0	0 2 0
To KINGSTON	0 2 6	0 1 6
To WIMBLEDON	0 1 6	0 1 0
To WANDSWORTH	0 1 6	0 1 0

No Fee or Gratuity will be allowed to be received by any Servant of the Company.

Times at which the Trains are appointed to arrive at the undermentioned Stations, until further notice:

DOWN.							UP.						
FROM Nine Elms....		8 A.M.	10 A.M.	1 P.M.	3½ P.M.	6 P.M.	FROM WokingComm².		7½ A.M.	10 A.M.	1 P.M.	3½ P.M.	7 P.M.
ARRIVE AT	Miles.	h. m.	h. m.	h. m.	h. m.	h. m.	ARRIVE AT	Miles.	h. m.	h. m.	h. m.	h. m.	h. m.
Wandsworth...	2¾	8 7	10 7	1 7	3 37	6 7	Weybridge....	5½	7 44	10 14	1 14	3 44	7 14
Wimbledon...	5¼	8 18	10 18	1 18	3 48	6 18	Walton	7½	7 51	10 21	1 21	3 51	7 21
Kingston	10¼	8 31	10 31	1 31	4 1	6 31	Ditton Marsh..	10	8 1	10 31	1 31	4 1	7 31
Ditton Marsh..	12¾	8 41	10 41	1 41	4 11	6 41	Kingston....	12½	8 10	10 40	1 40	4 10	7 40
Walton	15½	8 51	10 51	1 51	4 21	6 51	Wimbledon ...	17½	8 26	10 56	1 56	4 26	7 56
Weybridge.....	17½	8 59	10 59	1 59	4 29	6 59	Wandsworth...	20	8 35	11 5	2 5	4 35	8 5
WokingComm².	22¾	9 15	11 15	2 15	4 45	7 15	Nine Elms...	22¾	8 45	11 15	2 15	4 45	8 15

By Order of the Directors,
WM. REED, *Secretary.*

N.B. Omnibuses will convey Passengers to and from the Company's Station at NINE ELMS, near Vauxhall, from the following places, viz.

Spread Eagle, Gracechurch-street; Swan with Two Necks, Lad-lane; Cross Keys, Wood-street; White Horse, Fetter-lane; George and Blue Boar, Holborn; Golden Cross, Charing-cross; Universal Office, Regent-circus, Piccadilly.

Arrangements have been made with the London and Westminster Steam Boat Company, in consequence of which Steam Boats will be provided for conveying Passengers to and from the Station at Nine Elms, from and to the under-mentioned places, viz.

DYER'S HALL WHARF, Upper Thames-street; and HUNGERFORD MARKET.

OPPOSITE ABOVE: London & Southampton Railway Company's projected line of 1831, and the route taken in 1838. (Both TE) ABOVE LEFT: The first 'Kingston' station: a hut in a cutting near the Ewell Road bridge at Surbiton. (KM & HS) RIGHT: Advertisement and timetable for the new Vauxhall to Woking railway, 1838. (RR) OPPOSITE BELOW: The second 'Kingston' station at Surbiton, rebuilt 1840 on its present site in Victoria Road. BELOW: Suburban villas in Surbiton: The Crescent, Claremont Road, 1880. (Both KM & HS)

The changing face of Surbiton: ABOVE: King Charles' Road as a rural bridle path c1890, and the same road built up c1910; BELOW: the Ewell Road, c1910, and the cornfield on which it encroached. OPPOSITE: The growth of New Malden: ABOVE: Acacia Grove, pictured c1900, was one of the first streets laid out, in the 1850s; CENTRE: Blagdon road, c1910 (note Benjamin Looker junior's pottery in the foreground). BELOW: New Malden station had been much improved by the early 20th century. (All KM & HS)

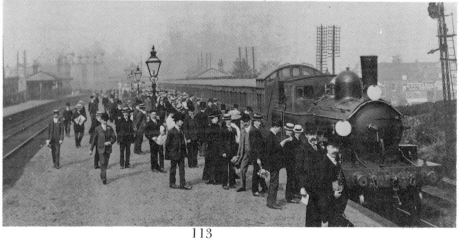

LEFT: Kingston and its surroundings before the coming of the railway. (TE) CENTRE: The growth of Kingston's suburbs after the arrival of the railway: the area in 1865, RIGHT: in 1897. (TE)

114

ABOVE: Kingston railway bridge in 1906; it brought the railway into central Kingston. CENTRE: Kingston's own central station, 1863, stood from the start on its modern site at the corner of Richmond Road and Wood Street. BELOW: The continued importance of river transport: barges carrying coal and timber at Kingston, c1910. (All KM & HS)

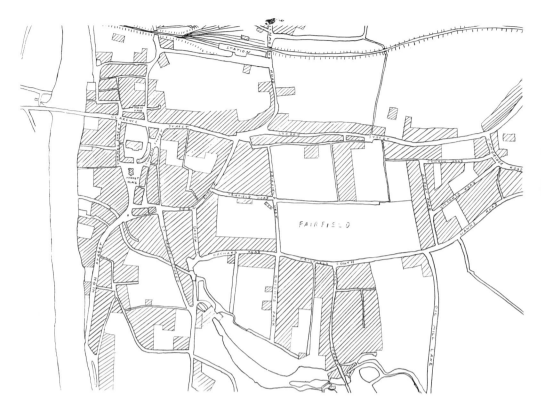

ABOVE: Kingston town post-railway, showing the growth of the built-up area by the later 19th century. (TE) BELOW: This horse-drawn omnibus served the Kingston area. (KM & HS)

ABOVE: The Epsom coach passes Bones Gate Inn, Chessington, c1900, and CENTRE: the horse-drawn delivery cart for Hodgson's brewery. BELOW: Batson's forge. (All KM & HS)

Post railway industry in Kingston: LEFT: Fricker's Eagle Brewery, RIGHT: the Marsh brothers' Down Hall flour mill, BELOW: Turk's boatyard. (All KM & HS)

ABOVE: Smith's candle factory, which moved to Oil Mill in 1895,
BELOW: Kingston shops included Wilcox the butcher, High Street.
(Both KM & HS)

W HEREAS an Act was passed in the Thirteenth Year of the Reign of King *George* the Third, intituled *An Act for the lighting and watching the Town of* Kingston-upon-Thames *in the County of* Surrey, *and for removing and preventing Obstructions, Encroachments, and Nuisances therein,* and certain Trustees were thereby appointed for putting the said Act into execution: And whereas the existing Borough of *Kingston-upon-Thames* is a Corporate Borough, and is one of the Boroughs named in the Second Section of Schedule (A.) annexed to the Municipal Corporation Act, and the Inhabitants of the said existing Borough are a Body Politic and Corporate, called and known by the Name of " The Mayor, Aldermen, and Burgesses of the Borough of *Kingston-uponThames:* " And whereas since the passing of the said last-mentioned Act the Town of *Kingston-upon-Thames* has greatly increased, and the Limits of the Town now extend far beyond the

[*Local.*]　　　　　　　　　6 Y　　　　　　　　　Limits

ABOVE: Part of the title page of the Kingston Improvement Act, 1855.
BELOW: The opening of Kingston Sewage Works at Downhall, 1888.
(Both KM & HS)

Apathy and Improvement

It required a major shift in attitude for the long-established Corporation to accept responsibility, not just for protecting local trade, but also for improving both environment and living conditions. Central government legislation first permitted and later compelled local authorities to improve public health and safety; the influence and expectations of local ratepayers increased the pressure and the problems caused by population growth demanded attention. By 1900 Kingston's inhabitants enjoyed properly lighted streets, a comprehensive system of sewage and rubbish disposal, plentiful fresh water, and an adequate police force and fire brigade. But progress was slow, hampered by complacency, apathy, ignorance and self-interest.

Kingston began the 19th century with a form of local government soon perceived as out of date. On the eve of the Municipal Corporations Act of 1835, which reformed urban government, Kingston was still an undemocratic 'closed' corporation of 57 freemen, elected from among the 273 free tenants of the Royal manor. Less than 3% of its 8,000 or so inhabitants could become members of the Court of Assembly which ran the town, and only existing members of that ruling body could vote for new members.

The Court of Assembly consisted of two Bailiffs, who led the Corporation; the 15 Headboroughs, or 'Fifteens', who theoretically acted as Constables in the town, and who made up the rank and file members of the Corporation; the Peers, members who had previously served as Fifteens; and the Masters, or Gownsmen, who were ex-Bailiffs. Each year, the Fifteens voted out two of their number, who then became Peers, and normally served as High Constables for the year, and voted in two more from the free tenants of the manor. The two new Fifteens served the office of Aleconners for the year. The Bailiffs were chosen annually from among the Gownsmen and Peers. The Fifteens selected four candidates, of whom one was then chosen by the existing Bailiffs together with two special borough officials: the High Steward, a person of social standing and influence, and the Recorder, a legal professional. The other new Bailiff was chosen by the Gownsmen and Peers themselves. The Court of Assembly, which controlled Corporation affairs and property, appointed the Town Clerk (for life), and every year elected officers like the Schoolwardens and Bridgewardens. The members and officers of Kingston Corporation thus formed an oligarchy which was not answerable to the majority of the people in the town, and had no reason to see itself as responsible for improving their general well-being.

This ruling body met about ten times a year. It accepted the accounts and considered the reports of different officials, for the Thames bridge, the grammar school and the various charities. It also discussed trade tolerations and matters of general interest, and had the power to 'make bye-laws and orders for the general government of the town'. But the Corporation itself did not have the power to levy general rates upon Kingston's inhabitants, so what it could afford was limited. Finances were such that most funds were tied up in trusts and had to be spent on trust objects, like the upkeep of the bridge. Kingston Corporation's non-trust income was not enough to cover any major programme of urban improvement.

However, the Corporation did show some concern for environment: in 1773 it obtained an act of Parliament 'for the better lighting and watching the Town of Kingston-upon-Thames'. This established the Bailiffs and other residents as a trust, to levy a local rate for the provision of lamps. By 1835, Kingston was well lighted by 80 new gas lamps. The trust also levied a rate for watching, to pay three night watchmen and one of the town constables to police the streets at night. It had powers to stop people throwing muck into the streets, and to make them build drain-pipes. But the Corporation did not use these powers much, and did not have the right to levy a rate to improve drainage. In practice, apart from the gas lighting, little enthusiasm was shown for improvements. Kingston Corporation protested to the House of Lords when a government report of 1835 described it as 'extremely inactive', and as 'rather harmless than useful to the town', yet there was much truth in the judgement.

The situation changed somewhat after the Municipal Corporations Act, which established Kingston's first 'openly' elected ruling body. The borough was divided into three wards, each of which elected six councillors to the new Town Council. The councillors then selected six aldermen, and the aldermen and councillors together chose the mayor, who led the Corporation. All adult males who paid poor rates had the vote, and were eligible for election to the Council. Local government was now more democratic and more likely to become responsive to local needs. As the act also abolished trade restrictions, the Council no longer had to spend time checking up on individual traders. Moreover, the Council could now levy a general rate for administration, and appoint salaried officials, including a treasurer. It was still not equipped to deal with the problems of unprecedented growth.

One of these was sewage disposal. As the population grew, the inadequacies became obvious. Many of Kingston's drains were uncovered ditches: these ran alongside the roads and discharged into local streams and finally, *via* the Town Ditch, into the Thames at Downhall. In the 1830s, a stinking open sewer ran down London Road and Clarence Street. Another ran down Kingston Hill and into the Latchmere Ditch, which also drained Canbury. The stench could be smelt from the top of All Saints' Church tower. Sewage from people's privies often drained into local cesspools. If these were not regularly cleaned, or if drains became blocked, sewage overflowed and seeped into the surrounding ground. This was an offensive 'nuisance' to those who lived nearby, and could contaminate the water in wells and streams, leaving people vulnerable to diarrhoea and cholera. Summer diarrhoea was commonplace among the poor. In the 1860s, a local doctor reckoned he regularly saw four cases a day, and was not surprised to have 17 cases on a Monday because there were always more to start the week. Infants, the old and the weak could easily die. Cholera struck in 1849, 1855, and again in 1866.

Kingston (like most British towns) was slow to get to grips with this. Even after 1835, the Council had no specific powers to improve sewage disposal, and for a while it did not apply for them. It did not set up a local board of health under the 1848 Public Health Act. Not until 1855 did the Kingston-upon-Thames Improvement Act place cleansing, drainage, lighting, paving and other urban improvements firmly under the control of the Town Council, and allow the Council to levy a range of rates, including a sewage rate and a general improvement rate. The act also made it easier for the Council to deal with such problems by extending the boundaries of Kingston borough to include the Norbiton area (though Surbiton stayed independent).

Even after 1855, when Kingston Council set up an Improvement Committee, it found it hard to take an overall view of the problem, while civil engineering had not yet developed proper drainage techniques. There was no immediate scheme for a borough-wide system. An Inspector of Nuisances was appointed, to report the faults, but no qualified Borough Surveyor, to plan systematic changes. Instead, drainage was dealt with piecemeal. Thus the Inspector, or concerned individuals, reported nuisances like the foul state of the Latchmere Ditch, or 'an offensive ditch at the back of Mr. Fuller's cottages in the Wanderings', and the Committee investigated. Either the Town Clerk then wrote to the person responsible — in July 1856 Mr Fuller was ordered to cleanse his ditch — or the Committee commissioned specific schemes for problem areas, like Latchmere and Canbury. But cottage owners like Fuller kept reoffending, and the attempt to drain Latchmere foundered in the absence of an overall borough plan. When the Canbury problem came up in 1859, Benjamin Looker junior suggested the appointment of a Borough Surveyor to plan a proper drainage system for the whole town, but had little support, and the Latchmere question was simply referred back to the Improvement Committee!

However, by 1862 the sewage problem was so pressing that the Council set up a special committee to consider the thorough and proper drainage of the borough. A comprehensive plan was made, to improve existing sewers, build new ones, do away with cesspools altogether — and discharge all Kingston's sewage, untreated, into the Thames. Work started on the scheme in 1864, and was finished by August 1865. By then the government was growing concerned at the pollution of the river. In 1866, an act of Parliament banned Kingston and other towns from discharging sewage into the river, so Kingston's new drainage system was in breach of the law. The Council felt hard done by. Yet Thomas Tindal Walker had warned councillors in 1858 that letting sewage drain into the river might constitute a nuisance and thus be illegal under existing law — the Council had simply chosen to ignore the likely pollution.

It was back to the drawing board. In 1867, the Council finally appointed a qualified Borough Surveyor, and considered different ways of disposing of Kingston's sewage. Eventually, in November 1888, the Kingston and Surbiton Sewage Disposal Works opened at Downhall Meadow. They were run by the Native Guano Company, using the so-called ABC process of sewage treatment, by which the sewage was deodorized and purified with chemicals, and the sludge used to make fertilizer. At last Kingston's sewage problem was solved. Yet Kingston had been beaten by New Malden, whose Local Government Board (established in 1866) had its sewage works open in August 1888.

A regular supply of clean drinking water was also important. Traditionally, Kingston relied on water from rivers, streams, wells and natural springs. As it became more densely populated, more houses had to share these sources, and the rivers, streams and shallow wells became polluted. Thus the establishment of the Lambeth Water Company's new works at Seething Wells in 1852, and of the Chelsea Company's works there in 1856, were welcome events. Both companies drew their water from the Thames, but purified it by passing it through filter beds. Clean piped water was supplied to houses whose owners or occupiers would pay. But many of the cottages where the poor lived, such as Young's buildings in Eden Street, were not supplied. The tenants could not afford it, and often landlords avoided the expense. In the slums of

Kingston's Back Lanes in the 1860s, households used water straight from the polluted Thames. Other poor tenants shared a communal tap. Even where piped water was laid on, the supply ran for only a few hours each day. Homes that could not afford water tanks had to store water in any available container; if the occupants were out at work when the water was turned on, they had storage problems. Fuller's cottages in the Wanderings shared a water tank so filthy that it negated much of the point of having mains water.

Kingston Council had no control over the privately owned water companies, and in the 1840s it was not generally recognized that polluted water caused cholera. When the link was scientifically established in the 1850s, the Council did little to persuade cottage landlords to pipe in mains water, though the 1855 Kingston Improvement Act gave it the power to compel them. When cholera returned in 1866, the Council paid the Lambeth Water Company to supply mains water to standpipes installed in the Back Lanes. The inhabitants were also allowed to use the water closets of the Old Bridge Street Ragged School, instead of their usual stinking communal privies. When the threat passed, the standpipes were removed and the privies reopened.

Only in the 1870s, when legislation placed a duty on local authorities to act against landlords and ensure a proper water supply to cottages did poor tenants begin to benefit. Disease then gradually declined. By 1911 a report on the health of Kingston said that its water supply was 'generally from the mains', though a few shallow wells still remained. By this time water closets were 'universal'. The death rate, at 13.9 per 1,000, was below the national average for small towns, and showed a steep — and welcome — decline against the death rate of about 36 per 1,000 of the 1830s.

Other matters related to public health included proper burial facilities and organized rubbish disposal. Burials were the responsibility of Church and parish, and it was the vestry of All Saints' which decided in the early 19th century that the original graveyard around All Saints' Church was overcrowded. An overspill opened in 1826, opposite the church in Union Street, where the Garden of Remembrance is now. As Kingston continued to grow, this too became inadequate. Medical theory blamed disease on 'pestilential vapours', of which crowded burials were a potent source, and in the end the Government ordered Kingston's town centre graveyards closed. A Burial Board was appointed to organize an out of town cemetery, and in 1855 the spacious site at Bonner Hill, then all fields, opened for burials. Bonner Hill cemetery serves Kingston today.

Under Kingston's Act for Lighting and Watching of 1773, rubbish disposal was in the hands of private individuals; the authorities simply had the power to prosecute offenders who let rubbish obstruct the streets. The 1855 Improvement Act gave the Corporation power to make bye-laws for the removal by occupiers or, if they did not do so, by the Corporation, of rubbish, ashes, dust, manure, filth etc., but Kingston Council did little. It only removed rubbish that had become a health hazard if someone complained, or in an emergency such as the cholera outbreak of 1866. However, by 1871 both Kingston and Surbiton paid contractors to remove dust and rubbish on the rates. In Surbiton, every house in the district was visited once a fortnight.

One local authority after 1836 shared responsibility for public health with Kingston Council, and was particularly responsible for the health and welfare of the poor — the Board of Poor Law Guardians for the Kingston Union. Poor relief previously was a matter for the town, which administered charitable bequests, and the parish, which since 1603 appointed overseers for the poor, levied a poor rate and supervised aid for the old, sick and unemployed. Kingston parish had had a Workhouse since before 1725; by the early 19th century this stood in the London Road, opposite its junction with Coombe Road. Here, paupers were looked after, and instructed in the habits of 'virtue, sobriety, obedience and industry'. Children were taught to read, write, add, spin and knit, and adults set to work. Doles of money, food or fuel were handed out to poor families in their own homes. This combination of 'indoor' and 'outdoor' relief was expensive, and in 1834 the Poor Law Amendment Act tried to ease matters by amalgamating parishes into Poor Law Unions, so that the poor rates of different parishes could be pooled.

The Kingston Union, established in 1836, put Kingston and Ham together with neighbouring parishes. Kingston's Workhouse became the central facility, and a new building to accommodate increased numbers was opened in Coombe Road in 1839, opposite what today is Norbiton Station. A medical officer was appointed, with responsibility both for the inmates of the Workhouse, and for those families who received relief in their homes. In 1842 a Workhouse Infirmary was set up, with places for 90 sick people, and in the next century this developed into Kingston Hospital.

The Poor Law Guardians did not always see eye to eye with Kingston Council. In 1864 they quarrelled over paying an increased rate for the new borough sewage system, arguing that already in 1840 they had covered part of the Coombe Road drain at their own expense. In June 1866 the Union Medical Officer, Mr Kent, compiled a report on the insanitary condition of parts of Kingston. Among the blackspots were the Back Lanes (in Waterman's Row, 'privies full and very offensive. No water supply except that which is obtained from the Thames by carrying'), and Young's Buildings in Eden Street, where 'nearly all the privies are full to the floor, and are frequently running over, and very offensive and detrimental to the health of the inhabitants'. The report was sent to the Council, but the Council was dismissive: it insisted it had the situation well in hand. Mr Kent felt insulted, and the Guardians were indignant.

However, when cholera hit the town in August, the Guardians and Council managed to work together. Thanks to the exertions of Alderman Gould, the Council at once appointed its own Medical Officer, Dr Price Jones, and a second Inspector of Nuisances, and instituted house-to-house visitations to detect sickness. An emergency system of rubbish disposal was introduced, and disinfectants ordered to cleanse streets and houses. The Guardians arranged for infected bedding and clothing to be burnt, and the free supply of medicines to the poor. Thus the threatened epidemic was forestalled. Yet Kingston Council did not retain its Medical Officer after September, and only appointed a permanent one after 1872, when it was compulsory anyway.

For the rest of the 19th century, the houses of the poor were a standing disgrace. In the housing boom that followed the railway, speculative builders hastily put up many streets of artisans' cottages which were inadequate in sanitation and water supply, and poorly constructed, with leaking roofs, and floors and walls that let in the damp. Such were Fuller's Cottages, off the Cambridge Road in Norbiton, and nearby premises in Asylum Road, Washington Road and Mill Street. Other slums, though often of older houses, included the Back Lanes by the Thames, and Young's Buildings. Overcrowding exacerbated bad housing. Because cottage building in the 1860s did not keep pace with growing numbers, rents doubled to 6s or 7s a week, which those who earned low weekly wages of maybe 12s found hard to afford. Tenants therefore took in lodgers, or people rented rooms or tenements rather than houses, and families lived in cramped, unhealthy conditions in one or two rooms. The Back Lanes were also notorious as the site of several dirty, ill-kept lodging houses, which made Kingston 'the dumping ground for all the disreputable characters in the neighbourhood'.

Kingston Council was slow to deal with its housing problems. Property, and the rights of landowners, were held sacred, and not until after 1868 did the Council have legal powers to make owners keep rented houses in repair, or to make builders build to a standard. Even then, its powers were often not used, partly because of opposition from its own 'cottage owning element'. When the Kingston-upon-Thames Improvement Act (1888) gave the Council powers to purchase land for street improvements, and the Housing of the Working Classes Act, 1890, ordered local authorities to demolish unfit housing and provide alternative accommodation, a real effort was made. A scheme was drawn up to improve the Back Lanes, off the Horsefair, and this was approved in 1891. It involved pulling down a number of tumbledown old houses and building better dwellings for some of those displaced, though the Council was not anxious to replace lodging houses for vagrants. By 1895, £20,000 had been spent on the Back Lanes project, but it was not completed because the Government wanted Kingston Council to build more replacement houses than the Council thought necessary. Kingston's Medical Officer of Health kept up the pressure on slum landlords, and by 1897 more houses in the Back Lanes and Norbiton had been put into repair, or demolished. Even then some landlords did the minimum of repairs to avoid demolition. Kingston's slums were much improved by 1900, but not completely eradicated.

Public safety became important too. Law and order was always taken seriously by those who feared disruption of trade and destruction of property caused by disorder and riot. However, until the late 18th century Kingston had no paid night police; all its inhabitants were meant to take turns patrolling the streets at night as members of the watch. The 1773 Act for Lighting and Watching allowed the trustees to appoint paid night watchmen and to pay one of the existing day constables. By 1835, Kingston town had three constables and three watchmen. However, these were not sufficient when extra people flooded in for the Assizes and the annual fairs, when Kingston Corporation paid for extra constables from the Metropolitan Police Force.

The Municipal Corporations Act compelled the new Town Council to set up a Watch Committee, and in 1836 this added five new paid constables, 'making the whole number with those at present on the watch 9 constables', and extended the boundaries of the watch to include Norbiton and Surbiton. The policemen were all to be clothed 'in an uniform manner with blue coats, waistcoats and trousers, glazed hats, oil skin capes and great coats. The night constables to carry for their protection, and that of the inhabitants, a cutlass, rattle, dark lanthorns and a staff', and should 'go their rounds silently, and without calling the hour'.

Kingston's early 19th century police force was adequate to deal with day-to-day crime. Ayliffe recalls Richard Cooke, the police inspector appointed in 1836, as 'a smart man, who was the dread of thieves and poachers', and one of the night watchmen, the 20-stone Charles Hanks, as a 'formidable figure to encounter', when armed with 'his huge stick in one hand and his horn lanthorn in another'. However, the Government was anxious to extend the area of the Metropolitan Police Force, and an act of Parliament of 1839 brought Kingston within the metropolitan district. The new police force took over in 1840, under protest from Kingston Council. In 1852, Biden judged that 'the town is well protected by the police and still better by the generally peaceable nature of its inhabitants', and crime does not seem to have been a major problem. Indeed, so strict was security at the opening of Bonner Hill Cemetery in 1855 that the *Surrey Comet*'s reporter was refused entrance to the chapel 'because he was unprovided with a blue ticket'! Traditional celebrations at which large crowds gathered and disorderly behaviour was usual were gradually phased out. From 1840 the police banned the Guy Fawkes' celebrations in the Market Place, and the riotous Shrove Tuesday football game was discontinued in 1867.

Thus Kingston began to conform to the higher standards of public behaviour expected in the more crowded Britain of the later 19th century. Better night-time street lighting helped the process along.

Kingston had had trustees for street lighting since 1773: they raised a lighting rate and put up oil lamps fixed to house walls or on posts. In 1833, the year that John Bryant set up the first gasworks in Kingston, the town began to convert the street lamps to gas. For once, Kingston's leaders were in advance of local opinion, which was suspicious of gas as dangerous to produce and bad for health. By 1835, when Bryant established his Kingston Gas Light and Coke Company, a government report said that 'the town and bridge are now well lighted'. The lighting rate was raised from 1s 3d to 1s 6d in the £.However, in the 1840s Kingston was reluctant to extend street lighting to Surbiton, which did not get street lamps till 1855. In both places, the street lights were at first not lit in summer, or on moonlit nights, but from the late 1860s in Kingston and from 1870 in Surbiton they were lit all the year round. The expansion of street lighting was good for John Bryant, who incorporated his business as the Kingston-on-Thames Gas Company in 1854, and continued to expand his works. He also supplied houses.

If Kingston was forward in gas technology, it was backward in fire-fighting. This was a parish responsibility, and the fire 'engine' (merely a water container on wheels) was kept first in the South Chancel of All Saints' Church, and after 1825 in a special building in Church Street. In 1836 the new Town Council decided 'that as the Fire Engines of the Parish of Kingston are much out of repair and as the same would be much better placed under the control of the managers of the Borough Police than in the hands of Parish Officers', the Council would ask the vestry's permission to take them over, which was granted.

In 1856, when it set up the first official, paid Borough Fire Brigade (previously it relied on volunteers), the engines were in only 'moderate repairs'. They were in a worse state eight years later. A report of 1864 lamented their 'most unsatisfactory and improper condition', and the brigade superintendent was suspended. Yet two years on the same man was still in post, only to be again suspended for 'failure to attend to his duties'. The public considered the service inadequate, and in 1870 William Roots established a private volunteer service, with its headquarters in London Road. This was in the forefront of technology because it used a steam fire engine; it was known as the Kingston Volunteer Steam Fire Brigade. Surbiton, whose Improvement Commission also wanted a steam fire engine, joined it in 1879. Kingston Council stuck with its increasingly antiquated equipment and lost the contest with the volunteers. The 'official' fire brigade was discontinued in 1881.

But even the more efficient Volunteer force was dangerously slow. It took 25 minutes to get the horses harnessed to the engine and to get this, and the hand-pulled hose cart, from the London Road to a nearby fire in the Market Place, and another ten minutes to get up enough steam to work the engine. Till the end of the 19th century, the intermittent nature of the water supply also hampered fire-fighting. Nor was the Brigade itself free from parsimony and complacency. In the early 20th century, its chief officer resisted the Council's call to replace the horse-drawn engine with a motor one. When in 1910 the Council won the argument, the Brigade acquired two new motor engines which could be mobilized in 30 seconds — an enormous improvement.

In 1852, Biden thought that Kingston had of late 'boldly progressed in the march of improvement'. It had a splendid new Town Hall, built in 1840, which much improved the appearance of the Market Place. Other improvements of the 1850s and '60s included moving the 'Coronation Stone' and making an imposing feature of it, enclosing the Fairfield with railings, and building Queen's Promenade, a raised riverside walk along the Portsmouth Road. All these projects made the town more attractive, but were largely cosmetic. In the streets nearby, many people still lived in damp, insanitary, tumbledown hovels with no running water. Much progress in urban infrastructure remained to be made, and much was made over the next 50 years. At last, by 1900, though some of its housing still left a lot to be desired, Kingston was decently lighted, drained, and supplied with water. Its sewage was safely disposed of, its rubbish regularly removed, and it had a responsible fire brigade and police force. Local government accepted responsibility for a range of public services. Kingston had finally entered the modern world.

LEFT: Communal pumps, like this one at Fountain Court, often supplied water to several houses in the 19th century. RIGHT: The new Union Workhouse, 1839: the Infirmary, here in the early 20th century, is now the oldest part of Kingston Hospital. (Both KM & HS)

Housing contrasts in Kingston: ABOVE: the ornamental lake in the garden of Norbiton Park, originally part of Charles Pallmer's pleasure grounds at Norbiton Place and BELOW: a slum cottage in Wood Street, c1898.

ABOVE: More slums — the 'Back Lanes', c1890. BELOW: The Shrove
Tuesday football game, banned 1867 in a public order drive. (KM & HS)

a Public Meeting

Held in the **GUILDHALL** of this **TOWN**, on Thursday, the **25th** of **July**, **1833**, of the **Trustees** of the **Watch** and **Lighting Act** of the said **Town**, and also of the **Owners** and **Occupiers** of **Messuages** and **Lands**, as well rated as liable to be rated or affected thereby, duly appointed to be there holden pursuant to the said **Act of Parliament.** *" To take the sense and wishes of the said Owners and Occupiers as to the Propriety of the said Trustees entering into any Contract for Lighting the Public Lamps of this Town with Gas, and if the sense and wishes of the majority should be opposed to it, then to take such steps as should secure such wishes from being frustrated".*

Charles White Taylor, Esq.

ABOVE: Opposition to gas lighting in 1833. CENTRE: Kingston Debtors' prison, also the Hand & Mace, was pulled down 1831 and a new debtors' prison built near the Market. BELOW: Kingston and Surbiton Fire Brigade, c1900, outside their London Road HQ. The tender was still horse-drawn. (All KM & HS)

Kingston improved: ABOVE: The New Town Hall, or Market House, 1840, designed by Charles Henman, cost £3,800 and the new Post Office, built 1875 in Brook Street, is pictured in 1906. BELOW: Canbury Gardens, opened 1890, and the Shrubsole Memorial, Market Place, commemmorating Henry Shrubsole, three times mayor. (All KM & HS)

The Pursuit of Virtue

Improvements in local services and living conditions did not take place within a spiritual vacuum. Religious life continued to be of great importance, even though the passions of previous ages were now more contained. Official suspicions of nonconformity still lingered, and occasionally led to a heavy-handed response. As late as 1858, the Baptist preacher Thomas Medhurst was fined for obstruction after preaching to the crowds on Queen's Promenade. But since about 1700, Protestant nonconformists had co-existed peaceably with the Anglican establishment for most of the time, and this continued.

In the early 18th century, when Daniel Mayo, youngest son of the 17th century clergyman Richard Mayo, led the Presbyterian congregation in Kingston, he fostered particularly good relations with the Anglicans. In the later 18th century, splits among the nonconformists led to the establishment of a Congregational church (1775), and a Baptist chapel (1790) in Back Lane (later Brick Lane and now Union Street). The new Congregational church converted William Ranyard, a member of a leading Kingston family, who founded Kingston's first Sunday School in 1798. The Quakers, an old established Protestant sect which used to be seen as socially subversive, had long been accepted as 'respectable'. From the later 18th century, suspicions focused on the Methodists, whose enthusiastic preaching and appeal to the lower orders provoked riots. However, from the mid-19th century Methodism ceased to threaten, and values preached in the Wesleyan chapels of Canbury and St James' Road were similar to those proclaimed from Anglican pulpits.

The established Church itself underwent an evangelical revival in the early 19th century. Kingston's vicar, Samuel Gandy, was an eccentric but committed clergyman who realized that All Saints' Church was becoming inadequate for the growing parish. He increased seats in the church by enlarging the galleries, and then turned his attention to founding new churches, galvanizing local people into raising large sums of money — St Andrew's, Ham, opened in 1832, followed by St Paul's, Hook, in 1838, St John's, Kingston Vale, in 1839, St Peter's, Norbiton, in 1842, and St Mark's Surbiton, in 1845. New parishes and vicars came with the churches; several of the vicars, like John Powell at Norbiton, were noted preachers and teachers.

Full religious toleration was established in 1828-9, when the laws preventing Protestant and Catholic nonconformists from holding civil office were finally repealed. In Kingston, this favoured Protestant nonconformists, as Roman Catholicism had been virtually non-existent since 1603. For many years anti-Catholic prejudice, fanned by two and a half centuries of propaganda, was a feature of local life. But a Catholic 'mission' was established at Kingston in 1847, and the first Catholic Church, St Raphael's, was consecrated in 1850. It was built by Alexander Raphael, on his recovery from illness, to fulfil a vow made to the Virgin Mary. Its existence encouraged the growth of a local Catholic community, and by 1894 there were enough Catholics in the area to warrant a new focus, St Agatha's.

Respectable Kingstonians of the 19th century shared a moral consensus firmly based, within a Christian framework, on self-help, hard work, temperate habits, individual responsibility and education. Morality and education were also seen as closely linked to public order. In 1840, when Kingston Council discussed a ban on Shrove Tuesday football, the game was described as 'subversive of good order and prejudicial to the morality of the Town'. Ignorance was commonly held to be the 'fruitful parent of moral evil': the cause of crime and anti-social behaviour. It was thus the duty of Kingston's citizens to improve the morals and education of the poor.

Kingston had long been concerned about the increasing number of poor people. When the parish Workhouse scheme of 1725 was established, it was stated that 'the poor of Kingston upon Thames are become very numerous and chargeable', and that it was 'very advantageous and necessary' that they should be 'sufficiently maintained and educated and taught to work' so as to inculcate 'habits of Virtue, Sobriety, Obedience and Industry and Labour . . . and to keep the Poor at work, and from begging about the streets and pilfering and other vices and Idleness'. The aim was to care for the poor in the Workhouse as one family, providing suitable tasks for all according to age and ability. The children were also to learn to read, write and count, and then put out as apprentices or servants, while the elderly were to be treated 'calmly and tenderly'.

A century later, Kingston's poor were still a charge on the parish, and the situaton was worsening. In 1817 the Bailiffs called a public meeting, and the Kingston Association for bettering the Condition and Morals of the Poor was formed. Its leading lights included the vicar, Samuel Gandy, and a local gentleman, Charles Pallmer, who was later MP for Surrey. The Association's aims were 'to better by every eligible means the condition and morals of the Poor, and for that purpose to enquire as minutely as possible into their wants, employment and habits — into the causes which promote bad or good effects upon them; and into the means of preventing one and promoting the other'.

The Association organized several schemes. A Savings Bank was established, where the poor could save their money, and see it earn interest. A Clothing and Bedding Society, subsidized by charitable donations, was set up. Poor folk contributed 3d a week, and received necessary clothes and bedding to double the value. A Medical Dispensary, funded entirely by voluntary subscription, allowed the charitable subscribers to recommend responsible poor families who, when sick, were attended free of charge by local doctors. Later on, the Kingston Provident Dispensary encouraged the poor themselves to contribute 1d per week in return for medical treatment when needed.

The Kingston Association also awarded sums of money each year to 'those among the poor who have distinguished themselves by industry, frugality, perseverance, &c' — these included servants of good character, and people who had managed to bring up large families without poor relief. As the main cause of 'the bad morals and conditions of the poor' was held to be 'the omission of proper observance of the Sabbath', the Association tried to persuade employers to pay wages on Friday, instead of Saturday evening. Then they could buy cheaper goods in the Saturday market might not spent their money in the pub on Saturday night, and would not have to shop on a Sunday, 'by which the duties of that day are neglected both by seller and buyer'.

However, the Association had little impact on the roots of poverty: low wages, high rents, too little work and the price of food. Unemployment and the need to pay the rent forced many families 'on the parish', especially in winter, and the receipt of 'doles' of money, food, clothes, shoes or coals, either from the old-established Kingston charities, or from the poor rates, continued into the second half of the 19th century. The establishment of the Kingston Union in 1836 reduced Kingston's poor rate to an acceptable level, but large sums were still spent helping poor families in their own homes even after the new Union Workhouse opened at Norbiton. Churches dispensed charity and ran coal and clothing thrift clubs; local branches of Friendly Societies and later the Trade Unions looked after their members when sick or unemployed, and the new Building Societies helped working people of modest means buy their own houses.

Education helped people to help themselves. By the 18th century Kingston had a variety of educational establishments. The most prestigious was the Grammar School. According to its statutes of 1670, 'children born in the Town shall be taught freely', and were to learn Latin, English, and 'good writing', as well as to be 'trained up in piety' through reading the Scriptures. In the 18th century, the Grammar School flourished, but many of its pupils were gentlemen's sons from outside the town, who boarded. After 1797, there was a renewed attempt to restrict the school's intake to the sons of Kingston's freemen; numbers slumped dramatically, and for much of the 19th century the standard was low. Nor was the school free for townsfolk: the 1832 statutes declared that each scholar should pay 15s per quarter, plus £2 to the master on admission. However, there was a growing demand for secondary education. In 1874, when Kingston's charities were reorganized, some of the money from the old charitable bequests was diverted to the Grammar School. New buildings and a new headmaster raised its reputation, and by the late 19th century Kingston Grammar School, then called the Queen Elizabeth School, was a popular choice among middle class Kingstonians who could afford fees of £10 10s per year.

Throughout the 18th and 19th centuries, private academies and dame schools flourished, patronised by the well-off. Poor children, if they were fortunate, also went to school. Some of Kingston's charities, before the reorganization of 1874, specified that their money should be spent on schooling for the poor. Thomas Tiffin's will of 1638 bequeathed £50 to buy land for income from rents, with which Kingston Corporation should 'yearly, for ever, cause to be taught, in some good school, to write and cast accounts such honest poor men's sons' as the bailiffs chose, and John Tiffin's will left more money the next year. The Tiffin charity rented a schoolhouse which, by the early 19th century, was in the Horsefair, and in the 1820s it was paying a schoolmaster (Thomas Spearing, after 1826) to teach 22 boys to read, write and 'cypher', and was clothing 18 of them. Six boys maintained by Brown's charity and eight by Harding's charity were taught in the same schoolhouse and by the same master as the Tiffin scholars.

Girls, too, were catered for. Brown's charity clothed 28 poor girls and employed a mistress to teach them reading and needlework. Fourteen girls were also educated on Belitha's gift, and eight on Harding's gift, and were taught with the Brown's girls; their mistress (Mrs Emms in the 1820s) had to provide the schoolhouse at her own expense. The Brown's girls also learnt writing and arithmetic from the Tiffins' schoolmaster. By the later 1820s the girls were probably educated in the same building as the boys, for Ayliffe remembers Thomas Spearing and his wife running a mixed charity school in the Horsefair. The charity children were distinguished by their different coloured 'uniforms'. Ayliffe says that 'there were a certain number of "Blue Boys" and an equal number of "Brown Boys", so designated because of the colour of their coats and caps; while the girls wore mob caps, white aprons and brown or blue frocks'. In the 1820s the boys paid for by Harding's charity wore green coats. From the account books of the Tiffin and Belitha charities, the charity children ceased to attend the Horsefair school during 1836-7; instead, their charities paid for their education at the Public School in the Richmond Road.

The Richmond Road School, founded in 1818, was the major legacy of the Kingston Association. At its inaugural meeting in 1817, it declared that as 'amongst the younger Part of the Poor, the principal causes of what is bad in their conditions and morals, are Idleness, Ignorance and Bad Language', it would be a good idea 'if a public school were established in the Town of Kingston, in which the time of the children of the Poor shall be employed in qualifying them for receiving instruction suitable to their condition, especially the precepts of religion and morals calculated to guard them against the pernicious influence of bad conduct in others'. The school, non-denominational and with separate girls', boys' and infants' departments, was supported mainly by public subscription — subscribers were then entitled to recommend the scholars — but also by a small weekly fee of 1d per child (in 1817).

Biden described the school in 1852 as 'well conducted'; it then had over 270 pupils. By 1888, it had 377 boys, 264 girls and 150 infants, and continued to flourish into the 20th century. Children who started in the Infants' Department, established in 1828, had no idea of letters or numbers, and in the winter were frequently absent through illness, chilblains, bad weather and 'also for want of shoes'. Yet they eventually learnt to read, write and count and moved up into the main school, which they left to go into service or other jobs.

Poor children also received an elementary education in Nonconformist schools, sponsored by the British and Foreign Schools Society, and in the Church schools, or 'National' schools, encouraged by the Anglican National Society for promoting the Education of the Poor. Norbiton, for instance, had a National school which started in 1838 in a cottage in the Wanderings, and developed in association with St Peter's Church after 1842. The St Peter's Church Schools, funded by a mixture of voluntary subscriptions and modest weekly fees of a few pence per child, moved into proper school buildings in the Cambridge Road after 1853, and were closed as recently as 1960. The All Saints' National School was built in Wood Street in 1873, and by the later 19th century there were other church schools in Surbiton, New Malden and Ham.

Though such schools were not free, the local vicar or other charitable souls might pay a child's fees if they knew the family. The Workhouse had its own school, where pauper children were taught to read and write, and where the girls learnt needlework and housework and the boys gardening and crafts. Apart from that, poor children might learn their letters at a Sunday School, or at the Ragged School, held in the evenings in a barn in Old Bridge Street for 20 years after 1855. However, school attendance, even at elementary level, was not compulsory till 1876, and before then many children had no education at all.

In 1870, Kingston decided it was sufficiently supplied with elementary schools not to need a School Board, so it did not set up any local authority or 'Board' schools which the law that year empowered it to build. Nevertheless, there was a strong feeling that more should be done, especially at secondary level. Moreover, an earlier (1861) inquiry into Kingston's charities suggested that money spent on 'doles' pauperized rather than truly helped the poor, and that it should go to education. A scheme was adopted in 1874 which used Kingston's charitable bequests to revitalize the Grammar School and to establish secondary schools. The Tiffin Schools for boys and girls were founded, aimed at lower middle class children, with fees of under £5 per year. The original buildings were in the Fairfield, and the schools opened in January 1880 with 36 boys and 46 girls. They were soon extremely successful, and had about 700 pupils between them by the end of the century.

Self-education was considered important for adult morals and opportunities. Frederick Gould helped found the Kingston Literary and Scientific Institution in 1839, to promote 'useful knowledge in Literature, Science and the Arts' among young working men. At its new building (1841) in Thames Street, members could attend lectures, classes and discussions, and use the Institution's library. Libraries were a characteristic feature of the 19th century: first private 'circulating' libraries, where people paid to borrow books and later, free public libraries, funded on the rates. Kingston had a famous circulating library run from 1850 by George Phillipson, who took over 'Seeley's Library' and ran his business from premises in the Market Place. Some of the churches ran libraries of religious and 'improving' books; at St Peter's, Norbiton, in the 1870s, parishioners paid ½d per volume. But there was no free Public Library in Kingston till 1882, when a reading room opened in an upstairs room in a hall in St James' Road. The library opened for lending in 1883, and had an 'intelligent and obliging librarian', Mr Baxter. By 1887 it had over 6,000 books.

Kingston was not a great centre for theatres, music halls or other places of entertainment in the 19th century, though there were halls where plays and concerts could be staged. Surbiton Assembly Rooms, one of the best known, opened in 1889. Yet Kingston gained a proper theatre in 1896-7, when the Albany Hall in Fife Road was converted into the Royal County Theatre. This became a cinema from 1917. The Kingston Empire, a music hall, opened on the site of Canbury House in 1910. Many working people spent their leisure in the pub — of which Kingston had many — and moralists deplored the results. Temperance societies, whose members pledged to moderate their intake of alcohol or abstain completely, flourished from 1840 in opposition to the 'alehouse culture', though an attempt in the 1880s to establish coffee houses as rivals to pubs was unsuccessful.

Leisure otherwise focused on clubs and societies. The Kingston Workmen's Club (1878) attempted to 'promote the social and intellectual welfare of the working men of Kingston'. It moved to new premises in 1879, and offered its members a games room, reading room, skittle alley, and a splendid concert hall and stage where twice weekly concerts were held. Earlier, the Norbiton Working Men's Institute staged entertainments, and in the 1860s its 'Penny Readings' raised money from amateur performances of music, singing and recitations.

Clubs founded to promote particular interests included the Kingston Debating Society (1886) and the Photographic Society (1893), and several sporting clubs for rowing, football, tennis and athletics. Regattas were held regularly on the Thames, and Queen's Promenade was a good place to enjoy the view. Walking was a favourite pastime. People were in the habit of visiting the woods on Coombe and Kingston Hills, to admire the views and the wildlife, and in 1853 there was a successful public outcry when the local landowner, the Duke of Cambridge, tried to close the public right of way at Warren Road. As the area became more built up, and the countryside dwindled, a few far-sighted schemes preserved and improved certain areas for the pleasure and recreation of inhabitants. The Fairfield, which in the 1850s was still 'an untidy waste', made dangerous at night by 'the roughs of Water Lane', was enclosed by railings as a public recreation ground in 1865, while Canbury Gardens, laid out in 1889-90 created an attractive setting for families to stroll on a Sunday afternoon.

Biden remarked severely in 1852 that vice and immorality used to be practised openly in Kingston, but admitted that his own century had already witnessed an improvement, and that the town's inhabitants had progressed in intelligence and prosperity. They received much encouragement from local churches, societies and schools. There was still ignorance, drunkenness and poverty in late 19th century Kingston, but the moral imperative of the age, with its stress on self-improvement, had already transformed the prospects of ordinary people. Frederick Merryweather was voicing a general belief when he said in 1887 that 'no previous half century has recorded such progress in those social and domestic circumstances which contribute to the health, and to the happiness, of mankind'.

The expansion of the Anglican Church in Kingston: LEFT: The nave of All Saints', 1847, showing the gallery at the west end. There were more galleries at the sides, which were extended as the population rose. RIGHT: St Mark's, Surbiton, established 1845 to serve the growing population of 'Kingston-on-Railway'. (KM & HS)

The toleration of Dissent: LEFT: The old Baptist Chapel, Brick Lane. Kingston's first Baptists met in a barn before building this chapel in 1790. It cost £402, and was 'the gate of heaven to many souls'. RIGHT: The new Baptist Chapel, 1864. BELOW: St Raphael's Roman Catholic Church, Portsmouth Road, built 1848. Alexander Raphael, its founder, delayed its consecration because he had dreamt he would die soon after. When it was finally consecrated, 1850, he died that November.

KINGSTON
PROVIDENT DISPENSARY,
GROVE ROAD.
ESTABLISHED JANUARY, 1865.

THE object of this Institution is to enable the Working Classes and poor persons by their own weekly payments, commenced in the time of health, aided by the contributions of other inhabitants, to ensure to themselves and their families efficient medical advice and medicine during illness.

The following very moderate WEEKLY PAYMENTS ensures to the Free Members, in case of illness, the very best medical attenuance and medicine :—

MEMBERS, male or female, over 12 years of age, ONE PENNY.

CHILDREN of Members, being under 12 years of age, ONE HALFPENNY each.

Where there are more than two children under 12 years of age in one family, all are included in one payment of ONE PENNY.

WIVES of Free Members are attended in their confinements on payment of a fee of 12s. 6d.

A Committee of 24 Free Members regulate the admission of Free Members, and receive their weekly payments.

The Committee of Free Members are entitled to attend and vote at all general meetings.

Three of the Committee of Free Members are Members of the Committee of Management.

Free Members are admitted every Saturday Evening from 8 to 9.

TO THE INHABITANTS

OF

KINGSTON AND ITS VICINITY.

THE prevalence of those principles and crimes which tend to destroy the order and comfort of society, has, within the last few years, excited the attention of the public, and led to an investigation of the causes which have produced these disorders. The numerous inquiries which have been instituted, have disclosed this important fact, that the greater number of those who have been convicted of having transgressed the laws of their country, were unable to read or write; proving beyond all doubt that ignorance is the fruitful parent of moral evil. It seems, therefore, a natural inference, that the most effectual remedy is to promote those improved systems of teaching, which at so small an expence, provide for the early instruction of the poor. In consequence of a desire to promote the moral advantage of that most numerous class of society, almost every town in Great Britain can already boast of institutions for the education of their poor; while Kingston possesses only a few confined channels for the dissemination of that knowledge, which enables those who possess it to read their Bibles. It appears that the Schools which are already established in this town are insufficient to perform their local share of this great national object; those which are free being very inadequate to receive that number of children which so populous a district as Kingston and its vicinity must always contain; and the others too expensive to allow the poor to derive much benefit from them.

UNDER these circumstances, it is proposed to establish a School, upon the improved systems of Education; and the following Rules are respectfully submitted to the consideration of the Nobility, Gentry and the Inhabitants of Kingston and it's vicinity, accompanied with this observation, that these Rules are not to be considered as fully adopted, but subject to the alterations of the Subscribers; being laid before the Public, only as a means of presenting the subject to their consideration previous to a General Meeting.

RULES.

I. THE Business of this Institution shall be conducted by a Treasurer, a Secretary, and a Committee consisting of 9 other subscribers, together with a female Committee to superintend the Girls; to be chosen annually by the Subscribers.

II. EVERY Clergyman and Dissenting Minister, subscribing one Guinea per annum, shall be entitled to attend and vote at the Meetings of the Committee.

III. A general Meeting of the Subscribers and Friends of the Institution shall be held annually, when the accounts as audited shall be presented, a report agreed on to be printed and circulated, and a new Committee appointed.

ABOVE: Kingston's old parish Workhouse, 1837, opposite the junction of Coombe Road with London Road. (KM & HS) LEFT: Advertisement for Kingston Provident Dispensary, 1865. (SC) RIGHT: Proposal for the establishment of the Richmond Road 'public' school, 1818. (KM & HS)

ABOVE: The 19th century Richmond Road school building was rebuilt 1907, and that building survives. LEFT: Bluecoat boy and CENTRE: Greencoat boy both attended a charity school in the Horsefair, but transferred to Richmond Road school 1836. RIGHT: Kingston Workmen's Club, Fairfield Road moved here in 1879 from a site near Kingston bridge. Burnt down 1886, it was rebuilt and continued to flourish. In 1908 it moved to London Road. (All KM & HS)

ABOVE: The playground at St Peter's church school (Norbiton national school). The building still stands in Cambridge Road. CENTRE: Kingston Grammar School, London Road: the new building of 1887. BELOW: The original Tiffin school, Fairfield (now St Joseph's RC Primary), taught boy and girls in separate schools. The girls went in 1889, the boys in 1929. (All KM & HS)

CORPORATION

PUBLIC BATHS

WOOD STREET

(Three minutes walk from Kingston, L. & S.W.R. Station; one minute from Thames Side).

These Baths are OPEN TO THE PUBLIC DAILY, and Tickets are issued and stamped up to half-an-hour of the time of closing as follows, viz :—

THE SWIMMING BATH

MONDAYS & FRIDAYS :

GENTLEMEN from 6.30 a.m. to 9 a.m., and from 2.30 p.m. to 9 p.m. ... ... } 6d.
LADIES from 9.30 a.m. to 2 p.m. ... ...

WEDNESDAYS :

GENTLEMEN from 6.30 a.m. to 9 a.m., and from 5.30 p.m. to 9 p.m. ... ... } 6d.
LADIES from 9.30 a.m. to 5 p.m. ... ...

TUESDAYS & THURSDAYS :

GENTLEMEN from 6.30 a.m. to 11.30 a.m., and from 4.30 p.m. to 9 p.m. ... ... } 2d.
LADIES from 12 noon to 4 p.m.... ... ...

SATURDAYS :

GENTLEMEN from 6.30 a.m. to 9 p.m. ... ... 2d.

SUNDAY MORNINGS :

GENTLEMEN from 6.30 a.m. to 9 a.m. ... ... 2d.

The above Charge of 6d. includes Two Towels and Bathing Dress.
In addition to the above Charge of 2d., a Penny extra to be charged for One Towel and Bathing Dress.

LIBERAL ARRANGEMENTS FOR CLUBS, SCHOOLS, &c.

Experienced Swimming Instructors for Ladies and Gentlemen are in attendance daily. All Swimming Lessons by appointment.

THE SLIPPER BATHS

Are open to Ladies and Gentlemen from 6.30 a.m. to 9 p.m. on Week-Days at the following Charges :—

First Class Warm Bath (Two Towels) ... ... 6d.
First Class Cold Bath (Two Towels) ... ... 3d.
Second Class Warm Bath (One Towel) ... ... 3d.
Second Class Cold Bath (One Towel)... ... ... 1d.
SOAP ONE PENNY EXTRA.

Any further information can be obtained of Mr. Gerald O'Rourke, Superintendent, The Baths, Wood Street, Kingston-upon-Thames.
1st March, 1898. By order of the Baths Committee. HAROLD A. WINSER, Town Clerk.

W. Drewett & Sons, Printers, Market Place, Kingston.

ABOVE: The new Tiffin Girls' School, built 1889 in St James' Road. LEFT: The new building (1841) of Kingston Literary & Scientific Institute. (KM & HS) Designed by Scott & Moffat, architects of St Peter's Church, it was spectacular in red and yellow brick, had a library, a galleried lecture room and reading room. Chemical experiments took place in the basement. RIGHT: Advertisement for Kingston Public Baths, 1898; the first iron pool (1882) that floated in the Thames by the Portsmouth Road, was replaced 1897 by the Wood Street Baths, superseded by the Coronation Baths, Denmark Road (1936). (All KM & HS)

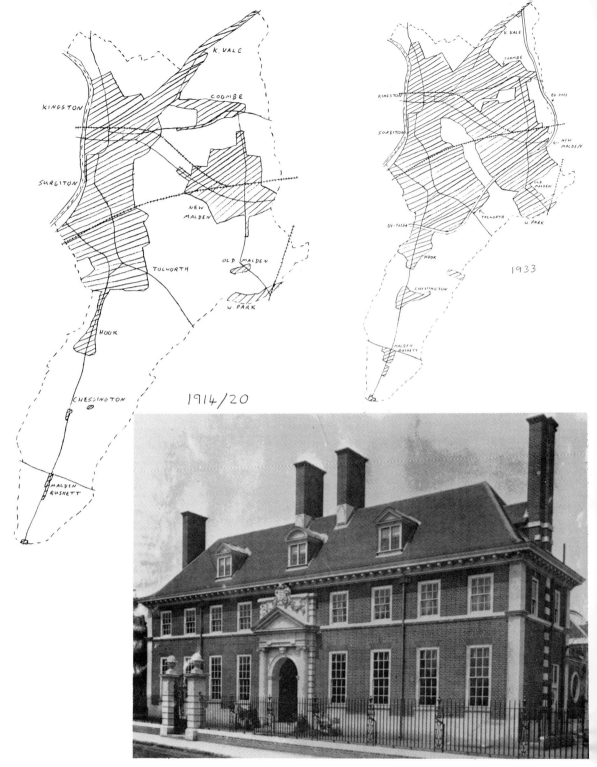

K. VALE

COOMBE

KINGSTON

SURBITON

NEW
MALDEN

TOLWORTH

OLD MALDEN

W PARK

HOOK

CHESSINGTON

MALDEN
RUSHETT

1914/20

K. VALE

COOMBE

BY PASS

KINGSTON

SURBITON

NEW
MALDEN

OLD
MALDEN

TOLWORTH

W PARK

BY-PASS

HOOK

CHESSINGTON

MALDEN
RUSHETT

1933

Early 20th century urban sprawl: Kingston and its suburbs LEFT: 1914-20, and RIGHT: 1933. (TE) BELOW: The new Public Library in the Fairfield, 1903, partly funded by the famous philanthropist, Andrew Carnegie. (KM & HS)

144

A Change of Identity

Between 1900 and 1939, Kingston faced an identity crisis. Population still grew, and the built-up area expanded. This accelerated the trend to urban sprawl. The local economy was changing and diversifying: Kingston had largely lost its dominant 19th century industries, and its role as a market town was less important. The town became more of a dormitory suburb of London. Kingston Corporation's freedom of action was increasingly restricted by central government directives, the borough had to accommodate the powers of the new Surrey County Council, and fight off attempts to absorb it into Greater London. Nevertheless, Kingston maintained civic pride and found a new role as a business and shopping centre. Despite the trauma of world war, the period also saw a steady rise in the standard of living.

On the eve of the First World War, the population of the Kingston area was about 68,000, compared to 55,625 in 1901. Kingston itself was a working class town; New Malden a notch up the social scale because it contained many 'one servant' houses; and Surbiton a wealthier, middle class suburb. There were still big houses with rich 'gentry' occupiers, especially on Coombe and Kingston Hill, and some tracts of land still belonged to the estates of large landowners and lay undeveloped. Already there was a strong feeling that green areas were under threat. The vicar of Norbiton wrote in 1903 that St Peter's vicarage, with its leafy garden, would soon 'hold the fort alone against the relentless advance of the builder'.

Kingston's economy was already varied by 1900. As local fields and market gardens were sold for building, fewer people were employed as gardeners or farm labourers. A new industry, the design and manufacture of aircraft, started in Kingston when the Sopwith Aviation Company was founded in 1912 at the corner of Canbury Park Road, but pre-war this was a small concern. In 1913 it employed six fitters and carpenters, plus a tea boy. A report of 1911 said that 'a considerable number of workers are employed outside the Borough, either in London, or in the wealthier districts adjoining Kingston'. Of those who worked in Kingston, many men were employed in the printing works, and many women in beer bottling, in the soda water works, and in laundries. Often these women were 'the keepers of the house, as the men are only casually employed, on the river etc.'

Of the girls who left Kingston's elementary schools between 1908 and 1913 to enter paid employment, the largest single category became domestic servants, and the second largest group went into the dressmaking, millinery or tailoring trades. Others became shop assistants, or worked in laundries or offices. Of the boy school leavers, a substantial number became junior clerks or office boys, or entered the printing or building trades, while others became engineers or gas fitters, or worked in motor car, 'cycle or carriage shops, in the candle factory or gasworks. But the largest single category was employed in different aspects of the retail and service trades, as shop boys, errand boys, van boys etc. This points to a trend that became more marked after the war: Kingston was becoming a shopping centre.

However, the First World War distorted normal development. People expected a quick victory in 1914 and at first there was much enthusiasm. Troops from Kingston's 'local' regiment, the East Surreys, who were based at Kingston Barracks, were cheered as they set off for the front, and a government recruiting drive launched from Kingston Town Hall raised 2,000 volunteers for the armed forces. As casualties ran into tens of thousands, a more sombre mood prevailed. The Borough Librarian began to collect the names of Kingston's war dead for a roll of honour. One was Andrew Stevens, a naval gunner who had attended All Saints' School and became the youngest qualified diver in the navy. He died, aged 23, in the North Sea off Zeebrugge when a mine sunk his ship. His mother, Alice, wrote: 'it was a terrible shock to me and also his fiancée and friends, for we were expecting him home any moment to get married, but heard of his death instead . . . I have lost one of the best sons a mother had.'

All areas of life were affected. Factories and shops lost workers, schools lost teachers, and public services were put under strain as men enlisted. By the spring of 1915, Kingston, Surbiton and District Fire Brigade had lost 12 firefighters: 'the loss of these 12 experienced men has been greatly felt, and more especially by no. 2 station, who have lost 8 of the 12 officers and men'. Conscription in 1916 exacerbated the labour shortage, especially as the war itself created an increased demand for military equipment. Some premises were compulsorily purchased for munitions factories, and local firms Sopwith's and KLG Sparking Plugs were forced to expand because of government demand. Sopwith's, whose planes were used by the Royal Naval Air Service, grew dramatically: it put up new buildings in Canbury Park Road, and leased a large new factory in Richmond Road, Ham, which was built with government money. By 1917 it employed about 3,500. Of these, 1,000 were women. Employers increasingly drew on female labour for jobs in factories and transport, while women also went to the front with the Red Cross as nurses and ambulance drivers.

The war caused food and fuel shortages. Existing resources were not fairly allocated, for rationing was only introduced in 1918. Prices doubled, and this caused hardship. People were encouraged to grow their own food. Kingston Council let out more land to tenants as allotments, and several areas, such as the Fairfield and Latchmere Recreation Ground, were dug up. Despite this, some foods like potatoes were virtually unobtainable for ordinary people, because profiteers sold them at high prices. When Bentalls bought potatoes direct from the Norfolk growers in 1917, and sold them at cost, thousands of Kingstonians queued up for hours.

Life was coloured by the concerns of war. People knitted for the troops and sent them food parcels. They could even hear the guns from the Flanders battlefields. Frank Marsella, who lived in Asylum Road, Kingston, remembered how 'we would be sitting there round the fire in winter and we'd hear the rattling of the windows and that told us that there was fighting going on in France . . . oh yes, the vibration reached Kingston. From the Front'. Wounded soldiers were cared for in the nearby Cambridge Asylum, and local children would push them up the hill in their wheelchairs. Kingston supported Belgian refugees: Kingston Museum held an art exhibition to raise money for them in 1915, and a little colony of refugee artists settled at Worcester Park. Bentalls staff ran a refugee hostel in Denmark Road, and Rowan Bentall remembered his mother organizing two large hostels in Avenue Elmers, Surbiton.

Kingston itself was hardly bombed at all, but people could sometimes see the

Zeppelins on their way to bomb London. Frank Marsella said 'we could hear the banging, and we knew London was going through it'. If he heard the anti-aircraft guns on Coombe Hill, 'then we knew they were getting very, very near'. People were warned of possible raids, and were meant to stay indoors until a policeman rode round on a bicycle with a bugle, sounding the all clear. Evacuees from London bombing came to Kingston. Once, an influx arrived from East Ham: 'and of course we had to take 'em as best we could, nobody refused shelter . . . even if we had to sleep on the floor'. Finally, in 1918, pride in victory was mixed with shock at the scale of human loss. Kingston's roll of honour remembered 623 men of the borough who had died in the Great War. The memorial in Church Street was dedicated in 1923.

After the war, military demand collapsed and the local economy slumped. Sopwith's cut back drastically, and in 1919 the labour market was flooded with ex-servicemen. Depression and unemployment were major national problems in the 1920s and '30s, especially in mining and heavy industrial areas. In Kingston, unemployment was not as severe, but still gave cause for concern. In November 1920 a deputation of the local jobless asked the Council 'for a speedy attempt to deal with unemployment in the Borough', and a special committee met. A local Labour party activist reckoned there were 281 unemployed men, with 538 dependents, in 1920; by September 1921 there were over 462 men registered as unemployed at the local labour exchange. This was only a small proportion of the borough's adult male population. Nevertheless, a public meeting in 1921 attacked the Council for 'failing to take adequate steps to deal with the serious distress existing in the Borough, owing to unemployment', and Kingston qualified as a 'distressed area' which could receive a government grant towards the cost of local works put in hand to provide jobs.

Until the mid-1920s, Kingston Council undertook regular winter programmes of road repairs and improvements, filter-bed cleaning and extensions at the sewage works, or the clearing of local recreation grounds, and employed the jobless to carry them out. It even added a few workmen from among the unemployed to its permanent staff. But it could not afford to do more. Those who sought work had to wait for an upturn in the economy. This happened to an extent after 1925, but by 1930 the numbers of jobless were again giving rise to concern. The Council reconsidered public works schemes, and the Mayor and other leading Kingston citizens launched a Rotary Club initiative to create jobs by encouraging people in work to spend more on goods and services.

However, to an extent Kingston bucked the national trend. Jobs were created in retailing as Kingston developed into an important local shopping centre for Surrey and Greater London. Jobs were also provided by the light engineering firms that survived or started up in the 1920s and '30s, and which expanded dramatically from 1936 once Britain began to re-arm. The building trade was another important employer. It had its own periodic slumps, for instance in 1938, but was buoyant for much of the period, both because of council house building, and because of the private 'estates' that developed Kingston as a desirable residential area. Finally, the transport industry employed many people. Kingston was on a good network of local trains and trams, and running these was more labour-intensive than now. In 1934, the *Surrey Comet* said Kingston was the most prosperous town in Surrey, while in 1938 the Mayor called it 'that famous business place called Kingston', and said that 'commercially we have progressed in a phenomenal manner' during the past half generation.

147

The General Strike of 1926 provided some short-term excitement but had no long-term impact. Electricity workers were called out on strike but managerial staff and volunteers manned Kingston Power Station round the clock. Transport workers came out and few trains ran, but volunteers ran the trams. Council workmen in sewage and waste disposal did not strike. Crowds of individuals flocked to the Town Hall to offer their help. By their efforts Kingston was adequately supplied with food and coal.

Inter-war Kingston was an important centre for light engineering. Though Sopwith's was forced into receivership in 1920 when aircraft demand slumped and the government demanded a huge tax bill for 'excess war profits', it was refounded the same year by Sopwith and his chief test pilot, Harry Hawker, as the H.G. Hawker Engineering company. This new company, known as 'Hawker's', remained a leading local employer. It made engines, cars, vans and motorcycles as well as planes, but its heart was still in aircraft design. Sydney Camm and the design team pioneered metal (instead of wooden) aircraft, and developed new bombers and fighters. The company was thus well placed to expand in the 1930s, when interest in military aircraft revived. By 1933 it employed over 600. In 1935, Hawker's took over Armstrong-Siddeley, and the famous Hawker Hurricane fighter plane made its first flight. In 1936, convinced that war was coming, Sopwith decided to manufacture 1,000 Hurricanes even before the Air Ministry placed its first order for 600. By 1939, Hawker-Siddeley's Canbury Park Road premises were working at full capacity, together with Sopwith's old-established site at Brooklands, near Weybridge, and his new site at Langley, near Heathrow. Kingston was, once more, a major producer of military aircraft.

It also produced motor vehicles. Between 1920 and 1948, Leyland Motors leased the former Sopwith's factory in the Richmond Road, and used it to make spare parts for Leyland cars, 'buses and lorries. The Kingston works also produced the 'Trojan' or 'Utility' car from 1923 until 1928, by agreement with the car's original designer, Leslie Hounsfield. In the 1930s, a 20-seater 'bus called the Leyland 'Cub' was built at Kingston, followed by the 'Lynx' range from 1937. A smaller firm, E. J. Newns of Portsmouth Road, built specialist cars and coaches at his Long Ditton works. He designed luxury 'armchair' coaches for foreign travel, in which each seat was like a separate armchair, beautifully upholstered to match the deep pile carpet on the coach floor! Motor accessories were manufactured by the firm of V.W. Derrington, established in New Malden in 1919, which moved to London Road in 1926 and flourished for the next 50 years. Kingston also had several garages, or 'motor works', which sold, serviced and repaired cars. Kingston Hill Motor Works employed 20 people by 1930, and had its own 'car ambulance' — a rescue vehicle with a pick-up crane.

One of the area's best known engineering firms was KLG Sparking Plugs, of Kingston Vale. It was founded, as the Robin Hood Engineering Works, in 1911 by racing driver Kenelm Lee Guinness. It manufactured Guinness's own invention, the sparking plug, which facilitated more powerful car engines, and hence faster cars. During the 1914-18 war a government contract to manufacture plugs for sea planes forced the firm to expand. It continued to flourish: by 1929 it employed over 600, and from 1937 it benefitted from Britain's rearmament programme. Smaller engineering firms included Nash and Thompson, established 1931, which made aircraft gun turrets. Kingston Gas Company supplied growing numbers, though the gas was increasingly used for cooking and heating, rather than lighting, as electricity became more popular. Kingston Corporation's Electricity Generating Station, established in 1893, went from strength to strength. Its 77 consumers had become 6,500 by 1930.

Turk's Boatyard, Gridley Miskin's timber company, Hodgson's brewery, Price's candle factory, and Kelly's printing works were household names. The Thames was still a commercial thoroughfare: besides timber, meat was imported in bulk and supplied to local wholesalers. Laundries continued to be large-scale employers of female labour. The printers Knapp Drewett and Sons published the *Surrey Comet,* and Vine Products manufactured British wines. Austin's jam-making and fruit-preserving factory in Cromwell Road employed about 100 in 1929, and dealt with 10-12 tons of fruit a day. More unusual was the Worcester Park Glove Repairing Company, based at New Malden, to whose Acacia Grove workshop gloves poured in 'from all corners of the globe', and Hadley's manufacturing opticians at Surbiton, where glasses were made to fit 900 different types of nose.

The building trade employed large numbers between the wars. W.H. Gaze and Sons was a family concern established in Union Street by William Henry Gaze in 1879. He built St Luke's Church, Kingston Public Library (1902), Surbiton Fire Station, and a number of Kingston Corporation's early council houses. By 1934, Gaze's employed over 1,000 men and was 'a large business concern with connections throughout the country'. Other building firms included those of H.C. Jones ('Mr Berrylands'), who was involved in the development of Berrylands and Tolworth, and of James W. Serjeant, who pioneered the use of breezeblocks.

For most of the period, the markets held at Kingston still drew the crowds, though they were no longer as important as in the past. The cattle market was held on a Thursday until 1918, and on Mondays thereafter, but the large numbers of animals crowded into the Market Place became a general nuisance, and in 1925 the sale of livestock moved to the Fairfield. Sheep, cattle, pigs and poultry were sold there until after the Second World War, though by 1939 the decline of local farming meant the cattle market's days were numbered. However, a general produce market was still held in the Market Place; after 1919 this took place every day, and became an adjunct to the town's general shopping facilities.

Kingston's reputation as a major shopping centre was confirmed, and by 1938 it was said that shopping was its most popular occupation. The town's shops acted as a magnet, not just to the inhabitants of Kingston's old suburbs, like Norbiton, but to the residents of the new estates of Tolworth or Coombe, and for the whole of Surrey. Kingston was 'the London of the suburbs' and had something for everyone. Poor people flocked into the town on a Saturday evening because at 6pm traders with surplus food stocks reduced their prices: you could buy a 3lb chicken from the meat market for 9d instead of 1s 6d. Some establishments, like Sainsbury's butchers in Fife Road, sold only top quality produce, and delivered to the big houses up Kingston and Coombe Hill. Kingston still had many specialist shops, especially drapers, tailors and shoemakers, and Nutthall's famous riverside restaurant survived till 1933. But 'department stores' were becoming increasingly popular: larger shops that sold a wide range of goods and made window-shopping a pleasurable treat. Kingston's department stores included Hide's, in the Market Place, and Marks and Spencer, which opened in Clarence Street in November 1932. The most famous was Bentall's.

The store was founded by Frank Bentall, who opened a drapery shop at 31 Clarence Street in 1867, and expanded by buying up neighbouring properties in Clarence Street and Wood Street. By 1907 Bentall's was described as the 'finest store and shopping centre to be found in Surrey'. Its departments now included china and glass, toiletries, stationery, fancy goods, silver, beds and bedding, and toys. It had electric light, and a 'Moorish' tearoom with 'Open Sesame' (automatic) doors. In the 1920s, Frank's son, Leonard Bentall, built a customers' car park in Wood Street, and set up the store's own electricity generating plant. By then Bentall's was a major employer. Its staff of about 100 (1904) had become 1,000 by 1925, and numbers rose again in the 1930s. A major programme of expansion and rebuilding provided much-needed local employment: 250 people were hired to build the Maurice Webb façade, and another 500 or so staff jobs were created. By 1939 Bentall's had over 2,000 employees. The remodelled store of 1935 drew massive crowds who marvelled at the escalators in the new Escalator Hall, and queued to take tea in the Tudor Restaurant. Throughout the period, Bentall's was the pillar of Kingston's reputation as a shopping centre.

Improvements in local transport helped Kingston's retailers. In 1906, the first trams came to Kingston. The Corporation had tried to get Parliamentary permission to establish its own tram network ever since 1871, but all its schemes had been turned down, and a disgruntled Council then opposed the schemes of the private tram companies. Finally, however, it was agreed that the London United Tramways Company should extend its lines to Kingston. The tram lines were laid in 1905, and electric trams ran the next year. Trams ran until 1931, when they were replaced by trolley 'buses.

Roads also improved. After 1900, there was a great increase in the number of motor vehicles, not only private cars owned by wealthy individuls, but passenger 'buses and delivery lorries owned by firms. By 1912, the Portsmouth Road carried roughly equal numbers of motor and horse-drawn vehicles, and the proportion of motor vehicles increased after the First World War. But it took a while for roads to become adequate. Ordinary compacted stone surfaces were dusty; the best surface was tarmac. Most of the Portsmouth Road was tarred by 1910, but many of Kingston's local roads were still surfaced with granite — which needed water carts in summer to lay the dust — or wood blocks, which swelled and became uneven in wet weather. However, by 1939 most roads had tarmac surfaces. They had white lines down the middle, and traffic signs were introduced to prevent accidents. Better roads meant that car owners from all over Surrey could drive to Kingston to shop, and once Kingston Corporation (1924) and Bentalls (1928) had provided 'motor parks' they could find somewhere safe to park.

However, within Kingston town centre, narrow streets and traffic jams were still a problem. The pressure was eased somewhat by the new Kingston by-pass, finished in 1927, which syphoned off through traffic from Portsmouth to London, but the by-pass itself soon attracted visitors and led to ribbon development along the line of the road. Housing estates were built at New Malden and Tolworth, and that increased traffic. If the by-pass did not solve Kingston's traffic problems, it created an even larger pool of customers, and helped the town develop as the focus of an ever-widening suburban area.

The Kingston area was promoted in the 1930s as an attractive place to live and work, or to live and commute. Private speculative builders laid out 'estates' at Berrylands Park (Thorogoods of Surbiton) and Greenfield Park, New Malden (Wates) in 1932, at Tolworth (Sunray estate, 1933), in the Latchmere/Ham area (Crouch, 1936) and on the slopes of Coombe Hill (Berg, 1933-6). Some of the houses on Coombe Hill were over £1,000 freehold, and you needed to be well off to buy them, but those on middling incomes could afford the deposit and weekly mortgage repayments on a £675 freehold or £555 leasehold house on the Tudor estate.

These had a hall, large sitting room, kitchen, three bedrooms, bathroom and WC. Smaller houses on the Sunray estate cost £399 leasehold, and a £25 deposit meant 'to keep out the riff-raff'. Bill Williams bought one of these houses in 1934, and could afford the weekly repayments of 22s 6d on a Sainsbury's van driver's pay of under £4 a week. For this he had a front room, back room, kitchen, three bedrooms, bathroom and lavatory. 'And those houses today . . . what they said when they built them was rubbish . . . they're still standing. And if you can get one, you're bloody lucky.'

By the mid-1930s, Kingston was quite well-off for affordable housing, and overcrowding was not a problem. Yet from the late 19th century until the early 1930s, there was a severe shortage of decent, working-class housing. The Housing of the Working Classes Act, 1890, gave local authorities greater powers to force landlords to improve the houses they let out, and to demolish buildings that remained unfit. A number of damp, insanitary, delapidated houses in the Back Lanes and elsewhere were pulled down in the 1890s, and lodging houses were strictly supervised. But house building did not keep pace with demand, and accommodation was expensive. Poor families had to rent small tenements or single rooms: in 1891, Kingston had 1,600 tenements of four rooms or under, housing 5,496 people. By 1914, cases of gross overcrowding — such as a family of four living in one room — were the exception, but 'several houses had more people in them than was satisfactory'. It was common for the main tenant to sub-let one or two rooms to a single person or married couple, or for two poor families to share a house. In Asylum Road, for instance, the weekly rent of 8s 6d for a small house was too much for many families, so they shared. Each family paid 4s a week; one family had the back room downstairs for living and dining, and the front bedroom for sleeping, and the other family had the front room downstairs and the back bedroom; they took turns in the kitchen.

The Government's Housing Act of 1919 was meant to tackle the shortage. It required local councils to build 'council houses', subsidized by the central government, which would be let to the working classes at reasonable rents. However, it was several years before Kingston Corporation's housing scheme became effective. It took time to find a suitable site: 21 acres between Cambridge and Gloucester Roads and the railway. Then the Council (with reason) worried about the cost of buying the land and building the houses; despite government subsidies, most of the expense fell on the local authority, and Kingston had to borrow £50,000 from Surrey County Council. Kingston Corporation wanted a guarantee that, if costs rose above what could be raised by a local rate of 1d in the £, the Government would foot the bill, but the Government was reluctant to promise. Thus in January 1920, when the *Surrey Comet* reported the Council's plans to build 199 houses (2 or 3 bedrooms, living room and scullery, and some with a parlour as well), the Council got cold feet and decided to build a smaller number to start with.

A year later work still had not begun, because of a quarrel with the Ministry of Health over the Council's plans for the new sewers needed. A public meeting in the spring of 1921 attacked the Council's tardiness. At last, in June, work started on the

151

first 12 council houses. By now, however, the Government was short of money for subsidies, and would not give Kingston permission to build more than 12! For a while, the Council gave up. In February 1922, when the 12 were ready, they were not let out, despite a waiting list of 346, but were sold to whoever could afford the £700-£750.

There matters rested until the 1923 Housing Act, with renewed promises of government subsidies, encouraged Kingston Council to try again. In 1924 it planned 70 new council houses on the Cambridge Road site, and these were built (in Douglas, Ernest, Densham and Rosebery Roads) by the autumn of 1925. At last council tenants moved in though, at weekly rents of 16s for parlour houses and 13s for non-parlour houses, they were still too expensive for the poorer families. More houses were built in 1926, and the Council also helped people afford homes by offering council mortgages on private houses under the terms of the Small Dwellings Acquisitions Act.

Though slow to get under way, the Council's housing scheme gradually reduced Kingston's housing shortage. Cases of overcrowding dropped form 57 in 1923 to 26 in 1925; in several cases the families in the most crowded accommodation were allocated council houses. By 1930 the Council had built 500 houses though, with over 700 applicants on the waiting list, there was need for more. Another 200 were built by 1934. During the 1930s the great explosion of private building brought the cost of buying a house on a mortgage down near the level of council rents. By 1939, Kingston had no slums, and more families than ever before could afford a decent home.

Throughout the inter-war period, Kingston Council took public health seriously, and gradually the town became a healthier and pleasanter place. The death rate fell from 14.06 per 1,000 in 1900 to 11.0 in 1930. Kingston's Medical Officer of Health inspected houses and ordered improvements. Drinking water was checked, drains and sewers monitored, the sewage works expanded and improved, and dust and refuse collected weekly and destroyed at the Corporation 'Dust Destructor' in Villiers Road. The Medical Officer notified the Council of infectious diseases, and tried to prevent them by vaccination, isolation and fumigation.

Kingston did not have its own isolation hospital, but the Council paid for fever cases to be looked after at Wimbledon, Molesey or Hampton. Smallpox cases went to the Surrey Smallpox Hospital, and TB patients were also the responsibility of Surrey County Council. The most serious epidemic was the influenza outbreak of autumn 1918, in which about 70 died. Half the schoolchildren caught 'flu, and borough schools closed for a fortnight. General medical care in Kingston was quite good. It was fortunate to have the publicly funded Kingston and District Hospital, as the old Workhouse Infirmary was renamed in 1922, for surgical and maternity cases and non-infectious diseases, and the Kingston Victoria Hospital, supported by voluntary contributions. After 1930, when Surrey County Council took over the former Poor Law institutions, Kingston Hospital was known as the Surrey County Hospital.

Council responsibilities increased in the 1920s and '30s, not only in housing, but in maternity and child welfare. That started by voluntary effort in 1915, and Kingston Council took over in 1919. A mother and baby centre gave advice and supplied free milk. Kingston also had a day nursery which looked after young children whose mothers needed to work. A School Medical Officer was put in charge of children's health. By 1925 there were two maternity and child welfare clinics in the borough (an ante-natal clinic, and a school clinic), and health visitors visited homes to give practical advice. Infant mortality fell, and child health and cleanliness improved.

Since the 1902 Education Act, Kingston Corporation (a 'Part III' authority) retained control of the borough's elementary schools, but was under the overall control of Surrey County Council for secondary education. Though the number of children attending Kingston's elementary schools fell 1900-1930, Kingston still had 3,884 children on roll in 1930 and employed 113 elementary teachers. In the 1920s, the Corporation ran the Richmond Road and Bonner Hill (founded 1906) Schools as all-age Council Elementary Schools, with Infants, Junior and 'Senior', ie 11-13, departments. It also controlled St Luke's Church of England 'Senior' Elementary school, St Agatha's Infants School (Roman Catholic) and the Anglican voluntary schools of All Saints' Infants, and St Luke's, St Paul's Kingston Hill, St Peter's Norbiton and St John's Infants and Junior. In the 1930s, a new element was added with the Latchmere Road Central School.

Since the 1918 Education Act, children were educated until 14, if funds permitted. Kingston's pupils were educated free till the age of 13 or 14, and could then leave for work (or unemployment!) or for the Technical College. They could also move, aged 11, to one of the borough's selective secondary schools (Kingston Grammar School, Tiffin Boys' or Tiffin Girls' School), if they could afford the fees or won a scholarship. Kingston was unusual in having such good secondary education; this, plus its excellent travelling facilities, drew pupils from a wide area. In 1929, over half those at Kingston Technical College came from outside the borough.

The Technical College, established in 1899 and extended thereafter, incorporated a School of Art, a Day Commercial School, a Junior Technical School and a programme of evening classes. It taught subjects such as engineering, commerce, building, law and accountancy. Kingston Grammar School had 330 pupils in 1929, and its buildings remained adequate. Tiffin Boys', with 486 on roll, outgrew its old building in the Fairfield and moved into new premises on the Elmfield site in 1929. Tiffin Girls', with 356 pupils, moved to St James' Road in 1889; in 1937 it moved again, to new premises in Richmond Road, and the Technical College adapted its old accommodation.

As local government expanded, Kingston Council's staff increased, though Kingston was still a small authority. Key individuals worked extremely hard. The Town Clerk, snowed under by the municipal housing scheme, for years ignored government directives for the reform of local building bye-laws; when he was found out in 1926, the poor man retired early with high blood pressure.

Council office accommodation had long been inadequate. Though in 1900 the official 'Town Hall', where Council meetings were held, was still in the Market Place, this was too small to house Council administration. In 1891, many municipal offices moved to Clattern House, an 18th century mansion at the south end of the Market Place next to the Assize Courts (built 1811). Kingston Public Library was also housed at Clattern House, until a new purpose-built library opened near the Fairfield in 1903. But the court and office premises became increasingly cramped, and in 1933 the Council decided to build anew. Clattern House and the Assize Courts were demolished, and the new Guildhall, incorporating law courts, municipal offices, Council chamber and committee rooms, designed by Maurice Webb, opened in 1935.

Kingston's councillors worked hard. Local government was not politicized, as it became after 1945, and most candidates stood on local issues, though party politics were not entirely absent. The Labour Party, for instance, lobbied the Council on housing and employment from 1919. It formally contested Norbiton and Canbury

153

wards in the local elections of 1925. The same year, Alderman Huckle said he had long been a Labour member of the Council.

Kingston Corporation had to work within the administrative framework laid down by statute. It was responsible for a smaller borough than today. Ham, New Malden, and Surbiton were under the control of their own Urban District Councils, which in 1894-5 replaced their previous Local Boards. Ham became part of Kingston borough in 1933, but New Malden and Surbiton stayed independent, and became boroughs themselves in 1936. Relations with Surbiton were at times uneasy, but Kingston preferred to be on good terms with its neighbours. The co-operation of Malden and Coombe was particularly important because much of Kingston's early council housing was over the borough border in New Malden.

It was also important for Kingston to be on good terms with Surrey County Council, established 1889, which moved into County Hall, Kingston (Penrhyn Road), in 1891. County powers affected Kingston in several ways. Surrey was the statutory authority for secondary education, but friendly relations allowed Kingston Borough's Education Committee to administer Kingston's secondary schools subject to certain controls. Kingston's Medical Officer of Health co-operated with the Surrey Medical Officer on the prevention and containment of disease. When the Poor Law Unions were abolished in 1930, the powers of the Kingston Union were transferred to Surrey County Council, so it was Surrey, not the local Poor Law Guardians, who then ran Kingston Hospital. However, Kingston was ever-vigilant to guard against erosion of its powers. In 1925, it successfully opposed a bill which threatened to make it surrender management of the borough's main roads to the County Council.

London, however, was the main threat to local independence. Kingston was within the Metropolitan Police District, but had no wish for closer links. When a Royal Commission on London government launched an inquiry in 1922, Mayor Finny argued strongly against Kingston being incorporated into the area either of the existing London County Council, or of any other central body for London. He said Kingston was running its own affairs well, and did not want London interfering. He worked hard to raise public awareness of Kingston's historical identity and tradition of independent local government. He stressed Kingston's association with the crowning of Anglo-Saxon kings, and himself wrote a play for the Athelstan millenary pageant of 1924. In 1927, he petitioned George V to change the borough's name from 'Kingston-upon-Thames' to 'The Royal Borough of Kingston-upon-Thames'. The King consented, and thus the Royal Borough was born. In 1938 another mayor, George Knowlden, launched a Kingston Civic Festival in an effort to raise civic consciousness. He lauded Kingston as a thriving business community with a 'great historic past', and a high level of present achievement, and exhorted Kingstonians to take pride in it: 'For, after all, if we can hold a firm town-consciousness for today, a bright and secure future is assured.'

Kingston in the 1920s and '30s was changing so rapidly that it needed its 'heritage' to buttress civic pride. As old buildings gave way to new, as housing estates replaced fields, and newcomers flocked to the area, the past was vanishing before people's eyes. The old, small market town serving an agricultural hinterland was gone; in its place was a thriving commuter and light industrial urban sprawl. Kingston, with one face turned towards London and one towards Surrey, on the whole welcomed the changes.

Places of pleasure in Edwardian Kingston: ABOVE: The popular riverside gardens of Nutthall's Restaurant (now Millett's store), Market Place, c1910 and Surbiton Assembly Rooms, opened 1889. CENTRE: The Royal County Theatre, Fife Road, photographed c1900. BELOW: The Kingston Empire, c1910-20, survives as the Reject Shop, Clarence Street. (KM & HS) RIGHT: 'The pity of war': Naval gunner Andrew Marmeduke Stevens, d1915, aged 23, and R. M. Ferris, d1916, aged 18. (KM & HS)

ABOVE: The original Sopwith factory in Canbury Park Road where
BELOW: planes like this Sopwith Camel were produced in Kingston
during the First World War. (Both BAe)

Bentall's, a Kingston institution, ABOVE: at the Wood Street/Clarence Street corner c1900, before the expansion of premises; CENTRE: after the expansion, c1910, BELOW: the Maurice Webb facade, 1935. (KM & HS)

157

Inter-war industry in Kingston: ABOVE: the Hawker's factory, LEFT: a Marsh Brothers' delivery van, 1937; RIGHT: Turk's Boathouse, Thameside, c1930; BELOW: the staff of Kingston Tannery in the 1930s. (KM & HS)

ABOVE: Kingston cattle market moved from the Market Place to the Fairfield in 1925. LEFT: The first tram in Kingston, on 1 March 1906, was driven by the mayor. RIGHT: Reinventing Kingston's past — two views of Kingston Market Place: late 19th century, and 1923. The small shop back left (Nutthall's 'Old Segar Shoppe') was built c1570, though the half timbering is Victorian. The shop to the right (now Next) is 19th century, a circulating library and bookshop which became Boots the Chemist in 1908. The carved and gilded 'Tudorbethan' front is a sham, added in stages from 1909. The second phase, in progress in the photo, took place in 1923, and was designed by Alderman Finny. (All KM & HS)

159

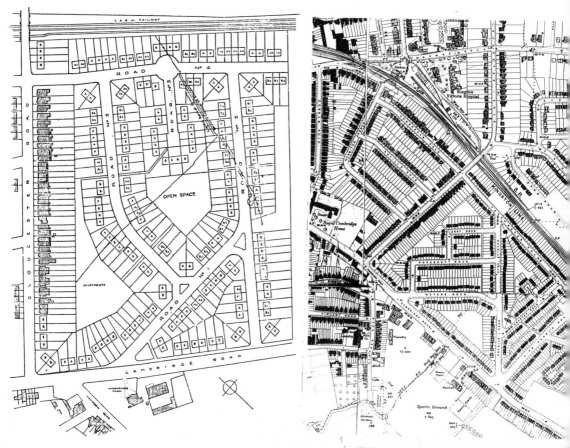

The Best in "TUDOR" HOMES

Inter-war council housing: LEFT: Kingston Council's plan for a housing estate, 1920. RIGHT: The housing as actually built, in new streets off the Cambridge Road. (KM & HS) BELOW: Private housing in the 1930s: Crouch-built homes on the 'Tudor' estate, Ham. (C) RIGHT: Kingston Guildhall designed by Maurice Webb, photographed in 1937. (KM & HS)

Civil Defence and Secrets

On 3 September 1939, normal life was put on hold as Kingston rose to meet the demands of 'total war' against Hitler's Germany. Civil Defence was the priority, because all-out air raids were expected, and gas attacks feared. Kingston Corporation had started to consider air raid precautions as early as 1935, and by 1938 a local scheme was in place. Air raid wardens were recruited, and shelters built. When war broke out, the Council set up an ARP Emergency Committee of four men, including the Mayor and the Town Clerk, which then put Kingston on a war footing. Although normal council services like education, road maintenance and refuse collection continued, the war put a halt to any new projects.

By December, Kingston's Air Raid Warden service was at full strength. There were 350 wardens, 80 full-time paid personnel, the rest part-time volunteers. The borough was divided into 16 districts, each with its wardens' post. Most of these were in sunken shelters, and all were manned night and day. The wardens supervised the borough's public air raid shelters, reported bomb damage, and were responsible with the police for enforcing the blackout. The latter was at first considered an 'onerous task', for many lights were reported. However, by December, due to the hard work of police and wardens, and the 'courtesy and helpfulness of the public', complaints were greatly reduced.

Kingston Council provided a number of public air raid shelters. Some were underground trenches, others surface shelters. The Fairfield trenches, originally built at the time of the 1938 Munich Crisis, could seat 2,700 people, those underneath Wood Street 1,200, and those in the Market Place 650. Other, smaller, public shelters were scattered around the borough, and each school had its own, which were available to the public out of school hours. Eventually, nearly 11,000 day seating places and 3,683 bunks were provided. The council also installed shelters for corporation flats, and supplied Anderson or Domestic Surface Shelters for householders to put up in their gardens.

The Auxiliary Fire Service, set up to help the regular fire service put out the fires started by bombs, consisted by 1940 of 64 full-time staff and 55 volunteers. They had 19 pumps and nine cars. There were two auxiliary fire stations, one based at the Alexandra Hotel, Park Road, and one in Penrhyn Road. There were also five 1st line action stations, which were continuously manned, and nine 2nd line action stations, whose personnel were completed by volunteers when the air raid siren sounded. During the Blitz of 1940, it became clear that still more fire-fighters were needed to combat incendiary bombs, so a Fire Watching scheme was set up. Local residents and business people were trained in the use of stirrup pumps, and street-based volunteer squads set up to supplement the fire services.

The Casualty Service, organized by the borough's Medical Officer of Health, had two first aid posts, one at the Victoria Hospital, Coombe Road, staffed by the Red Cross, and the other at the council's health centre, the Grange Road Clinic, staffed by the St John Ambulance Brigade. These helped people who were injured in air raids. To transport casualties there were 16 stretcher parties, each of five men, including a driver, which were based at depôts in Burton and Villiers Roads. There were ambulance depôts at Burton Road and the Fairfield car park.

A Decontamination Service (in case of gas attacks) and a Road Repair Service were on call in case they were needed after a raid. They had identical personnel, comprising Corporation workmen. A new building at the Villiers Road depôt had a room for cleaning and decontamination, and a store for protective clothing. There was also a Rescue Squad responsible for providing rescue parties, demolishing unsafe buildings and clearing debris. This consisted of four light parties of 11 men, and two heavy parties of nine men. They stood by in shifts; the night shifts slept at Villiers Road.

Kingston also had a centre for the Women's Voluntary Service (WVS), organized by Councillor Oldfield. The WVS operated a canteen, which in 1941 became the British Restaurant, at the Coronation Baths. This was useful for supplying food and hot drinks for emergency workers, and for people bombed out or evacuated during raids. The WVS also staffed two mobile kitchens. In 1941, a Housewives Section was established. A group of women in each street was trained in first aid and agreed to help with casualties, salvage or clearing up.

Kingston Council acted as permanent co-ordinator for all these services, and provided the Headquarters for the borough's civil defence. Two strongrooms in the Guildhall basement, belonging to the Town Clerk and the Medical Officer of Health, were adapted for use as a Message Room and a Control Room, and had special 'in' and 'out' telephone lines, including direct lines to the Police and Fire Stations, and to Group Control at County Hall. Information about air raids, casualties and damage all came through to this nerve centre, which was manned round the clock by a permanent staff supplemented by other members of the corporation staff in the event of an air raid warning. Senior corporation officers also supervised the Report Centre at night. The council also ran lectures and demonstrations, and in 1941 a special 'gas chamber' was set up at the Guildhall where people could try out their gas masks.

Poison gas attacks never materialized; it was air raids that tested civilian resolve. Kingston's proximity to London, and the presence of the Hawker's aircraft factory, made it a likely target for bombing. In the event, it was not heavily bombed compared to some other parts of London, but it had its share: 31 raids, mostly concentrated during the 'Blitz' of September-December 1940, and towards the end of the war in the summer of 1944. The bombs dropped between 1940 and spring 1944 were 'conventional' high explosive or incendiary bombs. From June 1944 Flying Bombs (V1s), which did more widespread damage, were used, and on 22 January 1945, Kingston experienced its first, and thankfully its only, V2 (Long Range) Rocket. This fell at the junction of Park Road and New Road, north Kingston, 'blowing away completely the houses at the point of impact, causing a large crater, and doing major damage to surrounding properties'. Eight people died and about 120 were injured. Over 2,000 houses were affected, including 33 demolished, and 80 so badly damaged that the occupants had to be rehoused.

Raids were signalled by sirens. There was an air raid siren attached to every police telephone box in the borough, and each box was manned by a police constable. As soon as enemy aircraft crossed the British coastline, a 'red' warning was given to the local police boxes so that the PCs on duty could switch on the sirens and sound the alarm. If a bomb fell, the local ARP warden informed Guildhall Control, and the emergency services were sent out. Fire services, ambulances, rescue and stretcher parties were all needed. Then roads had to be cleared of debris, buildings made safe or demolished, goods salvaged, the mess cleaned up. Those bombed out had to be found somewhere to stay, and any unexploded bombs made safe before those in the shelters could safely return home.

Air raids did not start until 1940, and it was New Malden, not Kingston, that suffered first. A Kingston police sergeant, John Page, remembered 16 August 1940. It was afternoon, and heavy cloud: 'There was a deep rumbling noise above and we realized it was heavy planes'. The planes passed over Kingston, but New Malden was heavily bombed, and all available Kingston police were driven over to help. 'It was chaotic. 80 people were dead, injured everywhere. The railway station badly damaged, trolley bus wires down, burst water mains, broken gas mains. Everyone implored not to smoke. The garden fences riddled with bullet holes. A milkman lay dead. I went into a house where a baby was dead, its mother trapped under beams of wood'. This was the worst raid of the war for New Malden: over 1,300 houses damaged, and a high proportion of the borough's total casualties sustained.

Kingston's first raid occurred at about midnight on Saturday, 24 August. Eight bombs were dropped on Clarence Street, Eden Street, Orchard Road and Avenue Road. Amazingly, there were no casualties, though at Avenue Road a family, including an old lady of 87, had a narrow escape when the front of their house was blown out and they were rescued from a first floor bedroom. All the emergency services were on the scene quickly. The old lady was taken to Kingston Hospital, the rest of the family billeted with the vicar of St John's while the council arranged temporary housing. The rescue party salvaged furniture and valuables, and by 3.30am the roads were cleared. Many people were evacuated for the night and at daybreak the wardens launched a search for unexploded bombs. From 8am those who could not go home were offered breakfast at the Coronation Baths, and by 9.45am the area was declared safe.

Later on, bombs caused much more damage. When a high explosive bomb made a direct hit on Hodgson's Brewery in September 1940, most of the buildings in Kingston town centre had their windows blown out or roofs damaged. The first three flying bombs of June-July 1944 damaged about 1,800 houses, and there was extensive damage to Kingston Hospital when a V1 landed in its grounds on 5 July. All the patients had to be evacuated. Altogether, in the V1 and V2 raids of 1944 and 1945, nearly 8,000 Kingston premises were damaged. The first two Kingston people to die in raids were killed in the fourth 'incident' of the war, on Wednesday, 25 September 1940. One was a woman, walking down the London Road, the other a soldier in the Fairfield trenches. From then on, fatalities became a grim part of life. Kingston suffered 67 dead in its air raids, about 129 seriously injured, and 207 slightly injured. In Surbiton, 53 residents died. New Malden had 90 dead, 161 severely injured, and 301 slightly injured.

Casualties were higher than they might have been because many people did not use their air raid shelters, which were often cold, damp and uncomfortable. Efforts were made to make them more appealing, for instance by installing heaters, but people never liked them, and continued to take risks at home. There were some lucky escapes. A George Road housemaid was in bed in her third floor room when a bomb dropped beside the house. 'The end wall fell out, and her bedstead wheeled across the sagging floor into space. The girl clung on and miraculously was not thrown out until the bedstead landed on the crater that the bomb had made, then the wire spring catapulted her clear of the bombhole unhurt'. A similar incident occurred in Clifton Road, but here 'it left a gentleman in distress, for there he stood in the toilet hanging on to the chain with his trousers around his feet — shouts of "Hang on, Bill don't let go, the Fire Brigade are coming!"'

As the raids continued, there were many individual acts of bravery. When a bomb fell at Elm Road in December 1940, the rescue party had to tunnel perilously through the debris to find survivors, and four people were awarded the British Empire Medal. On the whole, Kingston coped well. Civil Defence worked well, and in 1945 the Town Clerk praised all involved, saying that 'All jobs have been undertaken with good heart and enthusiasm'. Civilian morale remained high, and there were no reports of looting. A letter sent to the council after a V1 landed in Dysart Avenue in June 1944 mentions 'how wonderfully organized your many services were, with no overlapping, and all cheerful. I have heard nothing else but words of praise from the folks whose houses were bombed . . . if it wasn't for seeing the windows covered up with silk, one could never realize so much damage had been done, for all the roofs have already been retiled'.

However, the flying bombs and the V2 attack strained local resources to the utmost: the Council's War Damage Department could scarcely repair the extensive damage, and extra labour was drafted in. Shortages of materials made life even more difficult, and it was fortunate for Kingston that the war ended when it did. Despite the use of requisitioned premises and temporary huts to house those who had been bombed out, Kingston had a severe housing shortage by 1945.

Ironically, Kingston's greatest 'home grown' contribution to the national war effort, the production of fighter aircraft at the Hawker's factory, proceeded virtually uninterrupted. By September 1939, Hawker's had constructed 500 Hurricanes for the RAF. With the outbreak of war, production expanded. Between June and November 1940, 1,423 Hurricanes were built, and it was these that won the Battle of Britain. The planes were made in factories both at Kingston (Canbury Park Road), and at the new Hawker's site at Langley, near Slough (acquired 1936); coaches bussed Kingston workers daily out to Langley and back. Personnel increased to over 13,000, many of them women, and altogether about 14,500 Hurricanes were produced. At one stage 12 were completed each day. There was a constant need for more space. Kingston workers did night shifts to make maximum use of the premises, and other buildings in Kingston, like Bentalls garage, were used for storage or assembly work. The Experimental Drawing Office moved out to Esher, when some of the Canbury Park Road accommodation was bombed in 1940, but this, the only hit of the war, hardly affected manufacturing. Besides the Hurricanes, Hawker's also designed other aircraft — the Typhoon, and Tempest — and began to experiment with jet engines.

Many other local firms contributed, sometimes secretly, to the war effort. Parnell's Aircraft made turrets for bomber planes. The Leyland factory, Richmond Road, produced specialized vehicles for government use, and made tank units, developing a diesel power unit for the Mathilda tank. In 1940, part of the factory was turned over to bomb manufacture, and soon it was producing nearly 400,000 bombs per month. The rest of the works concentrated on tank units and, increasingly, on whole tanks, such as Churchills, Centaurs and Comets. As at Hawker's, many women were employed. Armature coils for radio sets were manufactured in a secret workshop set up by John Perrings on the upper floor of their Kingston furniture shop. At first the work was subcontracted from Hoover's at Perivale, but the Kingston workers (all female volunteers) became so skilled that they eventually took over completely. From 1943, Erskine Laboratories moved to Surbiton, and developed apparatus for advanced radar systems, while Siebe Gorman's Neptune Works at Chessington developed underwater breathing apparatus and made rubber suits for navy divers. (Navy frogmen also trained secretly for D-Day at Kingston's Coronation Baths.) Another Chessington firm, C.H. Coates Ltd, secretly made parts for the huge artificial ports, the so called Mulberry Harbours, which in 1944 were towed across the Channel to assist the D-Day landing ships.

The river at Kingston was important too. Individual small boats crossed the Channel in 1940 to help evacuate British troops stranded after Dunkirk. Kingston waterman Harry Hastings and his friend Bill Clark rescued about 900 men in *Tigris I*, which was normally a passenger boat. From 1942, boats for the D-Day landings were made in Kingston. Gaze's, the established building firm, were secretly contracted to the Admiralty to build landing barges and other craft, like water ambulances, for the planned invasion. Over 900 vessels were eventually constructed in improvised shipyards in Kingston Hall Road, the Bittoms, and Thames Ditton.

The fighting forces were much in evidence in wartime Kingston. There was the local regiment, the East Surreys, based at Kingston Barracks, whose men served in Flanders, Malaya, North Africa and Italy. Over 1,000 were killed, though not all of these were Kingston men. Others from the area joined the Navy and Air Force, and two RAF pilots from New Malden, Cyril Barton and Ian Bazalgette, were posthumously awarded the Victoria Cross for bravery. War deaths, though reported, were not dwelt upon in the local press, for it was considered important to maintain morale. Wartime censorship also suppressed information that might help the enemy. Thus the places bombed were not named — Kingston became merely 'another south-west surburb'.

Troops from elsewhere also came to Kingston. In 1939, Canadian troops were based in Oxshott Woods and, as PC Page reported, they 'would come into Kingston, get drunk and start a fight'. Once, 'the police van was full of these drunk and disorderly soldiers . . . when the rear doors burst open. Some escaped, and ran riot in the town.' One policeman had his ear bitten. From June 1942, an American base, Camp Griffiss, was set up in Bushy Park. It was codenamed 'Widewing', and was heavily camouflaged by netting to protect it from air raids. This was the headquarters, first of the Eighth United States Army Air Force, and then from 31 December 1943 of the United States Strategic Air Forces in Europe. From March 1944 it played host to General Eisenhower and the Anglo-American group which planned Operation Overlord, the allied invasion of Europe. Eisenhower, the Supreme Commander of the allied forces, also stayed at Telegraph Cottage, Warren Road, and some of the D-Day planning probably took place there, too. Richmond Park also housed an army camp. The huts were originally built to house East Surrey conscripts, but the camp's main wartime use was as a convalescence and rehabilitation centre for wounded or traumatized army personnel. This use ended in 1947, and the camp housed athletes for the 1948 British Olympics. The War Office kept the site, and in the 1950s it housed a unit of the WRACS, but finally, in 1966, the army left and the camp was demolished. The Park was also used in the war for Home Guard training, as a gun encampment, and as a site for decoy petrol tanks.

The secrets surrounding the precise doings of Forces personnel, and the details of militarily sensitive industrial design and manufacture, were on the whole well-kept. The C. & R. Laundry, which did Eisenhower's laundry at Telegraph Cottage, knew when the D-Day invasions had started, because Eisenhower's team suddenly left, but nothing was said. The slogan 'careless talk costs lives' was taken to heart, and local people were told to be vigilant against spies and 'fifth columnists'. Nor were fears about sabotage entirely fanciful. Stanley Rogers, who in 1939 was on guard duty at the Hawker's factory with the East Surreys, remembers that a gang tried to sabotage Kingston Gas Works, that pillar post boxes were vandalized (popular rumour blamed the IRA), and that Hawker's own security guards caught a spy on their premises. Ironically, there were apparent loopholes in central government security. Aircraft workers from Eire received two year permits to do war work in Britain, and could then go to Germany to do similar work there. When Sergeant Page told Special Branch, they merely said: 'We realize what is happening'.

The civilian population was expected to stand firm and frustrate the enemy in the event of an invasion and in 1940, when a German invasion seemed imminent, the Home Guard was formed to provide local defence. The Kingston Company, raised by Major Allen, had over 400 men but soon merged with the Molesey group. However, there were also two other Kingston companies, the Hawker Company and the Kingston Corporation Company, which was commanded by the Town Clerk, Major A.W. Forsdike. They all formed part of the 53rd Surrey Battalion in 1940.

Most local people were firmly behind the war, and supported it as best they could. However, not everyone felt the same. In the 1930s, there was support for Oswald Mosley's British Union of Fascists: a Kingston branch was set up in 1932, and had perhaps 500 supporters. Its 'Blackshirts' held regular Saturday evening meetings by Kingston War Memorial. Once war started, it campaigned for peace with Hitler until 1940, when the movement was banned and its leaders interned. Even then, fascist sympathizers could still be found. In July 1940 a factory worker from Portland Road appeared in court charged with praising Hitler and slandering the Royal family. He had tried to convert to National Socialism a man who had just left St Raphael's Church after mass. There were also a few pacifists. When 1,500 men from the 'class of 1907' registered at Kingston employment exchange for military service, 12 were conscientious objectors. Some pacifists tried to help the war effort in a non-military way. However, one man from Woodbines Avenue declared that conscription was as objectionable as German totalitarianism, and that he was doing nothing specifically to help Britain except keep alive the principle of non-violence.

Even among the majority which supported the war, there was some grumbling. The Mayor reported in 1940 that 'troops of irate women' had besieged Kingston's Food

Office because they had not received their ration books — they were told they had failed to fill in the application forms properly! Rationing, introduced in January 1940, put a strain on everyone. Bombing raids could cause tremendous stress: in 1940 a Surbiton woman gassed herself because she was so worried about air raids.

The war disrupted the lives of all Kingstonians. People lost loved ones, the marriage rate rose, and the illegitimate birthrate doubled. Some children never caught up on an education disrupted by frequent trips to the shelters: one pupil at Bonner Hill School remembers that, if the siren went during the day, the girls did not usually go back to school after the raid. In July 1944, some Kingston schoolchildren were evacuated to avoid the flying bombs. Many families lost homes and possessions in the bombing and had to live in requisitioned premises or temporary huts, while many young couples started married life with relatives. By 1946, 2,500 families were in need of homes.

When the war in Europe ended on 8 May 1945, expectant crowds gathered outside Kingston Guildhall, but nothing happened. Some streets held their own VE Day parties, but Kingston's official victory celebrations did not take place till 8 June 1946. There was heavy rain that afternoon, and the town presented a sorry spectacle: 'Flags and bunting flapped noisily in the deserted, rain-drenched streets'. But it had been fine that morning, when the same streets had been filled with cheering crowds for the mile-long victory procession, and it was dry again in the evening for the concerts, fireworks, and Finny's last pageant play in Canbury Gardens.

Yet already the mood was changing. The start of Finny's pageant was delayed because vandals had messed up its stage set and sound system the previous night. People were tired of effort, and no longer willing to make sacrifices. In the autumn of 1945, the focus of interest had shifted to domestic matters: to the general and local elections, and discussions about possible local government reorganization. By the time the 1946 victory celebrations were held, the Second World War had passed into history, and Kingston was already looking to the future.

NGSTON

ROTECT YOUR EARS GAINST BLAST

by calling at the Warden's Post in whose area you live, who will issue ear-plugs to you and your family on request. The Wardens' Posts will be open for this purpose to the public for ONE WEEK from **To-Day (Saturday)**, **5th October** to **Saturday**, **12th October**, between 10 a.m. and 12 noon and 2 and 4 p.m.

IS FOR YOUR BENEFIT

PLEASE CALL

ROYAL BOROUGH OF KINGSTON-UPON-THAMES

TEST YOUR RESPIRATOR

in the

GAS CHAMBER

AT THE GUILDHALL

KINGSTON-UPON-THAMES

Open Daily Mondays to Saturdays (Sundays excluded) 2.30 to 4.30 p.m.

Commencing date February 24th, 1941

A. W. FORSDIKE

TOWN CLERK

Civil Defence in action: advertisements and poster 1939-41. (SC)

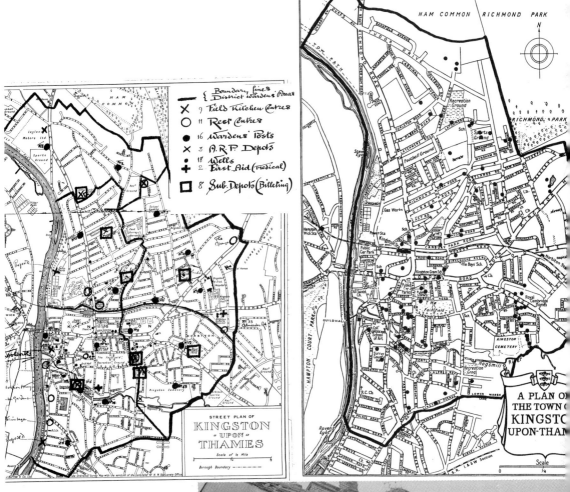

ABOVE: Civil Defence map of Kingston during World War II and where the bombs fell: RIGHT: conventional bombing incidents in Kingston, 1940-44 (mainly in the Blitz, 1940-1). OPPOSITE: V1 and V2 rockets dropped on Kingston 1944-5. The large black dot is the V2. BELOW: Effects of the Blitz in New Malden. (Virtually no photos were taken of Kingston) shops in Coombe Road.

BELOW: The rockets fell without warning: V1 damage at Van Dyck Avenue, New Malden. RIGHT: Local heroes included Flying Officer Cyril Barton, VC and Squadron Leader Ian Bazalgette, VC. (All KM & HS)

ABOVE: Launching a landing platform, c1943. (KM & HS) BELOW:
Working for victory: Machine shop at the Hawker's factory, Canbury
Park Road, showing capstan lathes.

You are to proceed at your utmost speed direct to the beaches eastward of DUNKIRK.

From the NORE proceed by Cant, Four Fathoms, Horse Bore and South Channels, or by any other route with which you are familiar, to pass close round North Foreland and thence to North Goodwin Light Vessel.

From NORTH GOODWIN LIGHT VESSEL proceed direct to DUNKIRK ROADS and close the beaches to the eastward. Approximate course and distance from North Goodwin L.V. S 53 E 37 miles.

NOTE: The tide set about N.E. and S.W. during the time of ebb and flood at Dover respectively. H.W. Dover 29th May is 5.30. a.m. and 6 p.m. B.S.T. On the 30th, about 6.45 a.m. and 7 p.m. — Maximum strength of tide about 1 to 1½ knots.

PRELIMINARY NOTICE

The **FUND**

that **EVERYBODY** has been waiting for

BENTALLS

Gives a lead to Kingston, Surbiton Malden & Districts

BY STARTING A

HURRICANE FUND

EVERY DONATION to the FUND will be DOUBLED ...
BY BENTALLS WHETHER IT IS A PENNY OR £1,000

ON VIEW FROM SATURDAY

A GENUINE GERMAN JUNKERS 88 AND THE BATTLE-SCARRED HURRICANE SIDE BY SIDE

Admission to View: Adults 6d. (3d. for Children)
THIS ADMISSION FEE WILL GO TO THE FUND AND WILL ALSO BE DOUBLED BY US

★ FOR THE BENEFIT OF THOSE CUSTOMERS WHO CANNOT VISIT THE EXHIBITION DURING WEEKDAYS—ARRANGE-MENTS HAVE BEEN MADE TO OPEN ON SUNDAY FROM 10 A.M. TO 8 P.M.—ENTRANCE IN WOOD STREET.

ABOVE: The Dunkirk evacuations, 1940: instructions given to those with small boats at Kingston. (KM & HS) LEFT: Helping the war effort: advertisement for the Bentall's Fighter Fund, 1940, which collected enough money to buy a Hurricane for the RAF. (SC) RIGHT: The Fascist alternative: Local Blackshirts selling their newspapers in Clarence Street, 1935. The man 3rd from left is Kingston BUF leader, John Nickolls. (JW)

171

Royal Borough of Kingston-upon-Thames

Programme of
VICTORY
CELEBRATIONS

FRIDAY, JUNE 7, at 8 p.m.
United Act of Thanksgiving and Dedication, All Saints' Churchyard (Clarence Street side). *Speaker :* The Bishop of Southwark.

SATURDAY, JUNE 8.
11 a.m. GRAND VICTORY PROCESSION of Military and Pre-Service Units; Youth and other Organisations, Decorated Vehicles, Tableaux, etc. Five Bands **Route :** Portsmouth Road—Guildhall—Eden Street—Brook Street—Orchard Road—Fairfield South—Hawks Road—Cambridge Road. Disperse Douglas Road.

**KINGSTONIAN FOOTBALL GROUND,
RICHMOND ROAD**
2.30 p.m. CHILDREN'S RALLY, SPORTS and MOUNTED GYMKHANA.

KINGSTON MARKET PLACE
3 p.m. Music by Band of East Surrey Regiment.
7 p.m. Alfresco Dancing. Basil Scammell and his Orchestra.

CANBURY GARDENS
3 p.m. Concert by The Kingston Orchestra.
6.30 p.m. Concert by The London Military Band.
8 p.m. KING EDRED'S CORONATION. A Historical Pageant Play to commemorate the Millenary of the Coronation of King Edred who was crowned King of England at Kingston in the year A.D. 946. **Over 100 Performers.**
9 p.m. ALFRESCO DANCING. Music by Band of The East Surrey Regiment.
Dusk. GRAND DISPLAY OF FIREWORKS (opposite Lower Ham Road).

WEDNESDAY, JUNE 12. Old People's River Trip. Kingston to Chertsey.

LEFT: 'Wings for Victory' week, 1943, raised money for Typhoons. (SC)
RIGHT: Telegraph Cottage, Warren Road, where Eisenhower stayed.
(KM & HS) BELOW: Programme for Kingston's victory celebrations, 1946. (SC)

Post War Visions

Since the war, Kingston has changed. Council estates and private developments have replaced Victorian streets and mansions. There has been an explosion of office building, and high rise blocks have transformed the townscape. Traffic has posed a major problem; the new relief road is the most recent attempt to solve it. Post-war Kingston has been dominated by town planning. The town is viewed as an organic whole, whose future development in terms of economic role and functions, infrastructure, and general physical and cultural environment must be mapped out in line with specific principles and an overall vision. The latter has altered with passing fashion; those who thought the vision of the 1960s a nightmare were relieved when it never fully materialised.

A major administrative change occurred in 1965 when Kingston, New Malden and Surbiton merged to form a new London Borough. This was still called the Royal Borough of Kingston upon Thames (though without the hyphens, to distinguish it from the previous one), but Kingston was finally brought within Greater London. Until 1986, when the Greater London Council was abolished, GLC guidelines, as well as central government directives, influenced local affairs. But this undermined neither Kingston's sense of community nor its economic prosperity. Kingston today is both a commuter town and an important regional economic centre. Some people mourn a loss of character but, now a university town, it is still a pleasant place and corporate awareness of its 'heritage' has never been higher.

The population of the original Royal Borough did not increase much between 1921 (39,479) and 1951 (40,172), and had actually declined a decade later. But New Malden and Surbiton were still growing, and after the war their populations overtook Kingston's. When they merged, administrative logic caught up with physical linkage. The new RBK had a population of about 142,000. This was 140,525 in 1971, and since then has continued to fall. It was 132,957 in 1991. Despite that fall, the number of households has increased. This is because of changing age and social structures — people are living longer, so there are more old people, living alone, and more one parent families. The need for more housing has not abated.

Since the war, the largest single land use has been housing. Development has been constrained and the environment protected by Green Belt policies, by the existence of Royal and town parks, and by designations of Metropolitan Open Land, but new homes have been provided by dividing old houses, and by infill.

Spacious gardens have been built on, large houses demolished and replaced by estates, as on Kingston Hill. The borough's housing stock increased from 51,500 in 1970 to 54,000 in 1980; most of it privately owned. Despite the rise in prices, which has made Kingston one of the most expensive Greater London boroughs, the proportion of owner-occupied housing (65% in 1981) has stayed well ahead of the national average.

However, the provision of council dwellings has been of great importance. In 1945, Kingston faced an urgent housing problem. Many homes had been badly damaged by bombing, and the Council was responsible for rehousing displaced families. Also, the demand increased as members of the forces, many of them newly married, returned home. At first, shortages and building restrictions meant requisitioned premises and temporary huts, but soon a major programme of council house building was inspired by need, and by a political and social vision.

Plans slowly went ahead, and the first few permanent post-war homes were built in 1946-7. The first large project was the council estate at Cambridge Gardens, where a block of 160 brick-built flats replaced the bomb-damaged Cambridge Asylum. These flats, officially opened by the Mayor in November 1949, were then the largest block in Surrey, and were hailed as luxury accommodation, with central heating and constant hot water. They cost £340,000, and rents ranged from 24s 5d to 51s 7d per week. Several other important estates followed. The Cumberland Lodge development on Kingston Hill provided 120 flats by 1952-3. The Kingsnympton Hall site, developed jointly by Kingston Council and Malden & Coombe District Council, finished by 1954, provided 320 units, mainly flats in 17 blocks named after Surrey villages, plus a school. The Chessington Hall estate was completed in stages: by 1956, 391 housing units were built, a mixture of flats, maisonettes and houses. There were many smaller developments too. Altogether, by April 1956, when the first main wave of post-war building ended, Kingston Council had built 361 permanent houses and 879 flats.

From 1957 to 1965, the rate of council house building slowed, but the temporary huts were phased out, and in 1960 the last requisitioned house was freed. In 1962 the Council planned the development of a large site off the Cambridge Road, consisting of several streets of small Victorian houses. The new development, the Cambridge Road Estate, was the council's most ambitious project so far, and cost £2.75 million. After five years of planning and land acquisition, construction started in 1968, and Stage I was completed by November 1970. This provided 603 dwellings, some in 17-storey tower blocks, to accommodate 2,000 people. Stage II accommodated 679 more people in 179 more dwellings, plus 40 old people's flatlets, some shops, and a tenants' social centre, completed by 1973.

The expense and disruption of the scheme and mounting criticism of high rise architecture militated against further developments like this. The Council continued to build smaller developments. Between 1970 and 1976 Council housing stock increased from 6,500 to 7,500 units. After 1979 the Government, anxious to save money, discouraged municipal building in favour of owner-occupation. This caused difficulties, as Kingston was expensive, and lower-income families found homes hard to afford. Economic recession exacerbated matters, and from about 1984 homelessness became a problem. The Council used bed and breakfast accommodation, but realized this was unsatisfactory. In the 1980s and '90s, Kingston Council adopted a range of strategies, including 'joint venture' schemes, whereby the Council and the private developers or housing associations collaborated to provide low-cost or rented housing on privately built estates. It also organized a private leasing scheme, whereby owners of private property leased their premises to tenants supplied by the Council. In the 1990s, council tenants have received grants to help them buy their own homes, thus releasing council properties for the homeless, and a Housing Advice Team tries to prevent homelessness.

The provision of social housing has recently become harder. Cuts in government subsidies have hit local authorities, and from 1990 they have been forbidden to subsidize social housing from local taxes. Kingston Council had to raise rents significantly in order to run its housing on a 'break-even' basis. Despite this, in 1992

174

council tenants voted by a narrow majority to keep the Council as their landlord, in preference to a housing association. The Council is still the main landlord, and manages about 5,600 dwellings, though housing management services will be subject to compulsory competitive tendering from 1997.

Despite the increase in homelessness, Kingston has maintained its prosperity. Unemployment has traditionally been low. In 1950, only 1% of those seeking work were unemployed. That had risen to 2% by 1978, but was still only half the Greater London average. During the recession of the early 1980s, unemployment rose to about 5%. It fell back to 2.6% in 1990, but rose sharply in the recession which followed and was exacerbated by the closure of British Aerospace's Kingston plant in 1992. In 1993 it reached its highest level (8.2% in April), and was still 6.5% in 1994. This is still low by London standards.

Kingston is still far more than a commuter town for London. About half the residents work outside the Borough, some of them in central London, others in different parts of Greater London and Surrey. Of Kingston's total workforce, about half commute into the borough, so Kingston is still an important centre of employment. The local economy has on the whole stayed buoyant since the war, but its structure has changed; there has been a marked decline in manufacturing industry, especially since 1971.

In the 1950s and '60s Kingston had a strong industrial base, grounded in engineering, and in 1971 about 26% of the borough's workforce was employed in manufacturing. Although British Leyland moved out when the lease expired on their Ham factory in 1948, Hawker's remained. It moved back into the Richmond Road premises in 1949, and took on some of the ex-Leyland workforce. For a while, its design department, administrative offices and machine shops remained at Canbury Park Road, but had moved to Ham by 1960, after a new building was put up there 1956-8. Hawker's, which became part of British Aerospace in 1977, continued to design and produce innovative, high quality fighter aircraft. BAe remained Kingston's leading industrial employer throughout the 1970s and '80s, and its Harriers saw service in the Falklands in 1982. Other important firms were Vine Products, of Villiers Road, which produced wine and vermouth, and Courages, which had taken over Hodgson's brewery in 1943, and which turned its town centre site into a bottling plant in 1951. Town gas was produced at Kingston gas works until 1955, and coal was shipped to it by barge. A new electricity power station (Station B) was opened at Kingston in 1948, and produced electricity into the 1970s.

Then the 1960s saw a number of closures, such as Cliffords Glass, which ceased production in 1965, the victim of town centre redevelopment plans and traffic problems. Kingston Tannery closed in 1963, and Courage's bottling plant in 1965; both sites were later redeveloped for shops and offices. From the 1970s industrial decline accelerated. Kingston Power Station, its plant outdated, finally closed in 1980. Vine Products relocated to the West Country in 1989, and its Villiers Road site is unlikely to be retained in industrial use. Kingston's largest employer, British Aerospace, closed in 1992 with the loss of about 3,000 jobs; its Richmond Road site will be used for housing. Manufacturing employment in Kingston borough 1971-6 fell by 21%, compared to a national average of 7%. In 1981 about 22% of Kingston's workforce was so employed; this had fallen to 15% by 1991 and by 1994 had collapsed to under 7.4%.

To some extent, Kingston's industrial decline reflects a national decline, but it has also been hastened by redevelopment programmes which, since the 1960s, have sought to 'smarten up' the town centre and to protect the residential environment. Industry, though not actively discouraged, took second place, and was increasingly restricted to designated industrial sites, outside the centre and often at the outskirts. Rising rents and land prices, traffic, delivery and parking problems and lack of ground space for expansion are other reasons. Kingston today still has manufacturing industry, especially in engineering and electronics, perhaps more than is often realized. From the 1980s this has been actively encouraged, and there are industrial estates at Canbury, New Malden, Tolworth and Chessington, but industry tends to be small scale. Traditionally, small businesses predominate but a few key employers have employed most of the workforce. One was British Aerospace. The borough's largest industrial employer today is the Racal Electronics group, which designs and provides electrical systems and services, including defence systems, and keeps Kingston at the forefront of technology. Its companies in the Kingston area (mainly in New Malden) employ approximately 1,500 people.

Many more firms in Kingston are involved in sales, distribution, servicing, design and consultancy, than are involved in production, while other firms are involved in service industries. Shop and office employment have a high profile in Kingston. Public administration is a major employer. Surrey County Council still has its headquarters in Penrhyn Road, Kingston, and Kingston Council expanded its office accommodation with Guildhall II in Kingston Hall Road in the 1970s. Private offices were encouraged from the 1960s, both by the Council's Comprehensive Development Area Plan of 1962-7, and by the Greater London Council's designation of Kingston as a 'preferred location for office development'. Between 1971 and 1984, the amount of office space in the town centre grew by over 80%: there were large office developments at Fairfield West, in Brook Street and St James Road, in Kingston Hall Road, London Road, and in Norbiton. By the mid-1980s, about 35% of all town centre jobs were office-based.

Office development in Kingston has been highly controversial. This is partly because in the 1970s it involved so much physical destruction and replacement, sometimes with high-rise blocks which dominate the townscape in a way many find unsympathetic. Partly it is because much office floorspace always appears vacant, which gives the impression of surplus. During the 1980s planners accepted only 'constrained' office development. More traditional styles and materials, and attempts to make offices blend in, have won local praise.

Shopping development has generally been less controversial, because Kingston has long been a shopping centre. However, 1960s and '70s developments like the shopping centres at Eden Walk and Fairfield West were not universally welcomed. They drove out small family shops, drove up rents, and aided the expansion of chain stores like Argos, BHS and Marks and Spencer. Yet even the latter did not halt Kingston's relative retail decline. Between 1961 and 1971, Kingston's shopping turnover increased less than either Croydon or Guildford, and by 1971 Croydon had replaced Kingston as the most important Greater London shopping centre outside central London. In an effort to revitalize Kingston, the Council sought to increase retail floorspace, to woo back small specialist shops, and to attract a major new department store.

This has had considerable success. Small specialist shops were attracted to the new Crown Arcade (1983), and to Adams Walk (1990). Kingston's shopping was boosted in the mid-1980s by the last phase of the Eden Walk shopping precinct, which provided a large new Boots store, and added another extension to M&S which made it one of the largest branches in the country. The major new retailer to the area was John Lewis. In 1983 they received planning permission to develop the Horsefair site, and their large new department store by the river, with attached car park and underground Waitrose, opened in September 1990. Bentalls rose to the challenge, remodelling its own department store (though preserving its characteristic Wood Street facade), and leasing off half its site for the new Bentall Centre, a large indoor shopping mall on four levels, with shops opening off a high central hall. The remodelled Bentalls store opened in July 1990, and the Bentall Centre in 1992. Together they, and the new Virgin Megastore in Clarence Street, have attracted much custom to Kingston, though the overall effect on shops elsewhere is still uncertain.

The upgrading of Kingston as a shopping centre has, since the 1960s, been part of an overall strategy. The first step was the Comprehensive Development Area Plan (CDAP), drawn up jointly by Kingston Council and Surrey County Council in 1961-2, and published in 1963. This was fiercely opposed by many local interests, but nevertheless adopted by the Council and finally approved by the Government in 1967. Besides promoting substantial shop and office redevelopment, the resiting of Kingston library and police station, and the extension of the Guildhall, it put forward a radical solution to what was increasingly seen as Kingston's main post-war problem — traffic.

By the 1960s the increased use of private cars meant that Kingston was choking. Much of this, despite the A3 Kingston by-pass, was through traffic, especially across Kingston bridge, so that the town centre at peak hours was clogged. This and a lack of parking space had an adverse effect on life and business. Kingston Council took two important steps: the introduction of parking meters to restrict on-road parking (1962), and a one-way road system clockwise round Clarence Street and Wood Street (1963), but its radical proposal was to build a raised ring road around the town centre.

Council planners, adopting a suggestion made by Bentalls, proposed a second road bridge across the Thames, north of the present one, to carry an east-west relief road for through traffic. This would be taken on a raised flyover above a major roundabout near Kingston station, which would provide for the intersection of the ring road with a north-south throughway. As part of the ring road, a new main road was to run right along the river bank south of Kingston Bridge. The relief and ring roads were designed to syphon off through traffic, and strategically placed 'interceptor' car parks on the road approaches would encourage visitors to leave their cars outside the inner ring. Much of the town centre, including the Market Place and Clarence Street, would be pedestrianized. Several streets and historic buildings would be bulldozed for the new road system, which would have isolated the town centre in a motorway-enclosed island. The estimated cost was £30 million, and it would have taken 20 years to complete! Though the plan had supporters — the *Surrey Comet* called it a 'brilliant scheme' and a 'blueprint for progress' — there was much opposition. At one stage the GLC called it 'an environmental disaster'.

The controversial road scheme never materialized. After 1965, the GLC was the body responsible for metropolitan roads, and its opposition eventually led to the scheme being scrapped in 1974. For ten years Kingston's Master Plan was held up while the road element was discussed. Some development did take place in line with the plan, such as the new police station, built 1966-8 in Kingston Hall Road, and the Eden Walk complex, where a multi-storey car park, shops and offices were built in three stages (1964-6, 1977-9 and 1985). However, much of it took longer to complete than expected because of rising costs, opposition to compulsory purchase and new government restrictions. Several sites purchased for redevelopment or in anticipation of the ring road lay derelict for years, and 'planning blight' harmed Kingston's image.

Between 1974 and 1979, Kingston Council and the GLC hammered out a new road plan. The planners of the 1960s had provided for unrestrained traffic growth, assuming the traffic would double between 1961 and 1981. 1970 planners decided that was environmentally undesirable; peak-time traffic increased by only 5%. They opted for a Relief Road which mainly used existing roads, but improved and upgraded them, and introduced a new one-way system. This still adopted the 'interceptor' car parks and pedestrianization of the centre.

The scheme received planning permission in 1981, and construction started in 1986. By July 1989 the new road system was in use, and Clarence Street was pedestrianized (the Market place was pedestrianized in 1983-4). The final touches came in October 1992, when a new linking road, Dolphin Street, was opened, and new 'bus lanes put into operation. Kingston's road and traffic problems are still not over, for Kingston bridge is now (1995) collapsing under the weight of traffic, in urgent need of repair.

The relief road was an important part of the Kingston Town Centre Local Plan of the 1980s, which replaced the CDAP in 1985. The new plan was designed to remove uncertainty and 'planning blight', to improve Kingston as a shopping centre, and to constrain office development. It protected Kingston's historic character, brought housing back to the centre and linked town more to riverside.

In the later 1980s, a Local Plan for the rest of the borough aimed to revitalize the 'district centres' of New Malden, Surbiton and Tolworth as shopping and employment centres, and to make their shops more attractive than out-of-town superstores, which were beginning to proliferate. New Malden was renewed by the Malden Centre (1987) and a new Waitrose supermarket in the old Town Hall building (1989). Tolworth was improved by a revamped Tolworth Broadway, launched in 1989, which included a new M&S store and car parking, and Surbiton in 1992 with upgraded Victorian style street lights and 'street furniture'. In 1991, a new Unitary Development Plan was drafted for the whole borough, with a priority to make the environment cleaner and more pleasant. Waste recycling and energy conservation, started in 1990, were now stepped up.

From the 1980s, the council has also improved borough facilities in two newly fashionable spheres, 'leisure' and 'heritage'. Kingston Council set the leisure ball rolling when it built a splendid new pool, the Kingfisher (opened 1984), on a prime town centre site, the Wheatfield, to replace the old Coronation Baths (closed 1980). This was followed by the Malden Centre, Blagdon Road, in 1987. The Kingsmeadow Athletics stadium provided a new ground for the Kingstonian Football Club. In 1989 the council also acquired Ravens Ait, an island in the Thames, used as a water sports and conference centre.

However, traditional entertainment has declined. Several cinemas have closed since the war, though the former Granada in Clarence Street, which became Options Nightclub in 1987, still has three screens. Kingston has not had a proper theatre since the closure of the 'Empire' in 1955. It was hoped in 1990 that a theatre might be part of the redevelopment of the Charter Quay riverside site, but the developer withdrew because of the recession. Nightclubs are popular, and Kingston is still well-off for pubs, but there is considerable support for the idea of a theatre and arts centre.

Kingston's libraries still flourish and, since the establishment of the Kingston Museum and Heritage Service in 1980, Kingston's heritage has been better protected and promoted. At first a Heritage Centre was set up at the Kingston Museum building in Wheatfield Way, but since 1992 the Kingston Local History Room has had its own base at the North Kingston Centre, Richmond Road. Kingston Museum was beautifully refurbished and internally redesigned between 1992 and 1994. The 1980s and '90s have seen a new awareness of the need to preserve Kingston's few remaining old buildings. The Central Library was refurbished in 1993, with faithful attention to period details, and the Market House, lovingly restored, opened to the public in 1995. Archaeology has unearthed much information about Kingston's past, and now there is usually a dig before town sites are developed.

Education is a traditional concern but, for 20 years after the war, Kingston Council lost much of its control over schools. The Butler Education Act of 1944 transferred control of Kingston's elementary schools to Surrey County Council. Schools and further education were run by the Surrey North Central Divisional Executive, on which Kingston Council had five representatives; the borough Education Committee ceased to exist. However, Kingston Council continued to be involved in Kingston Grammar School and Tiffin Boys' School because its members were foundation governors and trustees. KGS continued as a direct grant school, while Tiffin Boys' chose the status of a 'voluntary controlled' school.

In 1965, the newly enlarged Royal Borough of Kingston once more ran all its own schools and institutions of further and higher education. In the later 1960s, central government pressured local authorities to introduce comprehensive education, and from 1970-78 Surrey County Council converted to non-selective schools. Kingston's grammar schools were under threat, and KGS went independent in 1976, but Kingston retained selection. It continued to run Tiffin Boys' and Tiffin Girls' as selective grammar schools, and also built up and maintained a good range of primary and non-selective secondary schools. The system has always had its opponents, and in 1986 an Alliance council tried to introduce comprehensive education, but there was much local opposition and the party lost control of the Council at a by-election before taking action.

After the Education Reform Act of 1988, Kingston Council had to introduce both the new National Curriculum and Local Management of Schools. Some schools, including Tiffin Boys', have 'opted out' of council control altogether, and receive funding direct from the Government. Several schools are oversubscribed, and a recent court ruling, the 'Greenwich Judgement' (1988-90) forbids the Council to discriminate in favour of borough residents when admitting children into its schools.

From 1944 until 1965, Surrey County Council ran Kingston Technical College and the College of Art. Kingston Technical College offered degree courses and research facilities, and in 1957 Kingston was designated as the site of a Regional College of

Advanced Technology. From 1962, this College concentrated on degree work, and moved into new premises in Penrhyn Road; it merged with the College of Art (at Knight's Park) to become Kingston Polytechnic in January 1970. Meanwhile, a new Kingston College of Further Education was established in 1962, for courses below degree level. At first it occupied the old Victorian premises of the Technical College, but in the 1970s new purpose-built accommodation was provided in Kingston Hall Road, and KCFE, now called Kingston College, occupies them today.

Kingston Polytechnic amalgamated in 1975 with Gypsy Hill Teacher Training College, on Kingston Hill, and thus gained its Kingston Hill site. Since 1965, both the Poly and the College of Further Education had been run by Kingston Council. However, in 1989 Kingston Polytechnic became independent from the Council, and in 1992 it became Kingston University. Since then it has expanded dramatically.

Kingston Hospital has never been run by Kingston Council, and passed out of Surrey County Council's control after the National Health Service Act of 1946. Run as a National Health Service hospital under the local health authority, the Hospital expanded in the early 1960s. In 1991, it became a self-managing NHS Trust Hospital. Kingston Council remains responsible for social services. It runs sheltered housing units and day care centres, and community services like 'meals on wheels'. Kingston launched its Community Care Plan in 1992.

For thirty years or so after the war, local government expanded, but during the 1980s a radical change in government policy sought to curb public spending and undo the 'nanny' state. Many council jobs have been shed: the number of council employees has dropped from 5,811 in 1981 to 3,330 in 1994.

Local government from 1945 has become more politicized. The 1945 local elections were fiercely contested: for the first time in Kingston, Labour challenged the Tories in all wards. The result was a hung Council, and Labour influence on housing policies. However, the Tories regained control by 1949, and kept it till 1965. Labour was marginalized. In 1965, the enlarged Royal Borough of Kingston had 24 wards, 60 elected councillors, and ten aldermen. This was reduced in 1978, when aldermen were abolished, to 20 wards and 50 elected councillors. The creation of the new borough made no significant difference, because both Surbiton and Malden & Coombe borough councils had always been Conservative. The new RBK had a Tory council until 1986. During the 1980s, the main threat to Tory control came from the Liberals, rather than Labour, and it was the SDP-Liberal Alliance which took over in 1986. However, in 1987 they lost control after a by-election, mainly because of their education policy, and the Tories were back in power. This situation has only recently altered when the Liberal Democrats won the local election of 1994. They have decentralized the Council by setting up seven 'neighbourhood committees' to deal with 'local' issues, leaving fewer policy-making committees at the centre.

Despite Kingston's active political life, its identity as a national parliamentary constituency has come to an end. From being just a part of the East Surrey parliamentary division in the early 19th century, and of the Mid Surrey division from 1867, Kingston finally became a parliamentary constituency in its own right in 1885 and has always returned Conservative MPs. But it is a small constituency, and has just fallen victim to the rationalization of the Boundary Commission which, despite fierce local opposition, decided to abolish it in 1994. Some of Kingston's voters will now join the existing constituency of Surbiton; others will join Richmond voters in a new constituency, Richmond Park.

Kingston may count itself lucky to have retained its administrative identity as a separate borough. During a Boundary Commission enquiry from 1989, Surrey County Council wanted to absorb Kingston. Kingston resisted. The Boundary Commission's decision of 1992 leaves Kingston as an independent borough. Its boundaries will change only slightly: some of Ham goes to Richmond, and the A3 road, not the Beverley Brook, is the new border with Merton. But Kingston is still the smallest London borough, and may yet have to fight its corner against central government plans to reorganize it out of existence. For centuries, those in charge have tried, with considerable success, to protect the livelihood of residents; more recently they have tried to protect their environment and preserve their quality of life. If the Royal Borough disappeared, it would be a sad footnote to nearly 800 years of history.

1967

LEFT: Built up to its limits: the Royal Borough of Kingston upon Thames in 1967. RIGHT: Post-war council housing: these flats at Cambridge Gardens, built 1948-9, replaced the Cambridge Asylum for soldiers' widows, which was bombed in the war. BELOW: Brave new world? These tower blocks of the Cambridge Estate replaced Victorian cottages. (All TE)

181

ABOVE: Post-war industry in Kingston: British Aerospace, Richmond Road, showing the late 1950s facade demolished in 1993. (BAe) LEFT: Office development in Kingston: Fairfield West, built c1976. RIGHT: The Bentall Centre: Clarence Street, opened 1992. (Both TE)

ABOVE: The planners' dream: 1963 model of the new town plan for Kingston, showing the raised ring road. (KM & HS) Congestion relieved: LEFT: Kingston's growing traffic problems in the 1960s and (KM & HS) RIGHT: a pedestrianized Clarence Street, 1995. (TE) BELOW: The future — Kingston University, (formerly Polytechnic) Penrhyn Road site. (TE)

The Coronation Stone

In 1850, a large sandstone block, thought to be the coronation stone of Anglo-Saxon kings, was rescued by Alderman Gould from the yard of Kingston Assize Courts. It was then set up in a place of honour at the south end of the market, surrounded by 'Saxon effect' railings. According to Ayliffe, the stone was moved to the Assize courtyard from just outside the eastern entrance of the old Town Hall, when this was pulled down and the new one built in 1840. Children played on it, and horsemen used it as a mounting block.

Before it was moved to the Town Hall, the stone stood beside the parish church, on or near the site of St Mary's Chapel. *The British Directory* of 1793 says: 'Some of our Saxon kings were also crowned here; and close to the north (*sic*) side of the church is a large stone, on which, according to tradition, they were placed during the ceremony. Adjoining the same side was formerly a chapel, dedicated to St Mary'. Finny's excavations confirm that St Mary's was to the south of the church, not the north, so presumably the stone was to the south of the church too. Finny thought the stone was moved to the old Town Hall in 1825, when its former site was merged into the churchyard. This is plausible, though he cites no evidence.

The reference in *The British Directory*, 1793, is the earliest I have found which specifically mentions a coronation stone in Kingston, and links it with St Mary's Chapel. Manning and Bray (*The History and Antiquities of the County of Surrey*, c1804) do not refer to it, though they mention the portraits of the Saxon kings once kept in St Mary's Chapel. John Aubrey, in his 'Perambulation of the County of Surrey' (1673) describes the portraits (some of kings supposedly crowned in Kingston Market, and some of kings crowned supposedly in St Mary's Chapel), but has no knowledge of a coronation stone. Leland, in the 1540s, has not heard of it. In his *Cygnea Cantio*, 1544, he reports the contemporary rumour that the (three) Saxon kings crowned at Kingston were crowned 'in the midst of the market-place, a lofty platform being erected, that the ceremony might be seen from afar'. In his *Itinerary*, he says that Kingstonians claim 'certen knowlege of a few kinges crounid ther afore the Conqueste; and contende that 2 or 3 kinges were buried yn their paroche chirch; *but they can not bring no profe nor likelihod of it*', (my emphasis). This suggests strongly that no connection was made in Leland's day between a Kingston stone and the coronations. Nor is there any medieval or earlier documentary reference to a coronation stone at Kingston.

We may discount as a reference to a Kingston stone the oft-cited passage from John Speed's *Description of England*, 1627: 'At Kingston likewise stood the chaire of Majestie, wherein Athelstan, Edwin and Ethelred sate at their coronation, and first received their Scepter of Imperiall Power'. Speed says 'stood' not 'stands', and 'chair', not 'stone'; he is not referring to an actual artefact which in his day survived in Kingston (or, indeed, to one which used to exist there), but is embellishing his material with details from coronations of his own day, simply saying in a flowery way that kings were crowned at Kingston.

There is thus no mention of a coronation stone at Kingston before the late 18th century. It must be significant that the stone is placed by *The British Directory* near St Mary's Chapel at a time when this no longer existed, but does not appear in Manning and Bray's work, which illustrates St Mary's Chapel as it was before its collapse in 1730, on the basis of drawings made in 1726. The stone may have lain in St Mary's till the chapel fell down, or perhaps have formed part of its walls, but it does not seem to have been associated with coronations until after the chapel was in ruins. Maybe then the traditional association of St Mary's with the coronations, which developed in the later 17th century when the pictures of the kings were hung there, became transferred to a large stone from the building.

Of course, the stone could still have been venerated in the past as a holy object, either in Saxon or pre-Saxon times, before being placed in, or becoming part of, the Chapel of St Mary. It *might* have been used to crown kings on. But the tradition that links the stone with Saxon kings is of fairly recent coinage and, if the Victorians were correct in their guess that the stone was a coronation stone, it was a lucky guess, not based on any firm evidence.